# Enchanted Maidens

# Enchanted Maidens

## GENDER RELATIONS IN SPANISH FOLKTALES OF COURTSHIP AND MARRIAGE

*James M. Taggart*

PRINCETON UNIVERSITY PRESS
PRINCETON, NEW JERSEY

Published by Princeton University Press, 41 William Street, Princeton, New Jersey 08540
In the United Kingdom: Princeton University Press, Oxford

Library of Congress Cataloging-in-Publication Data

Taggart, James M., 1941-
  Enchanted maidens : gender relations in Spanish folktales of courtship and marriage /
James M. Taggart.
    p.  cm.
  Includes bibliographical references.
  ISBN 0-691-09453-5—ISBN 0-691-02852-4 (pbk.)
  1. Courtship—Spain—Folklore. 2. Marriage customs and rites—Spain—Folklore.
3. Sex role—Spain—Folklore. I. Title. II. Title: Gender relations in Spanish folktales of
courtship and marriage.
GR230.T34  1990                                                    89-37244
398'.355'0946—dc20                                                 CIP

Publication of this book has been aided by a grant from The Program for Cultural
Cooperation Between Spain's Ministry of Culture and United States Universities.

This book has been composed in Linotron Sabon

Princeton University Press books are printed on acid-free paper, and meet the guidelines
for permanence and durability of the Committee on Production Guidelines for Book
Longevity of the Council on Library Resources

Printed in the United States of America by Princeton University Press, Princeton, New
Jersey

      10  9  8  7  6  5  4  3  2  1

(Pbk.) 10  9  8  7  6  5  4  3  2  1

## TO COUNIHAN

*Who is the Blancaflor in my life.*

# Contents

*List of Stories, Their Tellers, and Their Communities*  ix

*Preface*  xi

**CHAPTER ONE**
Introduction  3

**CHAPTER TWO**
The Context  17

**CHAPTER THREE**
"The Innocent Slandered Maiden"  41

**CHAPTER FOUR**
Maidens and Thieves  59

**CHAPTER FIVE**
"Snow White"  77

**CHAPTER SIX**
"Cinderella"  93

**CHAPTER SEVEN**
Disenchanting a Princess  116

**CHAPTER EIGHT**
The Animal Groom  146

**CHAPTER NINE**
"Blancaflor"  165

**CHAPTER TEN**
A Cross-Cultural Perspective  200

**CHAPTER ELEVEN**
Conclusions  219

*Appendix: List of Supplementary Tales*  225

*Notes*  229

*Bibliography*  237

*Index*  245

# List of Stories, Their Tellers, and Their Communities

"The Innocent Slandered Maiden," by Florencia Herrero, age
sixty-eight (Garganta la Olla)      43

"The Innocent Slandered Maiden," by Narcisa Justo Perez, age
sixty-two (Serradilla)      49

"The Innocent Slandered Maiden," by José Díaz Sanchez, in his
early sixties (Serradilla)      53

"The Maidens and the Thieves," by Filomena Arivas Miguel, age
fifty-four (Navaconcejo)      60

"The Maidens and the Thieves," by Julia Perez, age fifty-one
(Navaconcejo)      65

"The Maidens and the Thieves," by María Fernández, age forty-
five (Piornal)      67

"The Maidens and the Thieves," by José Díaz Sanchez, in his
early sixties (Serradilla)      70

"Snow White," by Domitila Prieto Perez, age sixty-seven
(Piornal)      82

"Snow White," by Evarista Moreno, age thirty-three
(Cabezuela)      86

"Snow White," by Vito Flores, age seventy-four (Cabezuela)      87

"Cinderella," by Ulalia García Castaño, age seventy-eight
(Garganta la Olla)      95

"Cinderella," by Filomena Arivas Miguel, age fifty-four
(Navaconcejo)      101

"Cinderella," by Maximina Castaño, age sixty-eight (Garganta
la Olla)      106

"Cinderella," by Leandro Jimenez, age seventy-four (El Gui
jo de Santa Bárbara)      112

"The Griffin Bird," by Julio Lopez Curiel, age seventy-four
(Garganta la Olla)      120

"The Grateful Animals," by José Díaz Sanchez, in his early
sixties (Serradilla)      134

"The Grateful Animals," by Felisa Sanchez Martín, age seventy-
two (Serradilla)      140

"Beauty and the Beast," by Teresa Herrero, age twenty-four
(Garganta la Olla)                                                                  147

"The Soldier," by Julio Lopez Curiel, age seventy-four
(Garganta la Olla)                                                                  151

"Cupid and Psyche," by Juana Moreno, age sixty-five
(Garganta la Olla)                                                                  157

"Cupid and Psyche," by Zacaria Iglesia, age seventy-four
(Piornal)                                                                           161

"Blancaflor," by Florencio Ramos, age sixty (Navaconcejo)       170

"Blancaflor," by Gregoria Ramos Merchán, age sixty-eight
(Piornal)                                                                           190

"The Little Donkey Mother," by Fernando Vega, age fifty
(Santiago Yaonáhuac)                                                                204

# Preface

I BEGAN thinking about Spanish folktales while living with the Nahuat Indians in Mexico. The Nahuat in the northern state of Puebla have experienced Spanish and mestizo domination for centuries and tell many folktales of Spanish origin. Men told most of the tales I heard and expressed a complex worldview in their stories that fit their position in an ethnically and sexually stratified society. I wondered how men and women might represent gender relations in the folktales of a historically related Hispanic culture where the sexes have a different relationship. Spain seemed like a good place to gain a broader cross-cultural perspective because some ethnographies of Spanish villages present a comparatively egalitarian picture of relations between husbands and wives.

Stanley Brandes very graciously and generously suggested that I look in the rural villages of northern Extremadura, near Jarandilla de la Vera, for Spanish storytellers who might tell tales like those I had collected in Mexico. With a grant from the American Philosophical Society Penrose Fund, I went to Madrid in the summer of 1980 and met Fermín del Pino Díaz and Honorio Velasco Maillo, who discussed at length the state of anthropology and folklore in their country. Fermín pointed out the strong interest among such Spaniards as Luis Cortés Vázquez, who recalled hearing folktales in his childhood and later collected stories from oral tradition in order to understand his own culture. I went to Jarandilla, conducted a brief survey of the surrounding villages, and settled on the tiny town of El Guijo de Santa Bárbara. The Guijeños were warm and very generous and, to my pleasant surprise, women were accessible, friendly, and excellent storytellers. One such woman was Felisa Sanchez, who learned many folktales from here father-in-law, Leandro Jimenez. Felisa and Leandro told a number of stories that sounded very much like those in Nahuat oral tradition, including "Cinderella" and the famous tale of "Blancaflor," which describes in rich metaphorical language the power of a woman's love for a man.

The next summer, with a grant from Franklin and Marshall College, I went to Garganta la Olla, where I met Maximina Castaño, Julio Lopez Curiel, Florencia Herrero, and Guillermo Castaño, all of whom shared with me their tales and life experiences. The following summer, with more support from Franklin and Marshall, I went to Piornal, where Domitila Prieto Perez, Zacaria Iglesia, María Fernández, Gregoria Ramos, Emilia Moreno Calle, and Victoria Díaz gave me a fuller picture of

Cáceres oral tradition and society. At this point in my journey, I was struck by the women, who spoke in high-spirited voices that seemed much stronger and more accessible than those of their Nahuat sisters. Gradually it became apparent that male and female storytellers in this part of Spain carry out a dialogue through the telling of tales in which they exchange their impressions of gender relations in courtship and marriage.

With generous support from the National Science Foundation, I returned to Cáceres in June 1983 for a year of fieldwork to collect as many stories as possible from women and men for comparison with tales collected earlier from Nahuat oral tradition. By this time I had the opportunity to get to know more Spanish anthropologists, including Manuel Gutiérrez Estévez, who had conducted extensive fieldwork in both Extremadura and Campeche, Mexico. Manuel invited me to participate in two extremely productive conferences at the Universidad Internacional Menéndez Pelayo in Santander during the summers of 1983 and 1984. The conferences were a chance to exchange ideas with Spanish scholars and students interested in the expressive culture of their own country.

I spent the year in the field with my daughter Marisela, who was seven years old at the time, and we lived periodically in Navaconcejo and Cabezuela, Tornavacas, and Serradilla and then returned to Garganta la Olla, where we had spent the summer of 1981. In every village Marisela made friends, some of whom played a very important role in her life. We met Isabel García in Cabezuela, and she offered her care and affection to Marisela, who desperately needed the support of a "big sister." Isabel is from Ahigal, a community I never visited but that is represented by two of her stories (listed in the Appendix). In Serradilla we met Florencia Real Cobos, who carefully but gently combed the knots out of Marisela's hair every week and made both of us feel very much at home. Storytellers have been the informants with whom I have enjoyed warm friendships in Mexico and Spain. I thank them all for extending their hospitality, sharing their stories, and telling me about their lives.

I returned to Franklin and Marshall College in August 1984 to resume teaching and to order the stories and the ethnographic data I had collected in all of the villages. Many people helped me write this book by giving me their encouragement and their criticisms. George M. Foster and Lauris McKee made very helpful suggestions for revising the paper " 'Hansel and Gretal' in Spain and Mexico," which layed the foundation for this longer work. Ruth Behar and Michael D. Murphy carefully read my manuscript for Princeton and offered excellent suggestions for revision. Robert Laughlin and Norman B. Schwartz also read and gave me their valuable criticisms of an early draft. My sister Beatrice, who has always been an important source of support, used her considerable artistic talent to make the map and draw the illustrations. I thank Gail Ullman for her encouragement and careful handling of the review process and Lois Krieger for an excellent job of copy editing. Writing can be a lonely occupation, but I was fortunate to have had the loving support of Carole M. Counihan. She listened to many of the stories, gave birth to our son, Ben, and took time out of her busy academic schedule to read the "Hansel and Gretel" paper and make detailed critiques of several versions of this book.

Lancaster, Pennsylvania
March 1989

Enchanted Maidens

# CHAPTER ONE

# Introduction

SPANIARDS TELL many folktales that describe in metaphorical language how a maiden and young man emerge from their parental families and bond with each other in heterosexual love.[1] This book examines how women and men in one part of Spain carry out a dialogue through storytelling and grapple with some of the contradictions in gender relations that emerge in courtship and marriage. Young men and maidens in Cáceres villages enter the age of courtship under diametrically opposite social pressures. Men are socialized to be fearless and sexually assertive and simultaneously express a desire to marry virgins. Women are taught to guard their chastity and say they are justified in breaking courtships with men who make improper sexual advances. Yet Cáceres men, like their counterparts elsewhere in Spain, maintain that a woman with a history of broken courtships will have a difficult time making a good marriage. Men avoid women who have had prior courtships out of fear that once-courted maidens may have lost their virginity with their previous sweethearts. Men are expected to ask for and win the hand in marriage of a maiden, and women are socialized to fear the men who court them. Mothers and grandmothers tell young maidens stories that describe defloration on their wedding night as a brutally violent experience and their husband's family as cannibalistic thieves. Yet a woman is expected to consummate her marriage and live in permanent monogamy in a separate household with her husband. The filial loyalty of a woman is very strong because a daughter relies on her parents to help protect her from predatory men, she has close lifelong ties with her mother, and she frequently assumes the primary responsibility for taking care of her elderly parents. Yet men express a desire to break their wife's ties with her parents and expect their wife to care for them much as their mother had done prior to marriage. Men compete for many things, including women, and one man can take the honor of another by dishonoring that man's sweetheart, wife, or any woman in his family. The young man who comes to court a maiden represents a threat to her father, who stands to lose his own honor if his daughter is seduced and abandoned by her suitor. Some parents go to great lengths to block the marriage of their daughters to men of whom they disapprove. The conflict between a son and his father-in-law is a problem for a woman who may have to choose between her parents and the man who courts her. These contrasting social pressures are mediated through storytelling as men and women exchange tales about protagonists who represent maidens and young men at different points on their way to becoming husbands and wives. Male and female storytellers carry out an exchange of images through the telling and retelling of the same stories in which they alter the plots and story characters to present their views of courtship, share an awareness of the position of the other, mediate the fear in gender relations, and affirm their belief in a common model of marriage.

## THE PICTURE OF GENDER RELATIONS IN SPAIN

One of the perplexing problems in the Anglo-American ethnography of Spain is the portrayal of gender relations. The problem is an important one because Spain is the mother country to Spanish culture transplanted in the New World with the colonization of the Americas. Descriptions of all regional variants of Hispanic culture, including those of Spain, reflect upon Hispanics living in the United States (Fernandez 1983: 171). The accounts of rural Spanish gender relations vary depending on the ethnographer and the region. Husbands and wives work their land together as a team in many areas, but descriptions of their relationship vary from relative equality (Behar 1986: 15–16; Freeman 1970: 187–200) to a hierarchy of male dominance where the husband is the clear head of the family but also heavily dependent on his wife, who is the nurturer of her husband and their children (Kenny 1969: 55–75; Brandes 1975: 79–82, 112–120). The Mediterranean codes of honor and shame do not seem to govern relations between women and men in the northern Cantabrian region (Fernandez 1983, 1986: 74) and some parts of León (Behar 1986: 15–16).[2] Honor and shame play a greater role in defining the sexual conduct of women and men in certain parts of Aragón (Lison-Tolosana 1983),[3] Castile (Aceves 1971: 62–60; Kenny 1969: 76–94), and notably Andalusia (Pitt-Rivers 1966; Brandes 1980; Gilmore 1987a), where men are expected to demonstrate their manliness, and women must defend their chastity to maintain their feminine honor. In the agrotowns of Andalusia, gender relations among members of the agrarian working class are characterized by a great deal of difference, distance, and fear (Brandes 1980; GIlmore 1987a).

Cáceres is the northern province of Extremadura, and the villagers I observed in this part of Spain manifest many traits attributed to the relations between women and men living in the regions adjacent to Extremadura. When showing their concerns about honor and shame, they fit the descriptions by British and American anthropologists for Old Castile to the north and particularly Andalusia to the south. These descriptions tell of men and women moving in different worlds, masculinine identity differing sharply from feminine identity, men devaluing women, men fearing the power of women, and men competing with one another for and through women. Gender segregation is apparent when men sit apart from women in church (Pitt-Rivers 1966: 87–88) and when men walk separately from women and children in public religious processions (Pitt-Rivers 1966: 77). Maidens sometimes sit at different tables from bachelors at wedding banquets (Brandes 1975: 166), and men of all ages frequent cafés, whereas women sit near their homes in the afternoon sun mending and crocheting. Less visible is the gender division of labor in which men and women perform complementary tasks. Women and men know how to do many of the same things, and the lines in agriculture are "never so rigid that boundaries cannot on occasion be crossed" (Brandes 1975: 81). But women perform many domicile-based tasks and take primary responsibility for raising children. Andalusian men seem reluctant to spend "too much time in the home (*la casa*) because to do so would provide damaging questions about their masculinity" (Gilmore and Uhl 1987: 348).

Andalusian men express their separateness from women by stressing their own moral superiority and by giving voice to their fear of the power of women over men, particularly in sexual intimacy. Men stress their moral superiority by symbolically associating themselves with God and women with the devil (Brandes 1980: 80). The power of women is recognized in beliefs about feminine supernatural power directly related to women's sexuality. Julian Pitt-Rivers (1966: 189–201) reports that feminine supernatural power can bring about negative as well as positive results. Women have menstrual magic that can wilt flowers, kill bushes and trees, wound the backs of horses, and extinguish the fire in a lime kiln. They have grace (*gracia*), an inherent quality by which they can find lost animals, discover the name of a thief, determine if an absent person is all right and faithful, cause another to fall in love, protect one from natural disasters, and cure illness. Pitt-Rivers (1966: 196–197) asserts that men lack the inherent sources of supernatural power possessed by women and practice their magic by reading from books. Andalusian men in the town of Monteros voice in folklore their fear of women's power. Stanley Brandes (1980: 77) observed that Monteros men regard women as "seductresses, possessed of unsatiable, lustful appetites. When women wield their power, men cannot resist temptation and are forced to relinquish control over their passions."

The works that focus most closely on Spanish gender relations generally take the point of view of one gender more than another. Studies of Spanish masculinity emphasize the competitive male view of human relations and draw attention to men's fear of the power of women (Brandes

1980; Gilmore 1987a). Social anthropologists understandably work with informants of their own sex because many cultures of the world stress the difference between men and women and assign them to separate worlds. Stanley Brandes (1980: 13) noted that he could only "be considered a normal human being and thereby incorporated into Monteros society" by spending most of his time with men. Brandes aimed to study folklore, which he correctly points out is best observed in its natural context, and his presence among women might have dampened their spontaneity in expressive culture. Gilmore (1987a: xiv) had a similar experience and reported that he simply did not have access to women in rural Andalusia. As Brandes and Gilmore make clear, the focus on men is a field strategy that has definite advantages. Both men successfully became participant observers in Spanish culture and gained the trust and confidence of men by taking into consideration their concerns about other men taking away their masculine honor by dishonoring their women.

With the growing presence of women in anthropology and the radicalizing effects of feminism on anthropological theory, the female perspective has been increasingly heard. Some women have entered the field and studied the same societies earlier described by men; their results are remarkable. For example, Annette Weiner (1976) studied the Trobriand Islands, and because she had none of the male biases of Malinowski's original study of the same society, her results are quite different. Women have written many fine-grained works on Spanish culture and society (Freeman 1970, 1979; Harding 1975, 1984; Buechler and Buechler 1981; Behar 1986); some present a different picture and interpretation of Spanish gender identity (Buechler and Buechler 1981; Harding 1975) and gender relations (Freeman 1970; Behar 1986). But relatively few scholars of either sex have focused primarily on the mediation of differences between women and men in rural Spanish society.[4]

I came upon male and female storytellers when first carrying out fieldwork in Cáceres in 1980 and trying to find narratives like those I had collected earlier in Mexico.[5] Hispanic American and Spanish folklorists have collected folktales from men and women in many Spanish provinces since the early decades of this century.[6] My search for storytellers led me to women as well as men because both are accustomed to telling tales in front of one another in the villages of northern Cáceres. This book is based on sixty-eight Spanish folktales told by forty-two storytellers of whom twenty-five are women and seventeen are men living in eight villages. Twenty-three of their stories, translated into English, appear in this book, and forty-five others are list in the Appendix. I have also included for comparative purposes an English translation of a Mexican Nahuat folktale of Spanish origin to illustrate how groups within the Hispanic world tell the same stories differently according to the social and cultural context. Scholars may write me for copies of the Spanish and Nahuat originals of all folktales that are the basis of this study. The storytelling dialogue, reconstructed from an examination of the masculine and feminine stories, is one of several ways that women and men communicate with one another to reduce the distance and mediate the contradictions in their relationship.

## THE MEDIATION OF DISCORDANT THEMES

Cáceres Spanish society is highly monogamous, and men and women live in families where wives cooperate with their husbands in a complex division of labor. Relative to other societies in the Hispanic world, the tellers of tales in rural Cáceres express a high degree of faith in the conjugal bond, which is remarkably stable. Nearly all of the Cáceres tales of courtship and marriage told by women as well as men conclude with a couple marrying and living happily ever after. This faith in the conjugal bond is not shared by all cultures of the Hispanic world. Mexican Indians tell many of the same stories of courtship and marriage that originated in Spanish oral tradition, and they replace the happy endings with women betraying the men who love them. The differences between the Cáceres and Mexican Indian variants of the same stories are connected to contrasting configurations of family loyalties (discussed in Chapter 10 of this book).

The widely noted contradictions in gender relations create tension and fear between women and men that require mediation if a couple is to move toward intimacy. Although a woman fears defloration, she cannot return home to avoid consummating her marriage. A man and a woman normally begin their marriage in their own independent household, where the wife is expected to work with her husband in agriculture. New couples are expected to remain married for life in a culture that, until recently, did not allow divorce except under very special circumstances. Maidens and young men are expected to work through their contradictions and differences during the long period of formal courtship, in preparation for married life.

Studies of Spanish villagers of the same generation as the Cáceres narrators, however, present conflicting accounts of the mediation of gender differences during courtship. Julian Pitt-Rivers (1966: 84–98) concluded that the long, formal courtships and romantic love helped couples make the transition to married life in village Andalusia. Long courtships ostensibly allowed a man and woman to accumulate all the items necessary to establish a new household, but they also permitted the couple to get to know each other under the watchful eye of the maiden's parents (Pitt-Rivers 1966: 93). Numerous visits by the young man to the maiden's family undoubtedly served to break down the barriers of suspicion and build trust (*confianza*). Romantic love in courtship helped couples overcome their fears of each other, which developed out of the culturally defined differences between men and women. A man was expected to make a woman fall in love, which means create the necessary illusion (*la ilusión*) according to which both sweethearts feel they are "the most wonderful person in the world" in the eyes of the other (Pitt-Rivers 1966: 94). The illusion was created when a young man spoke to his courted maiden through her window, when the couple went for a walk, and when the young man visited the maiden in her home. To make a maiden fall in love was not always easy in rural Spain, as shown by the many young men who sang ballads to their maidens telling of the pain and doubts of love (see Lison-Tolosana 1983: 84–85). Some courting couples apparently succeeded in lowering their barriers because they remembered with nostalgia the time of their courtships when "everyone is happiest" (Pitt-Rivers 1966: 109).

Richard and Sally Price (1966a: 314–315) present a very different picture when they suggest that long and formal courtships during the early decades of the Franco regime perpetuated rather than removed the barriers to marital intimacy in Los Olivos, a village similar to the one studied by Pitt-Rivers. The Prices observed that courting maidens, who felt constrained to guard their premarital chastity in the eyes of their community, never really knew their sweethearts. Maidens and young men maintained a great deal of distance during courtship, setting the stage for a distant relationship once married. Recently married husbands spent their leisure time with men and had sex with other partners before their wife's first pregnancy.

Most of the Cáceres narrators were over fifty years old and have the values of the generation that courted and married at the same time as the couples in rural Andalusia studied by Julian Pitt-Rivers and Richard and Sally Price. An examination of their storytelling dialogue reveals some of the ways they believe couples can work through their contradictions according to a traditional model of marriage. All of the male and female storytellers expressed a great deal of concern with women's premarital and marital chastity. But they also describe a model of marriage based on sentimentality, and I suspect that sentimentality is probably an established part of the traditional model of marriage for many village men and women of this generation. Behar and Frye (1988: 28–29) discovered that older married couples, who came of age at about the same time in rural León, believe that marriage for sentiment literally means healthy children. They tell cautionary tales warning that those who marry out of pure economic self-interest set the stage for family tragedy. Although the Leónes men and women do not generally speak of marital love, they do emphasize the need for a husband and wife to understand each other (*entenderse*).

The men and women in the villages of northern Cáceres conveyed the message in their tales that a man and woman must conquer their fears, understand each other, and have faith in the power of a woman's love. The elders use storytelling as one of the ways of guiding their children and grandchildren, and the stories in their dialogue are metaphorical expressions of personal and collective experience that teach how to make compromises and accommodations in marriage and family life. The generations do not always understand each other completely, particularly in times of rapid social and cultural change, but I found that younger men and women, despite their modern values, were very interested in and valued what their grandparents said when telling a tale.

## THEORETICAL APPROACH

The stories as metaphorical expressions of experience offer an exceptional opportunity to understand gender relations in rural Cáceres. Metaphor is figurative language in which one thing is used to stand for another. Narrators in the Cáceres villages organize their experience in metaphorical form by describing the courtships and marriages of characters who live in other, often unspecified times and places. Storytelling is part of the culture, and narrators seem to enjoy talking about courtship and marriage in the language of folktales as a culturally approved means of reflecting on themselves and their world. Listening to stories about courtship is an opportunity to get to know Cáceres villagers in ways that are comfortable for the storyteller as well as for the observer.

Stories also present very complex problems of interpretation because as metaphorical statements they have many possible meanings. Narrators generally did not offer many clues when asked to interpret their own stories, because their metaphorical meaning is often unconscious or subconscious and the storytellers prefer to reflect on themselves through storytelling rather than in the direct description of their deeply personal experiences. Speaking in the metaphorical language of a story allows them to express deep feelings through the safety of fantasy. Consequently the language of stories invites many interpretations, which vary with the theoretical framework of the interpreter.

The Cáceres storytelling dialogue requires an eclectic method of interpretation because the male and female narrators told popular European folk and fairy tales embellished with individual touches that fit their specific backgrounds. They told tales that have remarkable plot stability over time and space, suggesting that they express widespread concerns about the human condition. Their stories resemble those Aurelio Espinosa

(1923, 1924), collected throughout Spain six decades earlier, in 1920 and 1921. They are regional variants of stories told in France, Italy, and England (Darnton 1984) and resemble many of the folk and fairy tales[7] in the Grimms' *Nursery and Household Tales*. The commonly known titles[8] and the Aarne-Thompson (Boggs 1930; Hansen 1957; Robe 1973)[9] tale-type numbers of the most popular stories are "The Innocent Slandered Maiden" (883A), "The Maiden and the Thieves" (956, 970), "Snow White" (709), "Cinderella" (510), animal-groom tales (425), dragon-slayer stories (300, 302, and 554), and "Blancaflor" (313). The stories contain panhuman archetypes for the Jungians (see von Franz 1982), express widespread Oedipal and Electra themes for Freudians (Bettelheim 1977), and are an art form dealing with beauty for Lüthi (1984), who interprets the fairy tales independently of their cultural context.

Each Cáceres storyteller tells a story differently; communities vary in their patterns of storytelling; and men tell the same tales differently from women. Folklorists (Dégh 1969; Georges 1969; Bauman 1986) have increasingly focused their attention on the complex relationships among the content of stories, the particular personalities of the storytellers, and the storytelling situations. The historian Robert Darnton has noted that French, German, and Italian folktales resembling the stories told by the Cáceres narrators "are historical documents which have evolved over many centuries and have taken different turns in different cultural traditions" (1984: 13). Darnton is particularly critical of mechanical Freudian interpretations, which identify psychic universals in folktale content. He notes that Freudian critics interpret fairy tales "like patients on a couch, in a timeless contemporaneity" (13). He correctly observes that narrators from specific cultures and historical periods tell the same stories differently because their worldviews change over time and space. One must approach the storytelling dialogue between men and women with an ear toward universals, while also recognizing the individual cast each narrator gives to his or her tale.

Maria Tatar (1987) has wrestled with the general and specific qualities of the Grimms' *Nursery and Household Tales*, and her conclusions are helpful for understanding how Cáceres women and men talk to one another through storytelling. Tater recognizes that the Grimms' tales bear the stamp of their times and the masculine voices of Jacob and particularly Wilhelm Grimm, who changed the stories in various published editions of their work. She also notes, however, that their fairy tales have a narrative structure like that which Vladimir Propp (1979) identified for Russian wonder tales. Tatar (1987: 55) further observes that many of the stories deal with dramatic family situations—including cannibalism, child abandonment, incest, and fratricide—which invite Freudian interpretations. To be sure, these situations are related to the hardships of family life that may have prevailed at the time the stories developed and began circulating in oral tradition. But the plots, when examined in their entirety, also express the struggles of childhood as recalled by adults. Tatar (74–75) notes that some tales resemble to a remarkable degree the family romances Freud (1968: 236–241) discovered in some of his neurotic patients who preserved and sometimes strengthened their childhood daydreams. Freud's patients saw themselves as stepchildren; they expressed hostility toward their siblings, replaced their father with men of high status, and obtained revenge in their fantasies. Tatar (74–75) notes many continuities between daydreamers and heroes in the Grimms' fairy tales, but cautions against taking the comparison too far. Whereas daydreamers reject their parents, fairy tale heroes experience parental rejection in such stories as "Snow White" and "Hansel and Gretel," illustrating how storytellers and story collectors censor expressions of children's feelings toward their parents.

The same themes in the Cáceres tales of courtship and marriage clearly invite a similar psychoanalytic interpretation. Bettelheim (1977) offers a penetrating psychoanalytical analysis of European fairy tales similar to the stories I collected in northern Extremadura. His interpretation stresses how the characters stand for children as they struggle to achieve maturity, resolve their Oedipal and Electra complexes, and transfer their affection from an opposite-sex parent to the man or woman with whom they bond in heterosexual love. Bettelheim's interpretations apply to the symbolic content of stories about courtship and marriage because courting men and women must separate from their parents and conquer their Oedipally based fears in order to live in intimacy during married life.

Bettelheim, however, does not consider how stories contain timeless themes expressed in specific ways by particular narrators. He does not compare masculine and feminine variants of the same stories to uncover the contrasting male and female points of view. He does not examine how men and women express their views of heterosexual love to one another through the telling of fairy tales. Few folklorists have considered how women and men express to one another through storytelling their similar and different views about parental separation and heterosexual love. Many recognize the importance of the narrator's voice in the telling of a tale (see Dégh 1969; Georges 1969; Bauman 1986; Rowe 1986; Tatar 1987; Bottigheimer 1987: 10–11), and some have examined how men tell tales differently from women (Baldwin 1985; C. Mitchell 1985). Folklorists, particularly those influenced by the theories of Mikhail Bakhtin,[10] have begun to pay particular attention to dialogue in storytelling, but few have considered how men and women grapple with their differences through telling tales of courtship and marriage to one another.

There are at least two requirements for a study of the storytelling dialogue. The first is a setting like the villages in northern Extremadura where women and men tell tales publicly and in the presence of one another. The second is a balanced interpretive approach that is sensitive to masculine as well as feminine concerns. Feminist scholars have drawn attention to the misogynist aspects of Freudian theory and the male-oriented nature of psychological anthropology, which has attempted to broaden psychoanalytic theory by its cross-cultural application. Chodorow (1978: 104–107) argues that psychological anthropologists have paid more attention to male than female developmental concerns. The focus on male psychological development probably originated with Malinowski (1929), who believed that only the relationship between fathers and sons varies cross-culturally and who took mothers and daughters for granted. Spiro (1982) radically revised Malinowski's ideas, but he did not examine the relationship between women in Malinowski's original study. Chodorow (1978: 104–107) believes that anthropologists attempting to offer cross-cultural generalizations about personality development failed to appreciate fully the relationship between mothers and daughters. Chodorow (1974, 1978) and Gilligan (1982) modified psychoanalytic theory to make it less male biased and more applicable to feminine as well as masculine concerns. Their work suggests not only how boys and girls separate from parents differently, but also how men and women develop conceptions of heterosexual relationships based on their contrasting early childhood experiences. It logically follows that women and men, who narrate stories of courtship and marriage, will express different views of the marital relationship. I have consequently balanced the more traditional masculine perspective of Bettelheim and Spiro with the feminine view of Chodorow. A more balanced approach is necessary because I focus on a dialogue through storytelling between men and women based on stories told by narrators of both genders.

I have approached the dialogue by asking male and female narrators to speak about their lives, linking their personal experiences to the content of their stories, and considering their tales as responses to the ideas that one gender has about the other. The contours of the dialogue, identified through a comparison of male and female stories with similar themes, fit many psychoanalytical generalizations about the development of gender identity, particularly if one considers the feminist reinterpretation of Freudian theory on mothers and daughters. The tales, however, also express how general psychological themes are adapted to family life in northern Extremadura. Family structure is bound to affect storytelling because narrators who tell the tales of courtship and marriage express values and models of conjugal relations learned in their families of origin. Emmanuel Todd (1988) identified four types of family systems in the regions of Europe that produced many of the popular tales like those told in the Cáceres villages.[11] Todd's work, although not focused on folktales, suggests a possible correlation between family structure and subtle but important aspects of ideology likely to become manifest in the ways narrators tell stories differently depending on their family background.

The rural Cáceres family is characterized by equal inheritance of land and houses by all children regardless of their gender, a strong conjugal bond, complex lifelong ties between mothers and daughters, weak ties between fathers and sons, and men who trade the nurturant care of their mother for that of their wife. This type of family is by no means universal in Europe, where Todd identifies three other family types with different relational configurations. Following Todd's line of reasoning, one would expect that different family systems would produce different models of parent-child relationships that become translated into similarly contrasting models of heterosexual love. One would also expect that women and men growing up in the rural Cáceres family would have very different perspectives on heterosexual love because women are the primary parents of boys as well as girls, and women have stronger filial ties than men.

## THE STORYTELLING DIALOGUE

Women and men work through their differences in storytelling prior to, during, and after courtship. Few courting couples spend their time sitting around the fire telling tales of heroes and heroines disenchanting maidens and young men. But many hear and tell common stories about courtship and marriage in mixed-gender settings in the home, among neighbors, and in work teams. Men and women carry out a dialogue in storytelling through which they share their different perspectives on love, family life, and gender relations. They tell the same stories but change them in subtle but clear ways according to their different male and female points of view. One can not directly observe the process of feminizing and masculinizing stories because the retelling takes place over a long period of time, storytellers do not always remember from whom they first heard a particular tale, and many narrators heard performances of the same tale from several storytellers before committing it to memory. The storytelling dialogue is indirect because it takes place through the language of metaphor and involves an exchange of views over a series of storytelling events. That a dialogue takes place, however, is indisputable when one examines many tales and notes consistently different male and female themes. Evidence of a dialogue consists of common stories known to male and female narrators, reports from men who said they learned their tales from women, and reports from women who said they learned their stories from men. I shall infer the contours of the dialogue by comparing masculine and feminine versions of the same stories.

In the dialogue through storytelling, older women communicate with younger women, maidens talk to one another, men and women exchange impressions, and men reinforce their own ideas about gender relations. The exchange of images takes place in the telling and retelling of stories that build on one another. The narrators, who hear of gender images in one tale, will modify those same images in another tale as they attempt to illustrate their views of gender relations and influence others. The stories feature heroes and heroines who represent the young men and maidens at different stages in the transition from daughters to wives and sons to husbands. The dialogue, when taken in its entirety, contains many exchanges that mediate the interlocked and contradictory male and female worldviews to facilitate cooperation and the development of intimacy in courtship and marriage life.

The chapters in this book follow the stages through which a man and a woman emerge from their parental families and bond in heterosexual love. The process is slow and complex, like the long and difficult courtships and the long and complicated plots of the stories themselves. The story considered first is "The Innocent Slandered Maiden," which describes a heroine caught in the clash between male sexual assertiveness and female defensiveness. The story considers the heavy costs to women who face male sexual predation and lose their moral reputation. Men tell the same story to acknowledge the problems of women, an essential first step in mediating the discordant male and female perspectives. They suggest less threatening ways of looking at men in their relations with women to mitigate fear in a culture in which men and women live according to different expectations for sexual conduct.

To protect maidens from losing their chastity and moral reputation, older women tell younger women "The Maiden and the Thieves," which warns maidens about the safe-appearing but dangerous sexual predators who might come to court them and remove them from the protective care of their parents. The older women personify their fears of men in the thief who lives in the forest. He is the seducer of innocent maidens; he will deflower a maiden with brutality and violence and will take the woman he marries away from her parents to live in the forest with cannibals. Men retell the same tales from the point of view of the thieves, affirming that they are really vulnerable and needy of women's nurturance.

Women grapple with their complex ties to parents, which remain strong throughout the life course in their telling of "Snow White," a story about a daughter's separation from her mother. The heroine is a maiden at a mature stage of development who is ready to conquer some of her fears of men. The women who tell this story present the male characters in less fearful and more human form: they give the heroine refuge in the forest after she has been cast out of her family and as she struggles to develop her independent feminine identity. Men retell the story to persuade women to trust them and marry them, a message that maidens, like the heroine, are not quite ready to hear.

Women tell "Cinderella" among themselves to communicate the idea that the illusion of love, as necessary as it is, may wax and wane during the course of courtship and marriage. They share their experiences as women who receive the compliments of love from a man while establishing their own independent feminine identity and dealing with a competitive mother-in-law unready to give up her role as the nurturer of her son. Men turn the story around and speak through the prince, who tries to create the illusion of love, illustrating that romantic love is very different for a man. It is brittle and can break suddenly, totally, and forever.

A man has a brittle conception of love because he fears that the woman he loves may betray him and he will lose his masculine honor. That fear develops in a competitive society in which one man can take away the honor of another man by dishonoring his sweetheart, his wife, or a member of his family. Every man has the potential to lose his own or take another man's honor, and a young man who comes to court a maiden is a potential threat to her father's honor if she is seduced and abandoned. Men express their view of male competition for and through women in dragon-slayer tales, which symbolically express the universal Oedipal situation in which a father and son compete for the affection and loyalty of the mother. Their stories recast Oedipal rivalry in terms of competition between a father and his son-in-law for the affection of a maiden. Women pay heavily for male sexual competition and recast the same stories to persuade men to settle their differences in order to avoid putting the woman in the difficult position of having to choose between her suitor and her father. Men tell women in the same tales that, although male competition is to be expected in a courtship, men can forgive each other if no one has dishonored the other by breaking the elaborate rules of courtship. Women suggest to men that they should see courtship less as a competitive struggle between two men and more as the creation of an alliance between a man and his courted maiden's mother.

Older women tell younger women, ready to make the transition from courtship to marriage, animal-groom stories to help them lay aside their fear of defloration and learn to bond with a man in heterosexual love. Their tales describe a gender division of labor according to which women show their love and devotion to men by healing rifts in the marital relationship, which testifies to the power of a woman's love. Men retell the same stories to express how they too can overcome their own sexual anxieties and they affirm the gender division of labor and their need for a woman's devotion.

Men and women address all of these discordant themes and the mediation of fear in the grand narrative of "Blancaflor," a very popular tale in Cáceres and Spanish oral tradition. The story presents a model of how women and men can form an alliance in courtship and marriage. Storytellers of both genders tell the tale to affirm their belief that they can transcend many of the contradictory and discordant themes in gender relations by accepting their differences and having faith in the power of a woman's love.

# CHAPTER TWO

# The Context

THE FORTY-TWO storytellers whose tales served as the basis for this book live in eight villages in northern and central Cáceres (see map).[1] Their villages are small, have declining populations, and demographically represent much of rural Spain.[2] El Guijo de Santa Bárbara, whose current population is 691,[3] and Garganta la Olla (pop. 1,133) are two small villages nestled on the southern slopes of the Gredos mountains, which divide northern Extremadura from southern Old Castile. El Guijo and Garganta are part of a string of towns along the Gredos foothills in a region known as La Vera. Immediately adjacent to the foothills is the Tietar River valley, where many from El Guijo, Garganta la Olla, and other communities sharecropped the estates of the large landowners to grow paprika, tobacco, and cotton. The Tietar flows southwest into the mighty Tajo, and in the Tajo River valley is Serradilla, a small agrotown (pop. 2,285) almost in the very center of the province of Cáceres. Above Garganta la Olla and to the west is Piornal (pop. 1,611), the highest village in the province of Cáceres. The tightly clustered houses of the Piornalegos are surrounded by open country that has little agricultural potential and serves primarily as pasture. The Piornalegos support themselves largely by farming the more fertile slopes in the Plasencia valley. In the bottom of that valley and along the banks of the Jerte River are Navaconcejo (pop. 2,000) and Cabezuela del Valle (pop. 2,286), two prosperous cherry-producing communities that have attracted a large number of Piornalegos. The Jerte flows from its source in the north near Tornavacas (pop. 1,524), a few kilometers from the Cáceres and Avila border. Beyond the Plasencia valley to the west is Ahigal (pop. 1,913), and beyond Ahigal is the region of Las Hurdes, where Luis Buñuel made his famous film *Las Hurdes* (Land without Bread) on rural Spanish poverty. The city of Plasencia, at the southern tip of the Plasencia valley, is the commercial center for all eight villages as well as other towns in the surrounding area. Paprika, tobacco, and cotton grown in the river deltas after the Spanish Civil War stimulated the economy of the region in general and Plasencia in particular. Eventually cherry and more recently raspberry production replaced paprika, tobacco, and cotton as the most important commercial crops produced in El Gijo, Garganta la Olla, Piornal, Navaconcejo, and Tornavacas. The agrotown of Serradilla has experienced the greatest

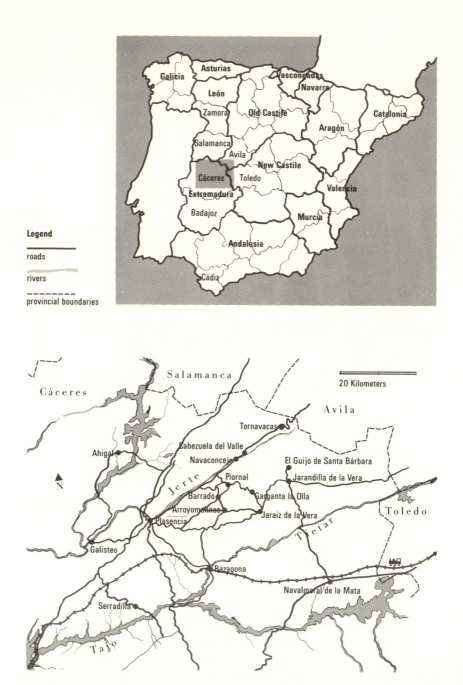

**Legend**

—— roads

~~~~ rivers

- - - provincial boundaries

amount of permanent emigration as wheat and truck farming lost their commerical importance.[4]

The eight communities are close to one another and have connections through storytelling described later in this chapter. They differ in their village economies and their internal class structures, and cover the range of rural manifestations of the Cáceres variant of Spanish culture.

## COURTSHIP AND MARRIAGE

One might expect the families of the landed aristocracy to court and marry very carefully to protect their wealth in many times and places throughout Spain. But Richard and Sally Price (1966b) describe marked differences related to wealth in courtship among families who courted during the first decades of the Franco regime in the classless village of Los Olivos in Andalusia. A look at the experience of Los Olivos couples, as described by the Prices, will help place the Cáceres narrators in historical perspective because they came of age at about the same time in Spain. Los Olivos men and women with the same amount of land tended to marry one another, the rich had longer courtships, and the poor experienced more broken courtships. Courtships became longer and more formal among poorer families in Los Olivos after the end of the Second Republic and during the first few decades of the Franco regime. Women after the Spanish Civil War may have promoted more formal courtships because they were insecure about finding a mate in a society that had lost so many men on the battlefield (Price and Price 1966a: 315). George Collier (1987: 181–185) and Jane Collier (1986), however, who did fieldwork in Los Olivos for intermittent periods from 1963 to 1983, also connect courtship to the political economy of rural Spain. The more formal courtships emphasizing premarital and marital chastity rested on the conviction that the position of one's children depended on their legitimacy, which guaranteed their inheritance. Those with the most property were more concerned with chastity and legitimacy, but the landless were still affected by the same moral code because they depended economically on the more propertied members of their communities and had to conform to their values. Conformity to the values of the landed elite became particularly apparent after the Spanish Civil War, when leftist families, less committed to the value of marital chastity, faced stigmatization by the wealthier members of their community.

Most of the male and female storytellers in the Cáceres villages are the rural poor who came of age before or during the early decades of the Franco regime. They share the value of premarital chastity for women and publicly manifest less conjugal intimacy than their children and grandchildren, who have a somewhat different worldview. The younger men and women I know, however, valued the stories told by their parents and particularly their grandparents, and a storytelling dialogue takes place across generational as well as gender lines. The stories older men and women tell about courtship and marriage have historically specific as well as timeless themes. An understanding of the values of their generation, as they were manifested in courtship, will help place their stories in the proper social and historical context.

Their long courtships, in which a young man (*mozo*) and a courted maiden (*moza*) moved toward intimacy, took place in accord with ideals of masculinity and femininity similar to those in many other parts of rural Spain. Many who observed rural Spanish social life when most of the narrators came of age describe the young man acting assertively in an effort to win the esteem of others with demonstrations of manliness (Pitt-Rivers 1966; Lison-Tolosana 1983). Carmelo Lison-Tolosana, whose fieldwork took place between 1958 and 1960 (1983: ix), describes how a man had to assert himself gallantly in his affairs with women. He had to steer a careful course between appearing too morally correct (*tonto*) and excessively aggressive and crude (*sinvergüenza*). He could not seduce innocent maidens, and he had to use discretion when conducting his affairs with women of more experience. To fail to find this middle course was to fail to maintain his moral reputation in the community. The posture of the woman was more defensive because she had to protect her honor (*honra*) by protecting her chastity. A maiden might engage in flirtations with gallant men as long as she avoided any hint of losing her virginity. A married woman had to protect at all times against the appearance of losing her marital chastity. If the maiden or married woman failed to maintain her moral reputation, she became a woman without shame (*sinvergüenza*) or a woman who failed to maintain her feminine honor. If a maiden was regarded as a *sinvergüenza* she had a very difficult time making a good marriage (Lison-Tolosana 1983: 316–334).

The Mediterranean codes of honor and shame, manifest in gender ideals and behavior, have a complicated history (see Persistiany 1966; Schneider 1971; Schneider and Schneider 1976; Davis 1977; Gilmore 1987b). Timothy Mitchell offers an interesting account of the historical origins and development of honor and shame in Spain. Drawing heavily on the work of Julio Caro Baroja (1957), Mitchell (1988: 41–46) asserts that most scholars located incorrectly the origin of the honor code in the individual when they should have started with the group. The codes of honor and shame were firmly established in medieval times, when households and lineages engaged in intense, often violent competition to be worth more (*valer más*) than the other. Honor and ignominy were hereditary qualities, and ignominious groups restored their honor by shedding the blood of those who affronted them. Shame (*vergüenza*) referred to several qualities, including respect for parents, elders, and kings; modesty; honesty; and piety—all of which helped maintain in-group solidarity and directed hostility toward others. Feuding between groups decreased between 1480 and 1530 as monarchs gained power, local groups lost solidarity, and honor and shame became individual concerns. The codes persist in villages today through socialization, a task largely in the hands of women, who spend much more time than men with young children (see Lison-Tolosana 1983: 333; Brandes 1975: 112–117; Gilmore and Uhl 1987).[5]

The evolution of male-female relationships was a complex process much like the complicated plots of the folk and fairy tales told in this and other parts of Spain. Cáceres men, in accord with the ideal of masculine assertiveness, were expected to take the initiative in courting women, just as male protagonists in stories take the initiative in disenchanting maidens. A maiden faced hazards if the man who courted her was too sexually assertive, if his or her parents did not approve of the match, and if a formal courtship came to an end before marriage. The male storytellers I know made it clear that a maiden from a broken courtship often remained single or married a man of lower social status. Broken courtships were problems for women of the same generation in many parts of rural Spain (see Price and Price 1966a) because men feared that women courted by other men had probably lost their virginity. Pitt-Rivers (1966: 96) noted that a young man could lose his honor in retrospect if he discovered that the maiden he courted had lost her virginity with another man. A maiden, however, could still be choosy about the man she married, and parents could prevent their sons and daughters from marrying partners they considered unsuitable by breaking off relationships before they turned into formal courtships. Knowing the point at which an informal relationship became a formal courtship was very important for maintaining a maiden's reputation.

Although few went to schools, because they had to work with their parents, young men and women had many other opportunities to get to know one another. Young men could meet maidens going to the fountains for water, attending church, taking strolls in the late summer and autumn afternoons, and working in the paprika and tabacco harvesting groups in the Tietar River valley. Maidens, concerned with guarding their moral reputation, stuck close together and spent little time alone with the young men of their villages. Gradually, however, they developed relationships that evolved into courtship and eventually into marriage. Most of the storytellers describe courtships beginning at dances held in many communities in conjunction with saint's day celebrations. Maidens were free to dance with many young men as the first step in developing a relationship that might turn into a formal courtship. Florencio Ramos, age sixty, from

Navaconcejo, said his wife probably danced with "fifty thousand," but he was the only one who became her official sweetheart (*novio*). Florencia Herrero, age sixty-eight, from Garganta la Olla, described how, as a young maiden, she rushed from working in the river valley below her community to attend the dances held in her village on the days of San Antonio and San Martín Bendito.

Segundo García y García describes how informal relationships began in his natal village of Ahigal during the early decades of the Franco regime: "When an individual finds a young woman pleasing, he invites her on Sunday afternoon to dance two, three or more times. If the maiden does not refuse, it is a sign she is not indifferent." Eventually, after villagers commented on the budding relationship, the young man says, "Listen . . . they say we are sweethearts." To that the maiden replies, "Well, if that is what they say, it's fine," and the relationship leading to courtship begins (García y García 1955: 49). Florencio Ramos (from Navaconcejo) said he began his first courtship by writing to a third party to discover if the maiden he wished to court was interested in him. He said: "When I was in the military, I wrote to a cousin of the woman I eventually married. Then the maiden said she loved me." Guillermo Castaño (from Garganta la Olla) said he wrote a letter of his intentions to his future wife, Petra, when she was working in Navalmoral de la Mata. When Petra replied to his letter, the two began making arrangements for their marriage, which took place on Christmas Eve in 1929. Guillermo probably knew how Petra would reply to his letter because Petra is from the same small village and the couple had many mutual friends.

However the relationship was initiated, the man in Cáceres was expected to assume a ritualized role asserting his intention to the maiden's parents to formally begin the courtship. The man looked for his bride (*buscar la novia*) by selecting a friend to accompany him, bearing a leather wine bag (*la bota*), and to ask entrance to the maiden's parent's house (*pedir la entrada en casa de la novia*). Marcela Vicenta Moreno describes the ritual as it was performed in Piornal and her description applies, with small modifications, to all eight Cáceres communities. Marcela's account begins with the appearance of the young man at the door of the maiden's parental home:

> The young man arrives and says, "Good evening."
>
> "Good evening," replies the maiden's father.
>
> "We've come here to ask for access [*entrada*] to your daughter [the hand of your daughter in marriage]," says the friend.
>
> So then [the father] goes and says, "Well, if they love each other, we don't have anything to say."
>
> Then the young man who comes courting says, "Yes, I've spoken with her."

She has welcomed me [*Ella me pone buena cara*]." Then he says, "Come take a drink from the wine bag."

And the father says, "No, not now. We don't have a desire for wines. It'll have to be left for a calmer time."

Well, the young man and his friend serve from the wine bag. Then they leave.

It was customary in Cáceres villages for the young man to take the initiative to visit the maiden, to whom he declared his intentions, in the evenings and on Sundays, when men normally did not work in the fields. Young men were expected to act gallantly with their courted maidens, who were expected to defend their premarital virtue. The woman's posture of guarding her virginity was undoubtedly one reason that maidens are depicted as enchanted in stories about courtship. Enchanted maidens are held prisoner in castles, fall into a deep sleep, or are turned into stone. Enchantment represents a state of unawakened sexuality and is often caused by the action of another. The one who enchants the maiden in stories could represent the members of the maiden's family, particularly her father and mother, who had the responsibility of making sure she kept her virginity during the long period of courtship.

Courtship was arduous and complicated, much like the long and complicated plots of stories about disenchanting maidens. Courtships normally lasted at least a couple of years, with many lasting longer. Florencio Ramos (from Navaconcejo) courted the woman he eventually married for a year and a half. Other couples faced unusual circumstances that led to much longer courtships. Benedicta Sanchez and Arsenio Cruz of Serradilla courted for six years, a period of time Benedicta considers excessive. She explained that their courtship was extended considerably because Arsenio was called to serve in Franco's army during the Spanish Civil War. No doubt, longer courtships frequently took place in Cáceres villages, as they did in other parts of Spain (Pitt-Rivers 1966: 93–94; Brandes 1975: 119).

One of the purposes of the long and complicated courtships in Cáceres was to prepare for the new couple's household, which involved the accumulation of property and capital. Preparations began with the accumulation of the trousseau (*ajuar*), which in Cáceres, as in other parts of Spain (Freeman 1970: 73–77; Brandes 1975: 164–171; Behar 1986: 104–121), consisted of items provided by both the man and the woman. The customary contributions were ritualized expressions of the roles of women and men in the sexual division of labor. The preparation of the maiden's trousseau began long before courtship, when she was ten to twelve years old. At that time she began, with the help of her family, to sew and buy sheets, quilts, and kitchen implements, including a glazed earthen pot (*puchero*) for making stews (*cocidos*), frying pans, glasses, caldrons of various sizes, lids, a copper kettle, and kerosene lanterns. The young man was expected to provide blankets and the bed. In earlier times, couples slept on straw beds (*jergas*) and the groom ritually fetched cornstalks to put into the mattress before marriage. The groom also had the obligation of finding a house, normally rented rather than owned. Some families helped the groom by providing a suckling pig (*lechón*), cured hams and sausages, potatoes, olive oil, and, nowadays, money. Few couples inherited land at the time of their marriage; married sons often sharecropped land owned by their father or father-in-law and worked as wage laborers during the early years of marriage. The division of the family estate took place much later, just before or after the death of the property owner.

Marriage in Extremadura was marked by a large number of complex rituals (see García y García 1955: 53–62; Foster 1960: 139–140). In Piornal and the other villages in Cáceres, the courting young man asked the maiden's parents if the couple could marry; they then set the date and published the banns of marriage. On the day of the publication of the banns, all of the relatives, godparents, and friends of the couple were notified to come with baskets of cheese and bread to feed all of the villagers. The next day the bride and her family had a meal in the house of the family of the groom, and they arrived with guitars or accordions to make the rounds (*ir a ronda*) through the streets of the village singing wedding songs. After the meal, the mother of the groom gave to the bride a large wicker basket for clothes, another basket for bread, and a round earthen jar with a spout and handle for water, a lid for the olive oil jar, a mortar and pestle, a broom, a *tajuela* used for kneeling when washing clothes in the river, and a towel. The dinner concluded when the guests walked arm in arm singing through the streets of the village as the family of the groom accompanied the family of the bride to their home. The wedding party rested until the day of the wedding, which took place after the period of the banns had ended (fifteen days).

The wedding day itself was filled with ritualized events beginning with breakfast in the homes of the families of the groom and the bride for all of their invited guests, the wedding ceremony in the church, a banquet, a dance, and a supper for a more select group than those invited to the banquet earlier in the day. Guests at the wedding banquet in Cáceres, as in other parts of Spain (Brandes 1975: 167), contributed money and gifts to the new couple, and in many villages this practice involved collecting money with an apple (*la manzana*). Segundo García y García describes the practice for his native Ahigal (1955: 55–58). He tells how young maidens, at the conclusion of the wedding banquet, "arm themselves with a long spit, sticking on it the biggest apple they can find." They traveled to the tables of the young men, who customarily sit apart from the maidens, and sing songs requesting and taunting the young men to contribute generously by sticking money on the spit or tossing coins into a small basin carried on a tray. A good collection can help a couple pay for the costs of the wedding banquet and complete preparations for their household. Florencia Herrero of Garganta la Olla married in the year of hunger in 1941 and received thirty-five duros in her *manzana*. Thirty-five duros equals 375 pesetas, which in 1941 in Garganta represented thirty-four days' wages for Florencia's husband, who earned eleven pesetas a day working for her father.

The wedding ritual continues into the night and the following morning. After the wedding supper, the groom takes the bride to their home to put her to bed. Marcela Vicente Moreno (from Piornal) gave the following account of what happens next, based on her own experience as she likes to tell it to her neighbors:

> There they sit on chairs with the bed all messed up. Their friends had messed it up. Then the bride cries and cries, as happened to me whan I married. Nevertheless, afterward the groom says to her, "Let's make the bed. If we don't, we won't have anything else to do but sleep on the floor." So then, well . . . he gives a kiss to the bride. They close the door, and she stays there with the groom until the next morning, if God wishes. Well, don't you know? On the following day, the godparents of the marriage bear the expenses. They go to wake them in the morning. They take them hot chocolate and *churros* [fried pastries] for breakfast. Afterward the bride and groom go have lunch in the house of their godparents. The godfather bears the expenses of the entire day: lunch, dinner and supper.

### Postmarital Residence

The ritualized accumulation of property by the bride and the groom enables most couples to set up their own independent households on the first day of their marriage. I conducted a census of household composition in Garganta la Olla to identify the patterns of postmarital residence. Garganta was chosen as the site of the census because the storytellers of that community told a great many of the tales on courtship and marriage considered in this work, and I spent more time in Garganta than in the other villages. According to the results of that census, most couples actually did reside neolocally from the time of marriage, particularly in recent times because the greater affluence of contemporary couples makes it easier to accumulate the items for a new household. Out of 221 married couples living in Garganta, 133 have always lived neolocally in households that are independent of the parents of both spouses.

A number of couples, however, remain attached to their parental families after marriage, and their patterns of attachment described statisti-

cally probably reflect the configuration of masculine and feminine sentiments in the family. Young married women generally remain more
attached to their parental families than do young men (see Table 1).
Among younger attached couples who are just starting out, more reside
with the parents of the wife (matrilocally) than with the parents of the
husband (patrilocally). Moreover, more younger couples live independently in houses owned by the parents of the wife than the husband.

The close ties of women to their parents continue throughout the life
course because older married women more than older married men assume the primary responsibility for the welfare of elderly parents unable
to care for themselves. Although most elderly parents rotate among all
their children to share the burden of their care, those who remain permanently attached to one child place themselves in the care of one of their
daughters much more often than in the care of one of their sons (see Table
1). The cold statistics on Garganteños household social composition express very warm and complex ties between daughters and parents

TABLE 1
Postmarital Residence of Married Couples in Garganta la Olla

| Patrilocal Couples | no. | Matrilocal Couples | no. |
|---|---|---|---|
| Young couples currently with the parent(s) of the husband | 5 | Young couples currently with the parent(s) of the wife | 11 |
| Couples living in house owned by husband's parent(s) | 5 | Couples living in house owned by wife's parent(s) | 6 |
| Elderly parent(s) living with a married son | 2 | Elderly parent(s) living with a married daughter | 11 |
| Couples who used to live with the husband's parents but now live in independent domiciles | 14 | Couples who used to live with the wife's parents but now live in independent domiciles | 16 |
| Wife from another town and husband from Garganta | 5 | Husband from another town and wife from Garganta | 7 |
| TOTAL | 31 | | 51 |

throughout the life course. The patterns described statistically for Garganta fit the life experiences of several Cáceres narrators, experiences that are described in later chapters in order to illustrate how storytellers introduce autobiographical material into their stories. Most narrators have always lived neolocally; but some started out matrilocally and a few lived patrilocally. The tendency toward matrilocality in Garganta and other communities appears elsewhere in Spain (Pitt-Rivers 1966: 101–102; Buechler and Buechler 1981) and probably reflects similar emotional ties in the rural Spanish family. Pitt-Rivers noted a tendency toward matrilocality for the small Andalusian community of Alcalá, where the "emotional tensions inherent in family life assert themselves, and the identification of the woman with the home overrides the principle of patriliny" (101–102).

The different emotional ties of women and men to their parents are entirely in accord with the ideals of femininity and masculinity manifested in courtship and in stories about courtship and marriage. Women, who have a defensive posture in courtship, remain attached to their parents, who guard their moral reputations. Moreover, women, according to Cáceres ideals of femininity, are selfless in their nurturance and care for others. Judging from the life histories of the narrators and the statistical patterns of household social composition, women are oriented to the nurture and care of others from maidenhood to the end of the life course. Feminine narrators recalled how as maidens they prepared food and cared for children, and how as older women they nurtured elderly parents in addition to working with men and other women in agricultural labor. Their roles in the nurturance and the care of others tie them closely to other family members, as is shown in statistics on household social composition.

Just as male protagonists in stories travel long distances away from home to disenchant a princess, so it is that men appear to be more independent of their parental families than women during courtship and marriage. Men, however, are the beneficiaries of the nurturance and care of women throughout their life course. They are in the care of their mother and sisters as unmarried young men and pass at marriage into the care of their wife. There are a number of reasons why a man's attachment to his parental family does not result in a higher frequency of patrilocality. Stories circulating among women in Cáceres oral tradition describe considerable tension between women when a maiden takes over the nurturant and caring role of her husband's mother at marriage. Thus neolocality or even matrilocality may prevent the tension between mother-in-law and daughter-in-law observed in many societies in which patrilocality is more common (Foster 1948; Lewis 1951; Nutini 1968; Vogt 1969; Chang 1970).

The tendency toward matrilocality over patrilocality may stem from the desire of sons to avoid their father as well as the wish of daughters to remain close to their mother. Michael Murphy (1983a, 1983b) offers an interesting interpretation of father-son conflict in urban Seville that helps explain the preference for matrilocality over patrilocality in rural Cáceres and other parts of Spain. Murphy refers to Pitt-Rivers's (1966) distinction between honor as virtue and honor as precedence to explain father-son avoidance, one form of which is a preference for any postmarital arrangement other than patrilocality. A man protects his honor as virtue when he maintains the moral reputation of his women and he protects his honor as precedence by demanding "the display of deference from inferiors" (Murphy 1983b: 653). Honor as precedence is what creates a conflict between fathers and their adolescent sons leading to various forms of avoidance, including neolocality or even matrilocality. The father attempts to maintain his moral reputation by demanding deference from his son, who struggles to establish his own reputation for manliness by showing independence. Marriage generally marks the passage of an adolescent into adulthood, but the vestiges of an earlier struggle create a strong preference among married men to live apart from their father even if that means living with the family of their wife.

Men nevertheless remain attached to their parental family in ways not apparent from statistics on household social composition. Many young married men sharecrop their parents' land, which they will eventually inherit many years later. The actual division of land takes place late in life, frequently near or after the death of parents. Florencia Herrero of Garganta la Olla recalled how her family called in a notary to witness her father, fallen from a stroke, nodding his head in agreement to a bilateral division of his property. The actual division did not take place until after his death, many years later (see Florencia Herrero's account of the division in Chapter 5). Neolocally married men, such as Juán Julian Recuero of Serradilla (whose "The King Don Damadá" is listed in the Appendix), worked as a partner with their father in the harvest of wheat and other crops.

## Recent Changes

The social pressures for formality in courtship apparently decreased in rural Spain with the collapse of the labor-intensive agrarian economy in the 1960s.[6] Many couples turned to wage labor outside of their community and relied less on the landed aristocracy or the propertied elite, who reinforced the value of premarital chastity (J. Collier 1986; G. Collier 1987: 181–185). The traditional moral order of the early Franco period came to an end because many families no longer saw themselves dependent on the inheritance of a landed estate. Censure by the wealthy meant less when the landed elite lost its relative economic importance and its power to enforce its strict moral code on others.

The collapse of the traditional agrarian economy affected the ideals of marital intimacy perhaps more than courtship among women who came of age in the 1960s. Women of courting age before as well as after the collapse were free to enjoy themselves as long as they were reasonably careful about their sexual modesty (Price and Price 1966a; J. Collier 1986: 103). Jane Collier (1986: 103) observed the sharpest change among modern married women, who do not see public manifestations of modesty as contributing to the future of their children. They no longer dress in drab clothing, they take greater pride in their appearance, and they no longer accept the traditional gender segregation in marriage. Women of different generations do not understand one another's point of view; older women believe that enjoying themselves means squandering their children's inheritance, a belief their younger counterparts do not share.

Older Cáceres men and women generally agree that morality is changing. Florencia Herrero (Garganta la Olla) and Florencio Ramos (Navaconcejo) said that premarital chastity does not have the same value today that it did in the past. Florencia Herrero declared that no one cares at all about premarital chastity anymore, and Florencio Ramos said the same thing a little differently.

> They say today they don't care about [chastity] because two become sweethearts, and someones says, "But she was the sweetheart of Fulano! He probably slept with her all he wanted." Her new sweetheart says, "What's that to me? I've also slept with eighty, and so on and so forth." But in those days it wasn't that way because the woman with whom you got involved was the woman you married. And one did not want the other to have been with anyone, and the other did not want the first one to have been with anyone else either. That was then.

I observed contemporary courtships and marriages that conform to the values of the storytellers' generation, making me suspect that older men and women exaggerated the degree of change in their communities. Elders in areas where I have done fieldwork in Mexico as well as Spain generally romanticized the values of past generations. To be sure, villages have discotheques playing modern popular music, young men and women question their parents' values and chafe at parental control, and some openly flaunt village morality. Many village couples, however, still court under the watchful eyes of a maiden's parents, young men still formally announce their intention to change a relationship into a courtship, and couples still marry in the church. Few family planning centers distribute birth control information, and maidens feel vulnerable to pregnancy if they have sex before marriage. Young women who remain in villages still face strong pressure to be sexually modest, and many of their counterparts, whose values differ most from those of their parents and grandparents, probably migrated out of their communities with the collapse of the rural agrarian economy. In a personal communication Ruth Behar noted that many of the twenty- and thirty-year-olds from rural León live together, do not marry, and do not baptize their children. I suspect that some emigrants from the Cáceres villages follow the same pattern, but I did not come across them in my study.

The Cáceres family changed in some subtle but important ways after the older storytellers came of age. Older couples in Garganta were more heavily dependent on their parents for financial support right after their marriage despite the widely held ideal of setting up an independent nuclear family household. Patrilocality occurred more often in the past; several older couples from Garganta reported that they began their marriage living and working with the family of their husband (see Table 1). Nearly as many older couples in Garganta resided patrilocally as matrilocally in the first years of marriage, and most who started off with their husband's family said that they sharecropped with their husband's parents. Many sharecropped land with their parents, growing tobacco, paprika, and cotton in the Tietar River delta after the Spanish Civil War.

One can readily understand how newly married sons would establish their greater independence from their father after changes in the rural agrarian economy created new wage-labor opportunities and permitted young men to acquire more easily the resources necessary for establishing an independent household. Father-son conflict, arising from the desire of each to maintain his personal reputation for masculinity (Murphy 1983a, 1983b), probably drove many young men who came of age in the 1960s to rent or even buy a house when the opportunity arose. Mothers and daughters, however, have a different kind of relationship, one that does not hinge on honor as precedence; consequently the rate of matrilocality has remained about the same over the generations covered by the census of Garganta la Olla households. Daughters today, like their counterparts of yesterday, still rely on their mother for help, particularly for the care of young children.

Despite all of the changes, men and women in the Cáceres villages still face many of the same issues when they approach marriage. Today as well as yesterday, a man must establish his position in society, temper sexual assertiveness with gallantry, come to terms with his fear of women, and transfer his devotion from mother to wife. A woman must conquer her fear of men, be willing to endure defloration, develop an independent identity from her mother in a society in which mothers and daughters still have a great deal of interdependence, shift her loyalties from her parents to a spouse, and contend with a jealous and critical mother-in-law. Courting men today, just like their counterparts of earlier generations, still must meet the approval of a maiden's father and particularly her mother. Florencio, age sixty, and his son Bernardo, age thirty-four, both courted women whose mother persuaded her daughter against the match. The older narrators tell many stories addressing timeless as well as generationally specific themes in their storytelling dialogue.

## STORYTELLING

One of the ways young men and their courted maidens learn about courtship and marriage is by listening to stories that circulate in oral tradition. Although there are no stipulated occasions for telling the stories, most appear to circulate in intimate settings within families. They pass between families when school chums gather or neighbors relax on sunny afternoons and warm evenings. They travel between villages when families of one community settle in another, when men and particularly women work in teams (*cuadrillas*) to harvest paprika and tobacco, and when sharecroppers from different villages grow paprika, tobacco, and cotton in the Tietar River valley.

Storytelling is not an overtly competitive activity. I observed no organized storytelling contests in any of the Cáceres villages, although organized contests featuring other kinds of folkloric performance do regularly take place in Plasencia during tourism week in the summer. I know of no liars' contests featuring storytelling from the seven villages like those that exist in other European countries (Mark 1987). Storytellers seem to perform their tales to entertain and transmit culture from one generation to the next.

### Storytelling in the Family

Most of the storytellers who could remember said that they learned the tales they knew from close family members. The experiences of the narrators from the seven villages where I collected tales are similar to those of other narrators from different parts of Spain. Larrea Palacín (1959: 16–18), who took the care to report on the origin of tales in the repertoires of Andalusian storytellers from Cádiz, noted that most said they too had learned tales from their close family members, particularly parents and grandparents.

A few of the Cáceres narrators are like Mercedes Zamoro Monroy of Cabezuela ("Cinderella"), age seventy-six, who said she learned her tales from an aunt who read her stories from books, Mercedes committed the stories to memory and then told them to her daughters when working in the kitchen. Mercedes is unusual, however, because most narrators said they learned their tales from close relatives who had heard them from others rather than read them in printed sources. Women and men mentioned parents and grandparents more frequently than others as the sources of their tales. Because few parents and grandparents of living narrators in the seven Cáceres villages went to school, it is likely that most of their tales have circulated in oral tradition for a number of generations.

Storytellers often mentioned learning their tales while sitting in small, intimate mixed-sex gatherings next to the kitchen hearth or the brazier (*brasero*) around the small round table (*camilla*) in the kitchen or dining room.[7] Felisa Sanchez Martín (from Serradilla) said: "When we were young, since there was no television, people gathered, men the same as the women, sitting at the fire, and there everyone told us what they knew. And that is how I learned from them." Florencio Ramos (from Navaconcejo) also said that he learned his tales by the warmth of a fire. He spent his childhood in a large dwelling called "the Factory," which housed several families who owned or rented portions of the building. The second floor contained a very large open room where several women of different families made their kitchen hearths. Florencio said:

> I learned all the stories there because they took me to that house when I was two years old. There I entered my age group. That is to say, from the time I arrived there, I lived for nineteen years and passed through my childhood. There were old women who lived there. There were at least seven, eight kitchens, and then, at the end of the day everyone gathered around one. And with an oil lamp, there we were all lighted. And then the women there, one would tell an anecdote, another would tell a story, another something else. One would say, "Look here, the daughter of Fulana is pregnant." Another [would say], "Her sweetheart left her." They spoke of all those things there. And the boys, since they had their ears so perked, then more than now, they put the tales in their heads and that is the way it is.

Storytellers mentioned other intimate family settings as the places where they learned the stories in their repertoires. Narcisa Justo Perez (from Serradilla) said that she learned "The Innocent Slandered Maiden" from her husband, who put their children to bed by telling them stories. Julio Lopez Curiel (from Garganta) said he learned his tales from his grandmother, with whom he slept as a child. María de Pilar Corrales Sanchez (from Serradilla) acts out a modified version of "Hansel and Gretel" when playing with her three-year-old daughter, María José. She recalls: "When I tell her that the children's mother is ill, and the children go into the forest for firewood and they have no blankets, and they make a fire, María José says that her mother has a headache, grabbing her head. 'And then they see a light,' and she points to her eyes with her finger. 'And the little house was of chocolate and caramels, and they eat a window,' and she points, running to the window."

Juán Julian Recuero described how he learned the tale "The King Don Damadá" from his uncle in a hut (*choza*) in the hinterland of Serradilla and gives some perspective on the length of time the story has circulated in oral tradition. He said: "This story my uncle Primitivo Gíl told me. We were in the country and since there the nights are so long in the hut, one is caught up in telling stories. And Tío Primitivo said his grandfather told it to him and his grandfather's grandfather told it to his grandfather. He had a house there where they lived on the plain, which is quiet out there. The house had a back door. And he says smugglers came there, to the house of his grandfather's grandfather. The smugglers came and entered through the back door, and no one knew. And his grandfather's grandfather told stories so the children would not know the smugglers were there."

It is interesting that Marciano Curiel Merchán, who collected stories from the region in Cáceres in and around Trujillo, and who was from Garganta la Olla, noted that he learned the popular story "La Flor del Lililón" from a woman servant who told it by the warmth of the fire on the long nights of winter. He wrote: " This story, forty years ago, I heard it told various times, being a child, when a servant of my home, who, by the loving [warmth] of the fire and on winter nights, told it to my brothers and to me in my natal village, Garganta la Olla, a lovely little town, nestled in the heart of the very beautiful region of La Vera of Plasencia" (Curiel Merchán 1944: 187).

## Storytelling between Families in Villages

Although stories appear to circulate in intimate settings and as part of particular family traditions, villagers have many opportunities to learn stories that do not necessarily circulate among the members of their own families. Eugenio Real Vázquez (from Serradilla) said he learned his tales when he went to school. He was sixty-five-years old when I knew him and he recalled how he learned his versions of "Snow White" and "Blancaflor" when he was much younger: "That was when were were kids. We arrived at school; we were a bigger group then. Because in those days, there was a tradition of stories and things because we gathered as friends on the corner, when we were fourteen, fifteen, or sixteen years old. And there one told one story and the other another one and so on." Evarista Moreno (from Cabezuela) said she also learned the story of "Blancaflor" in school. She was thirty-three when she told me her stories and she recalled how she learned her tales as a young girl: "It was in school that we told it. We were going to school. The girls were in a group, and we told one another stories."

Neighbors of the same villages tell one another stories when sitting in front of their homes in small groups on warm afternoons and evenings, after the midday meal and before the late evening supper. Elderly women, a few younger married women, and children gather in small groups in the early afternoon. The women sew and crochet and sometimes tell stories, sing *romances*, tell anecdotes, or just comment on the news of the day. Warm weather brings most out of their homes, but women in Garganta gather on the porch of the town hall to enjoy the afternoon sun throughout the year, even in cold weather.

Two storytelling performances in Garganta, one by a woman and the other by a man, illustrate some of the variation in narrative events among neighbors. On a late summer afternoon, I came to the house of Florencia Herrero, age sixty-eight, while she was telling her version of "Hansel and Gretel" to a group of small girls whose ages ranged from about eight to eleven. Florencia was sitting in a chair flanked by other neighbors, who were mending and crocheting. Florencia is married but has no children of her own and told her tale to neighborhood girls who were sitting at her feet. Each listened intently and looked up to Florencia as she delivered her tale in a soft but animated voice, keeping her eyes on her work. No one interjected a comment, and all waited quietly until Florencia reached her conclusion. Then several asked questions about details of the plot that they did not understand.

Neighborhood groups become more sexually integrated at nightfall when young men return from work in the fields and older men come home from their card games in the bars. On an evening in the summer of 1981, Julio Lopez Curiel, age seventy-four, told his version of "The Soldier" in Garganta. Tío Julio is regarded by his neighbors as one of the best masculine storytellers in his community. The storytelling event took place because Tío Julio heard I was in the village to collect stories. Word about my interest in storytellers had spread from his wife's sister, in whose house I was living at the time. Tío Julio walked slowly to the neighborhood, which included men returned from work in the fields, as well as women. Someone offered Tío Julio a chair at the highest point on the sloping ground. In a booming dramatic voice, he narrated "The Soldier," which took about twenty-five minutes. His delivery, like that of Florencia, was primarily a monologue because he did not invite comments from the audience. On other storytelling occasions, however, Julio engaged the members of his audience in a dialogue by posing questions requiring brief answers indicated by a yes or a no or the nod of the head. For example, when telling his version of "Snow White," Julio located the action of his story on a well-known road from Garganta to Jaraíz and asked his audience if they knew exactly the spot he was talking about. Julio and other narrators frequently size up an audience and periodically ask questions as part of their delivery to make sure their listeners understand every aspect of their narratives. It is common for all storytellers to ask members of the audience if they know the meaning of infrequently used words. It was clear to me that Julio's tales had a dramatic impact on his listeners because they broke their silence at the conclusion of his stories and remarked to one another on Tío Julió's incredible memory and skill with words.

## Storytelling between Villages

Stories pass from village to village in northern Cáceres through a number of channels: (1) storytellers from one village have permanently settled in other villages; (2) narrators have temporarily migrated to other communities where they work in teams (*cuadrillas*) composed of young men and women from a variety of different villages; and (3) many from communities with little available arable land have sharecropped outside of their communities on land made fertile through irrigation made possible by the construction of dams after the Spanish Civil War.

Navaconcejo has a large contingent of Piornalegos, who have introduced their stories into Navaconcejo oral tradition. Many Piornalego families moved to Navaconcejo to sharecrop and eventually bought land for producing cherries. Twenty-three years ago Filomena Arivas Miguel ("The Maiden and the Thieves" and "Cinderella") and her husband moved from Piornal to Navaconcejo, where they first herded goats and then sharecropped land and raised suckling pigs owned by others, splitting the profit with the owners of the animals. Eventually they, like many other Piornalegos living in the community, including Valentina Prieto ("Cinderella"), were able to buy their own house and land for raising cherries, the most important cash crop in the region.

Stories circulate among neighboring villages when young men and women from different communities join work groups to harvest paprika and tobacco in Jaraíz. Children, boys as well as girls, accompany their parents, and some reported learning tales from older women in the paprika and tobacco harvesting groups. Zacaria Iglesia ("The Wager on the Wife's Chastity" and "Cupid and Psyche"), for example, went with his adoptive mother to Jaraíz, where he learned most of the tales in his repertoire. With the introduction of cherry and raspberry production, few depend as heavily on wage labor in paprika and tabacco cultivation as they did in the past. Nevertheless, women described their migrant labor experience with detail sufficient to reconstruct storytelling situations among paprika and tobacco workers.

Paprika powder is used widely in Spanish sausages and soups and comes from a sweet pepper (*pimiento*) grown in Jaraíz and along the banks of the Tietar River. Paprika is harvested in September, October, and into November by work groups consisting of twenty-five to thirty men and women. Many recruits come from El Guijo, Garganta, and Piornal, as well as from other villages in the region. Women primarily told stories because their role in the sexual division of labor in the paprika harvesting and processing teams permitted them to sit in groups for long periods of time.

Men harvest the paprika and take it to the second floor of the drying barns, where every morning they open the slats in the barn walls and build fires on the ground below to dry the peppers. The dried paprika is piled in a big mound on a tarpaulin and the women gather around the mound and remove the seeds, later used for planting. Men smash the husks with a hammer in the first stage of grinding the paprika into a fine powder. The telling of stories—some very long narratives—the singing of *romances*, and the exchanging of jokes and anecdotes often takes place among groups of ten, fifteen, or twenty women as they sit around the mounds of paprika removing the seeds. In good weather, the women sit under the trees and in bad weather on porches or in the barns.

Many Garganteñas and Piornalegas joined work teams as young girls (*mozas*), and some continued to work until several years after marriage. A great deal of contact between storytellers of different villages took place in the paprika processing groups of Jaráiz. Domitila Prieto Perez from Piornal ("Snow White" and "Cinderella") worked in paprika processing teams in Jaráiz from the time she was twelve until three years after her marriage. Filomena Arivas Miguel, who is from Piornal but has lived in Navaconcejo for twenty-three years, worked as a maiden in the paprika and tobacco teams, where she met many other maidens from Garganta la Olla.

Women likewise told long narratives when working on teams removing and plaiting the leaves of harvested tobacco. Normally men cut and load the tobacco and take it to the drying barns in September and October. They suspend the crop on wires, where it dries until the first rains in autumn. At that time, the women remove the leaves, which are easily stretched, and plait them into bundles ready to be taken to the storehouses for classification. When sitting in groups of seven or eight, they plait the leaves and tell stories or sing *romances*, joke, gossip, and exchange anecdotes. While some women worked on tobacco-harvesting teams as maidens, others, such as Domitila, said that they worked as married women because tobacco began to replace paprika in the region.

Stories also circulate among storytellers of different villages with the temporary migrations to the lowlands made fertile because of irrigation from dams constructed after the civil war. Many from Garganta, including some renowned storytellers (Tío Julio, Guillermo Castaño, Ulalia García, and Juana Moreno), sharecropped paprika, tobacco, and cotton near Galisteo, Bazagona, and Talavera de la Reina (Toledo) alongside others from a number of different communities in Cáceres. Guillermo Castaño specifically remembers hiring workers from Serradilla. Several from Serradilla recalled encountering people from Garganta in sharecropping regions near Galisteo and elsewhere.

Families, peers, neighbors, co-workers in paprika and tobacco work teams and groups of sharecroppers have overlapping membership. For example, Domitila Prieto Perez (from Piornal) sat outside her home on warm afternoons with her neighbors, who were former members of paprika- and tobacco-processing groups that migrated to Jaraíz. Tío Julio and Guillermo Castaño (from Garganta) sharecropped in Galisteo. The overlapping members of different groups have a sense of a complete and well-told story, and listeners frequently remark after the conclusion of a tale that they have heard the story in a similar or a different form.

## Storytelling and Tale Variation

The nature of the storytelling process contributes to family variants within communities and community variants within regions. When close family members tell tales to one another, they appear to work toward a consensus of the story plot greater than that found among peers and neighbors, who circulate the same stories less frequently. For example, when Bernardo Ramos told a variant of "The Fisherman" in front of his father, Florencio Ramos (from Navaconcejo), from whom he learned the tale, Florencio interrupted his son to correct his memory on one of the details of the plot. On this occasion Bernardo began the story and his father finished it. On a subsequent storytelling occasion when Florencio was not present, Bernardo told his version of "The Fisherman," which closely resembled the tale his father told earlier.

Neighbors who are members of different nuclear families probably hear different family versions of the same stories less frequently and thus probably arrive at a weaker consensus. When Gregoria Ramos Merchán (from Piornal) narrated her long version of "Blancaflor," her neighbors waited quietly for her to finish and then burst into an animated discussion of their different recollections of the plot of this widely known tale. To justify any differences between her version and those of her neighbors, Gregoria replied that she had recounted the tale precisely the way it was told to her. This experience was repeated with a number of other storytellers when they performed among neighbors who were not members of the same nuclear family. Just as there are family variants within a village, so there are variants circulating within particular communities. For example, Eugenio Real Vázquez and José Díaz Sanchez (from Serradilla) told variants of "Blancaflor" that contain elements of the plot not found in variants of the same story told by masculine storytellers from El Guijo de Santa Bárbara and Navaconcejo.

There is no question that Spanish storytellers, like their counterparts from other cultures (Georges 1969; Bauman 1986), tell their tales in different ways depending on the storytelling context. María de Pilar Corrales Sanchez (from Serradilla) tells a variant of "Hansel and Gretel" to her three-year-old daughter, María José, that is very different from the one that Florencia Herrero (from Garganta) told to the young girls, whose ages ranged from eight to eleven. Storytellers consider certain tales appropriate depending on the audience, although this varies with the personality of the individual. Natividad Corrales (from Serradilla) did not consider "The Wager on the Wife's Chastity" a story appropriate for telling to her children, but Narcisa Justo Perez (also from Serradilla) did. Older women in all of the Spanish villages where I collected tales considered themselves privileged to tell spicy stories, as long as young maidens and other men were not in the audience. Younger women appeared to censor the content of spicy stories when telling them to me. The stories considered in this study are tales that narrators considered entirely appropriate for a mixed audience made up of men and women of different ages.

### Storytelling between Women and Men

Storytelling occasions in families, among neighbors and peers, and in paprika- and tobacco-harvesting groups are sufficiently integrated along gender lines to permit an indirect dialogue between women and men through storytelling as narrators take tales heard from a person of one gender and change them according to their own concerns. The dialogue through storytelling is only one of many ritualized exchanges between women and men that folklorists and anthropologists have described in rural Spain. Brandes (1980: 136–157) gives a fascinating account of the ritualized exchanges between women and men during the olive harvest in Andalusia. Men and women engage in banter with clear sexual innuendo sometimes expressing gender antagonism. Sexual innuendo and gender antagonism can be found in the folkloric exchanges between men and women in the Cáceres villages as well, although I did not make them the focus of my study. The most prominent examples I observed appeared in a revived Carnaval ritual in Garganta that involved public displays of transvestism like those in other parts of Mediterranean Europe (Counihan 1985).

The exchanges between the genders through storytelling are indirect.

The dialogue through storytelling takes place over a long period of time and does not involve a direct confrontation of women's and men's points of view like that which occurs during the olive harvest of Andalusia or the Carnaval. A woman will hear a story from a man on one storytelling occasion and tell the same story on another after she has forgotten precisely how the man originally told the story to her. Men and women introduce small, incremental changes to story plots, character development, and expressive language as they masculinize a story told by women or feminize a story told by men.

There appears to be a marked difference to the way men and women perform a story. Tío Julio delivered "Hansel and Gretel" in a style different from that of Florencia Herrero or any other woman who told a tale on any storytelling occasions that I observed in Garganta. Moreover, he clearly modified the story content in ways that resemble other masculinized stories collected from men in Garganta and the other villages. By careful comparison of the content of parallel stories, one can see how tales told by women and men differ in the use of language and in the depiction of parallel courtship and family situations.

## The Collection of Stories

The study of the ways women feminize stories normally told by men and the way men masculinize stories normally told by women requires the comparison of a number of stories with similar plots. I could not have obtained a sufficient number of tales to carry out a meaningful comparison had I limited the collection of tales to spontaneous storytelling situations. It was necessary to solicit tales from narrators to record all of the stories they were willing to tell. I generally recorded tales in storytelling situations that were similar in all seven communities. Usually stories were recorded among groups of adult neighbors warming themselves in the afternoon sun or sitting around a table in the dining room or the kitchen. I made it my practice to sit with groups of neighbors and wait until one seemed ready to tell a story to the tape recorder in front of peers. I obtained a few tales from men in bars who regularly sat together to play cards, talk, and drink wine. In most instances, storytellers performed in front of others who had heard them tell the same tales before. A very small number of tales were collected in interview situations where narrators told their stories to me with no one else present. I recorded all stories that narrators considered themselves competent and willing to tell in public. A small, hand-held tape recorder was used to collect the stories, and I transcribed the texts while in the field. Native speakers of the Cáceres variant of Castilian Spanish corrected the transcriptions. Those who helped correct the transcriptions came from Ahigal, Garganta la Olla, Navaconcejo, and Plasencia. This study focuses primarily on tales dealing with courtship and marriage, but I collected many other narratives dealing with other themes.

CHAPTER THREE

# "The Innocent Slandered Maiden"

JULIAN PITT-RIVERS (1966: 112–221) and Carmelo Lison-Tolosana (1983: 331–327) noted for rural Andalusia and Aragón, respectively, that the maiden and young man enter courtship under diametrically opposed social pressures. The young man is socialized to assert himself sexually to establish his manliness, and the maiden is taught to guard her premarital virginity to protect her feminine honor. Lison-Tolosana (1983: 331–333) describes the social pressures compelling the young man to be a Don Juán and the maiden to resist his *Donjuanismo* as complementary positions, each requiring the existence of the other.

Most observers of rural Spanish village life conclude that women are in charge of socializing of children, and many have noted how parents, particularly mothers, have very different expectations for their sons and daughters according to the sharp contrasts between masculine and feminine adult behavior (Brandes 1975: 112–117). On the one hand, mothers carefully guard the modesty of their daughters, and on the other, they encourage their sons to be assertive in their manliness. Lison-Tolosana wrote of his native community of Belmonte de los Caballeros in Aragón: "The mother, so jealous in guarding her daughter's modesty, is openly satisfied when she learns that her son is successful with girls and is regarded as a Don Juan; *huele a hombre*—he smells like a man, she says" (1983: 333). The contrasting expectations of the Aragonesa mother apply equally well to mothers in the villages of Cáceres.

The interlocked themes of male assertiveness and female defensiveness create tensions in gender relations that can clash in courtship in rural Cáceres. Florencia Herrero, a sixty-eight-year-old woman from Garganta la Olla, illustrated the clash with an anecdote about a virtuous courted maiden who defended her modesty with a young man just before their wedding was scheduled to take place. This anecdote illustrates Florencia's belief that contemporary morality is changing in Garganta la Olla, and through it she asserts her own moral values by idealizing the conduct of past generations. She said:

> I heard a very old woman—she was very old when I was young—say that in those days the friars were in the hermitage of San Salvador. They were in their prime then when the bride and the groom had to go up to the hermitage for the firars to discipline them, to examine them, as one used to say. They had to go

up at night to where the firars were. It seems the weddings always took place then around San Andrés when the money from the paprika harvest was collected. There would be two or three, six or eight couples. But one time it was the turn of one couple and they were alone. Upon arriving at a plot of land, an orchard that is called "La Medrana," he was saying some words that were a little roguish. And it seems she didn't like them because in those days, of course, modesty and purity were guarded so much. It was not like it is now that there is no chastity whatsoever. Chastity was guarded a great deal then. And as she went on in that mischievous situation, with him saying things to her, they had to carry a lighted candle in their hands. Then she dropped back. She dripped wax on a rock and left the lighted candle there. He was thinking that she had stopped to urinate or something. He did not dare to go down to her, but upon turning the corner at the place called "the Saddle Tree," he saw she wasn't coming. She left the candle there, went to the little house of the Torrontueros, and spent the night. With that, the young man, who saw she hadn't come up, went back and couldn't find her. He had to come home and tell his parents. They went out looking for her all night but they didn't find her until morning.

The position of the young maiden defending her modesty according to the ideals of femininity is complex because if she breaks her courtship, she may reduce her chances of making a good marriage. Men in Cáceres, like their counterparts in other parts of Spain (see Pitt-Rivers 1966: 96), say that men generally avoid entering into a courtship with a woman who has had a history of broken courtships because they fear the woman has lost her virginity with another man. Florencio Ramos of Navaconcejo described his view of maidens with broken courtships, a view that is shared by many men in all of the villages I know in northern and central Cáceres. He said: "When I was a young man, the maiden who made herself the fiancée of a young man, and it was one month, two months, one year, two years that he went into her house and they went here, they went there, and then he withdrew, well, then it cost that maiden a great deal of work to hook up with anyone because, of course, it was said he had walked with her. Do you know what I mean?"

According to Florencio, a broken courtship does not affect the moral reputation of the young man in the same way it affects that of the maiden. Florencio went on: "The man, not having children, would never lose anything. The man, almost in reverse, almost gains fame because they label him a man who is alive with women. The man, yes, the man almost always gains fame with that." The major exception occurs when the courted maiden becomes pregnant and does not marry her sweetheart; then both the maiden and the young man who has broken his engagement with her stand to lose a great deal. Florencio explained it in the following manner: "Now, if by chance he is careless, he has a child with the sweetheart, and he leaves her, he also has done very badly. Afterward no one wants him. The maidens will all flee from him. The family of another maiden would say to her, 'That so and so.' Because one sees that this one was the sweetheart of Fulana, and he made her a girl or a boy, and one then sees he left a wretch. And then the other maiden would hold herself back and, of course, would not want him. Understand? But if he did not have a child, he would not lose anything. The one who would lose would be the maiden. The maiden would lose a lot, a lot." Florencio further explained what he meant by using an example. "Here in front lives one who has a good deal of money and she had a boy. Some say that it was with that one who was her sweetheart and her sweetheart later withdrew and the woman, of course, was left with the boy. She had to raise him and no one said anything, as is natural, to that woman. And she had a lot of money. And then after much time had passed, a poor unmarried man appeared who didn't have anything; he was already an old bachelor. And she married him."

Florencia Herrero ended the anecdote described above without saying whether or not the maiden from Garganta la Olla who defended her pre-marital virtue actually went through with her marriage. She left the ending up to others, who can speculate about the consequences for a virtuous maiden who ends a long courtship in a culture in which men are suspicious of women once courted by other men. Florencia illustrates one possible scenario in her telling of the popular folktale "The Innocent Slandered Maiden" (AT 883A). The feminine protagonist in this folktale also defends her premarital virtue, but she discovers that women who keep their chastity may pay heavily for male sexual predation because they may lose their feminine honor. This tale has considerable continuity over space and time probably because it addresses widespread and timeless themes in gender relations. A number of narrators in other Cáceres communities told variants of the story, and their tales will be discussed later in this chapter to illustrate how women and men tell the same story differently. The tale has continuity over time because the Cáceres variants share many elements of plot and character development with a story Aurelio Espinosa collected from an unknown narrator in Ciudad Real in the early 1920s (1924: 199–202). The stability of this story over time illustrates that although Florencia Herrero believes that sexual morality is changing, some of the same themes persist in gender relations over six decades of Spanish history.

## "THE INNOCENT SLANDERED MAIDEN," BY FLORENCIA HERRERO

Once there was a couple who had a daughter, just one daughter, and were very well off. They put her in a convent to give her an education. One day when she was in the convent—I don't know if someone was pursuing her or what—

she threw herself out of the window and left. She got herself a job as a servant in a house that had a store. And she understood the business very well because her parents had a store too. They were delighted with her. And a captain who went there a lot fell in love with her. She was very beautiful. He asked her, "Do you want to go to the movies with me?" She said, "Yes, I'll go." Although she was troubled, she was a happy person, and she married him.

After they were married, the captain's assistant fell in love with her. And every day the assistant brought her milk and did her shopping because captains have their assistants do those things. She had a child, and the child was very small. Then one time the assistant asked if he could make love to her. She said no, and he tried to take her by brute force. So she threw herself out of the window and escaped. And after she threw herself out of the window, the assistant decided the only thing to do was grab the child and throw it against the wall of the room. He killed the child, then went running to the captain and said, "My captain, my captain, your wife has gone crazy. She killed her child. See for yourself. It's in the room. She threw it against the wall and killed it. Then she took off." The captain went looking for her but couldn't find her.

Instead of dressing as a lady, she dressed as a gentleman and called herself Sugar Plum [*Periquillo*]. "Now I'll have to go begging again," she thought. "Let's see what'll happen." She went to her parents' town. And as the fates would have it, the captain and her father were good friends, and so they were all there together. And she got herself a job in her parents' home. Her father asked her, "What's your name?" She said, "My name is Sugar Plum." And her father was very contented, very happy. He said, "Oh, we've been grieving because our daughter died some years ago." She asked, "What happened to her?" He said, "They took her to be educated by the nuns. They wrote us that she hadn't been ill or anything, only that she died, and we went to the burial. Since then we've been grieving a lot. We haven't reopened the store." She said, "Why don't you open it? I'll clean up the dust and everything." So joy filled the house again. The captain continued coming around and—my God!—they saw each other every night. And the captain, her husband, joined her father. And the assistant joined them. Her insides were stirred up, and she said, "Good, someday I have to arrange to bring to light what happened to me."

Then she said to her father, "Don't you think, sir, that you ought to invite the Captain and his assistant to supper soon because you get along so well with them?" He said, "Oh, yes, Periquillo." She said, "And I'm going to make the supper." He said "yes" because she was a good cook. She made dinner and supper, and her father said, "Take it easy, Periquillo. Let my wife make it." "No, no," she said, "I want to do it." But she did it to please him because she didn't tell them they were her parents. After she made supper that evening everyone went into the dining room. She said, "Well, gentlemen, let's have supper and then tell some stories afterward." After they had eaten she asked, "Did you like supper?" Her father said, "You bet, a lot." Another said, "You'd better believe

it. What talented hands this Sugar Plum has." He said to the store owner, "It's too bad you don't have a daughter. You, Sugar Plum, could marry her." She said, "Fine, but as you know, it's good to hear a story after supper. Each one has to tell his own." One of them said, "As you wish, Sugar Plum." She said, "I'm going to go first. But I'm warning you, he who has to urinate, leave now, eh. And if one of you has a desire to relieve himself, no one can go out the door anymore because I'm closing it. So if someone has to relieve himself, do it in his pants. No one can leave." Then she began telling her story. "Gentlemen," she said, "once there was a father who had a daughter. And they took her to a convent. It turned out there was someone who wanted to take advantage of her in the convent. So she had to leave. She jumped out of the window and left." "Oh, but Sugar Plum," said the captain, "tell more. This happened to me." And the assistant said, "Open the door, Sugar Plum. I have to pee." She said, "Wait if you have to pee. I said no one could leave after I started to tell my story." She continued: "Then she walked until she came to a town. When she came to the town, she started working as a clerk, as a servant in a house. The captain was a customer there. He went there and because he was such a frequent customer he fell in love with her. The two were married after he fell in love with her. And they had a child. But the captain had a soldier who was his assistant. This assistant fell in love with her too." The assistant said, "For God's sake, Sugar Plum, open the door. I have to pee badly." She said, "Wait if you have to pee." And the captain said, "Tell more, Sugar Plum, tell more. This happened to me." She said, "Then one day he insisted so much, and she didn't want to, that he tried to make love to her with brute force. He wanted to take advantage of her. Well, she jumped out the window again. But as for the child who remained in the crib, the assistant grabbed it, threw it against the wall, and killed it. Then he told the captain a lie." "Oh, my! Tell more, Sugar Plum, tell more. This happened to me," said the captain. "For God's sake, Sugar Plum, my guts really hurt me! I have to relieve myself very badly," said the assistant. "If you have to relieve yourself, do it in your pants. But no one leaves here," said Sugar Plum. And her father and the captain said, "Tell more, Sugar Plum, tell more. This happened to me." She said, "Then she went off and came to the house of a gentleman. In the house of that gentleman is where I am today. And here I started working. I'm Sugar Plum. But I'm your daughter. I'm your wife. And you're the one who wanted to take advantage of me. Now I'll change clothes. You'll see who I am when I change my clothes." So in another room she put on the clothes she wore when she left the captain's house. Then they grabbed the assistant and shot him and the captain . . . "*Colorín colorado*," this story has come to an end.

Florencia's formulaic ending—"Colored linnet, this story has come to an end" (*Colorín colorado, este cuanto se ha acabado*)— is used by many narrators and has the effect of shaking her listeners out of the fantasy world of her story and back into the real world of their own lives. The heroine in her tale is like many actually virtuous maidens, including the one in her anecdote, who have faced the improper sexual advances of ungallant men. The story, unlike the anecdote, contains bitter irony because Florencia implies that a priest may have pursued the innocent maiden in a convent where she was sent by her parents for an education. The irony of the first episode is that the slandered maiden faced sexual predation in a place—a convent—where she should have been safe from threat of seduction. A priest as attempted seducer of a virtuous maiden appears in another Cáceres version of "The Innocent Slandered Maiden," discussed later on in this chapter, and is in many other stories told by women as well as men. The priest as seducer is a common symbol of the safe-appearing but dangerous man, a character widespread in Cáceres oral tradition. The priest appears safe because he has taken a vow of celibacy, but he is dangerous because, in the opinion of Cáceres women, he has the same natural urges of other men. The frequent appearance of this character in stories told by men and particularly by women expresses women's fear of safe-appearing men and implies that no men are to be trusted.[1]

The selection of a priest as a symbol of an untrustworthy man is an expression of anticlericalism that developed out of a long history of tension between religious orthodoxy and village belief. Ruth Behar (in press) has explored the historical roots of anticlericalism in the Leónes village of Santa María, which appears to have many things in common with the communities of the storytellers from northern and central Cáceres. Those who live in Santa María, like their counterparts in Cáceres, have strong egalitarian values that conflict with the hierarchical model of society represented by the church. Many of the parish priests are native sons whom villagers regard as equals, and some priests have assumed attitudes of superiority and attempted to force their orthodoxy on rural communities in ways that deeply offended the villagers. In Santa María, the struggle between parish priest and village over orthodoxy became particularly intense during the early decades of the Franco period when many of the Cáceres narrators, such as Florencia, came of age. Behar notes that the parish priest, who served Santa María after the civil war, punished villagers for uttering the common blasphemous and scatological expressions "I shit on God" and "I shit on the Virgin" by making their users attend mass while kneeling in the front row of the church or else pay a stiff fine. Moreover, one priest discovered the names of the blasphemers by using his uncle as an informer! The long history of opposition between church and village, which appears to have been particularly acute during the early decades of the Franco era, consequently contributed to a refusal to regard priests as the "bearers of true faith" (Behar in press: 23). General anticlericalism coupled with priests' reputation for breaking the rule of celibacy (Behar in press: 19–20) undoubtedly lie behind Florencia's and other narrators' selection of a priest as the first man who attempts to seduce the innocent slandered maiden.

The events following the innocent maiden's flight from the convent illustrate what can happen to a woman who defends her feminine honor from a sexual predator. It turns out that her parents were not curious about what actually happened to her. They receive a letter telling them of her death but providing no details; they are not told that she had become ill. They attend her funeral without investigating any further and then begin grieving her death. The reaction of the innocent maiden's parents probably illustrates how, when faced with the attempted seduction by a treacherous man, women feel abandoned by even those who have the primary responsibility of guarding their premarital chastity. The innocent slandered maiden's flight from the convent could easily stand for the actual flight of innocent maidens slandered by the members of their community (see Lison-Tolosana 1983: 333). Although I know of no cases of slandered maidens fleeing from Garganta la Olla, the maiden's departure from the convent in Florencia's story illustrates the difficult position of women who may be innocent but nevertheless face gossip about their sexual conduct.

The maiden's marriage to the captain and the second attempted seduction by the captain's assistant further illustrate in the dramatic language of a story the tremendous costs of male sexual predation to women. Florencia illustrates the costs by depicting the captain's assistant brutally murdering the heroine's child by throwing him against the wall when she refuses the his improper advances and defends her marital chastity by jumping out of the window. The subsequent events illustrate how a woman as a woman is totally powerless to defend her reputation against slander. The assistant lies to the captain about the death of his son, the captain makes a weak attempt to find out what really happened by looking for but failing to find his wife. So the heroine must dress as a man, change her name to Sugar Plum (*Periquillo*), and return to her parental home to restore her reputation with her father and her husband and bring the assistant to justice. She succeeds by returning to her grieving parents, who coincidentally are good friends of her husband, and setting the stage for bringing the truth to light. She extracts a confession by telling the story of her life while still dressed as a man, and only after the truth comes out does she change back into woman's clothing.

## Feminine and Masculine Versions

Men as well as women tell the tale of "The Innocent Slandered Maiden," and the comparison of their versions illustrates some of the ways the genders view male sexual predation differently. It is ideal to compare masculine and feminine variants from the same storytelling community, where men and women are likely to have heard the same tales from one another on a variety of storytelling occasions. Below are two additional variants from Narcisa Justo Perez and José Díaz Sanchez, who are both from Serradilla, are about the same age, and know many of the same stories circulating in the oral tradition of their community. They told closely related versions of the slandered maiden tale, illustrating their respective points of view. A comparison of their stories reveals some of the contours of the dialogue through storytelling between women and men. Narcisa Justo Perez, a widow of sixty-two, learned her version of the tale from her late husband, who used to tell their children stories to make them go to sleep. Her tale is consequently a feminized version of a story originally told by a man.

### "THE INNOCENT SLANDERED MAIDEN," BY NARCISA JUSTO PEREZ

Once there was a couple who had two sons and a daughter. They had a very beautiful garden, and the father told the daughter to water the flowers in the garden every day. And a priest fell in love with her. She asked herself, "Is this priest chasing after me?" Speaking bluntly, he asked her to make love with him. She said no, under no circumstances. Then she said, "Well, if you do what I say, then, yes." He said, "I'll do anything you say." So she told him, "Please bring me a bucket of water from the well." And as the gentleman was fetching the bucket of water from the well, she grabbed him by the legs. Splash! She threw him into the well, and she left. She said, "My God! I've drowned the priest! Oh, my God, I've drowned him." So she told her parents. The authorities came, took him out of the well, and he was alive. And the priest sentenced her to die and demanded they bring him her eyes. Oh, what a frightening idea! And her father said yes. She'd done a very horrible thing, a very bad thing against righteousness. He'd do it.

One day her father told her two brothers, "You have to go kill your sister. You have to take her and kill her in the highest mountains. And you have to bring her eyes wrapped in a piece of paper." And the younger brother said to the older one, "Are you going to kill our sister?" The oldest said yes. The younger one said, "Well, I won't." His older brother asked, "But why?" "Because I won't. I saw a dog whose eyes are just like our sister's; we're going to kill that dog, take out its eyes, and bring them to father. The priest will see them and he'll think we really killed her."

They dressed their sister very beautifully, as if she were a bride. And they went away in the car, and once they were in the highest mountains—it was at night, very late at night—the youngest brother said, "Well, sister, the moment has come." And the older brother said, "Let's kill her." The little one said, "No! I won't kill sister. We'll kill the dog whose eyes are a lot like sister's. They're the same, and I won't kill sister." And his brother said, "Well, we won't kill her," even though he wanted to. They killed the dog and wrapped its eyes in a piece of paper and got into the car and said to their sister, "Look, you make your life any way you can. You can never go back to town, never, because you know what you've done. And father told us to kill you."

So she started walking. She walked and walked and she spotted a light in the distance. She said, "I must go where that light is. Let's see what I can do there." She came to a hut. A few shepherds were there, and their dogs charged her. They barked at her until the shepherds called them off. The shepherds saw a very beautiful young woman who was dressed all in white. And she said, "Will you please give me lodging tonight? I'm lost." One of the shepherds said, "Yes, lady, we'll give you lodging." She spent the night there. The next day after breakfast she said, "I have a favor I'm going to ask of you." "You tell us what it is," said the shepherds. She said, "Exchange my dress for the clothes of a shepherd." "But why do you want to exchange this dress of a lady for the clothes a shepherd? Your dress is so beautiful, and the clothes of a shepherd are very ugly." She said, "I want you to do this favor for me and I'll be very grateful from the bottom of my heart." The shepherds exchanged clothes with her because they had daughters.

And she said, "How shall I earn a living?" Dressed as a shepherd, she went to the closest town and passed through the plaza. And she went to the town hall and said, "Don't you need a secretary?" And a boy came out onto the balcony and said to her, "Are you a secretary?" She said, "Yes, sir. I'm a secretary." He said, "Wait a minute while I ask my father. Let's see if he needs one." He told his father, "There is a man here who comes dressed as a shepherd. He asked if we need a secretary." "What's he like?" The boy said, "He's very handsome." The father said, "Let's see, tell him to come up." And the "man" went up. The boy's father gave him a sum. He added it up. They gave him another one. He added it up. And he did everything they told him to do. The boy's father told the gentleman, "You stay here with us." It was shameful that he lived with them dressed as a shepherd because he went everywhere with the son. "Let's buy him the clothes of a gentleman." And he went with [the mayor's son] to the taverns, the casinos, and everywhere. And one day the young man said, "I have to know if you're a woman or a man because you're very handsome." That is, the man was very handsome. And he had the hands of a woman. Well, one day the mayor's son got him very drunk and the two of them went to bed in the same room, but each one in his own bed. And then, because it was summer and it suited the shepherd, he slept uncovered from the waist up. And the mayor's son went over to his "brother." He called out, "Brother." He touched him so. He said, "Careful you don't get in trouble. Your honor is intact." And now "the boy" had her work cut out for her because it was known she was a woman. She wasn't a gentleman. And after two or three days, the mayor's son told his father, "The gentleman we have here isn't a shepherd.

She's a lady. She's a young woman. Keep it a secret that she's a young woman. Don't let anyone know. I took it upon myself the other night to see if she was a woman or a man. And she's a woman." Now that his father knew it, they went to the store. They bought her women's clothes and all was well. On top of that, the young man fell in love with her.

The young man went into the army. And he spent a lot of time, many years, without writing his father. The maiden stayed with his parents and had a child. And his parents grew weary of her. But she had her child and had no recourse but to pick up again and leave. She left, and as she crossed a bridge at night, she met some thieves. They took her child. One of them said, "Give us your child or we'll kill you. One or the other. No matter what, you have to give us the child because we'll kill you if you don't." "Oh, my God, blessed Christ. Don't kill me, don't kill me. I'll give you the child, if that's what God wants." She gave the child to them, and she went on to the next town. She came to a store and said, "Please sell me the clothes of a mess steward." "A mess steward? Did you say mess steward?" She said, "Yes, yes. I want the clothes of a mess steward." "For whom?" he asked. "For me." They sold her the clothes of a mess steward. She went to the soldiers' barracks and asked the head of the barracks, "Do you need a mess steward?" And he said, "I don't know if the captain needs one. I'll go ask him." He asked the captain, who said, "Let's see what he's like." "He" appeared. And the captain said, "Come in. Would you dare make me supper? Even though it'll be just for the two of us." The young woman recognized him, and he recognized her, but neither one let the other know. The captain said, "Will you dare make me a good supper? Even though it's for just the two of us?" She said, "Well, let's see." The captain told his assistant, "Don't serve me supper tonight. I'm going to have supper with the mess steward." Well, there they were having supper, and he asked her, "Do you know who I am?" She said, "Yes, I know who you are." He said, "The child I left with you, where do you have him?" She said, "The child you left me with? Your parents abandoned me. And when I saw I was abandoned by your parents, I had no other recourse but to take the child and leave home. I was crossing a bridge with him at night, and some thieves took him from me. So you can see the life I've led." He said, "Let's get married." She said, "As you wish." He told everyone in his company that on such and such a day they would be married. "But during the wedding banquet you have to tell me all you blame, all who have wanted to harm you. Then they'll go to the hangman's noose." When everyone was eating during the wedding banquet, the captain said to his wife, "Now you're going to tell me all who have been your enemies in life. It's all the same to me if it's my father or yours, or whoever it might be." She said, "One who looks like this gentleman propositioned me and ordered me killed. Another man who looks a lot like this one was my father, who told them to kill me. My older brother, who wanted to kill me, is this one. My younger brother told him no. He said take a female dog, take out its eyes, and wrap them up in a piece of paper to give to our father so he might see them. And another who looked like that one, who might be the parents of this one, I found myself hated by them." She said, "I had to leave home. Let them go to the hangman. And some thieves who looked like them, they took my child. They killed him." So then they all lived happily and threw their bones at our noses.

Narcisa closes her tail with a formula different from the one used by Florencia but with the same effect of shocking her audience out of the fantasy world of her story and back into reality. Her mention of "bones" refers to the bones from the wedding banquet, and the "noses" belong to the spectators, including the storyteller herself. Many Cáceres storytellers use this closing formula in their folktales of courtship and marriage that conclude with the successful resolution of a conflict in gender relations as the main male and female protagonists end up living happily as a married couple. Narcisa, like Florencia, develops her picture of conflicted gender relations by describing an innocent maiden who enters the age of court-ship, faces safe-appearing but predatory men, and loses her moral repu-tation despite defending her premarital virginity. This narrator makes more explicit the identity of the first seducer as a priest, a detail Florencia implied but left unstated in her version of the story. The innocent maiden in Narcisa's tale, like her counterpart in the story by Florencia is forced by the attempted seduction to leave her hometown. The circumstances of the innocent maiden's flight and events following, however, depict a dif-ferent scenario for a woman who confronts a sexual predator. In Nar-cisa's tale, the heroine's father and older brother go along with the priest's sentence of death and his gruesome demand for her eyes as proof of her execution even though the maiden defended her virtue. The father and older brother's attitudes illustrate how, in the eyes of women, men tend to believe other men rather than women in their accounting of events. The heroine never tries to explain why she pushed the priest into the well because it is futile for a woman to attempt to influence the opinion of men about the moral conduct of women. Because men believe other men, women like the heroine are in a difficult position because they are vulner-able to male slander. There is bitter irony in Narcisa's tale because the heroine is taken to the highest mountains wearing a beautiful white wed-ding dress on the very day she is to be executed for defending her honor but going against the moral order by pushing the seducer-priest into a well.

Narcisa's heroine ends up abandoned in the forest by her brothers, and she changes her identity by trading her white wedding dress for the drab clothes of a shepherd. At this point she moves temporarily in the circle of men, first getting a job as the mayor's secretary, and then going with the mayor's son to cafés. All goes well until the mayor's son discovers her true feminine identity. Again, even though her honor is temporarily intact, the heroine is vulnerable because she loses her premarital virginity with the mayor's son and bears his child without the benefit of marriage. Her vulnerability as a woman living outside of the moral order becomes particularly apparent when the father of her child goes off to war and apparently forgets about her. Finding herself hated by his parents, she abandons their home with her infant, and while crossing a bridge in some dark place, she loses the child to thieves. The loss of the heroine's child is a detail that Narcisa and Florencia both put into their stories in order to dramatically illustrate the high cost for women of male sexual predation and slander.

The heroine in Narcisa's story must restore her reputation by dressing once again as a man. Narcisa, however, illustrates through the actions of her protagonist that even a woman dressed as a man cannot restore her moral reputation by acting alone. Her heroine must gain the help of another man to bring the truth to light. When the army captain recognizes her as the woman he loved, he arranges for the heroine to identify all who harmed her at their wedding banquet. By virtue of his support, all those who did her harm—the priest, her father and older brother, her parents-in-law, and the thieves who stole her child—go to the hangman.

José Díaz Sanchez told a different version of the same story, illustrating how men vew the difficult position of women created by male sexual predation and male slander. José, a married man in his early sixties, said he learned this tale from his grandmother. There is no way one can reconstruct the original version of the tale because José learned it when he was ten or eleven, and his grandmother died many years ago. It is possible that the original version may have had many elements in the plot shared by the feminine variants told by Florencia of Garganta la Olla and particularly by Narcisa Justo Perez, who, like José, lives in Serradilla; but José's version differs from theirs in clear ways that reflect a masculine worldview.

### "THE INNOCENT SLANDERED MAIDEN," BY JOSÉ DÍAZ SANCHEZ

Once there was a king who had a daughter. The daughter fell ill and she was so ill that the king said, "It's better to take her out of here." He called a servant and said to him, "Tomorrow you take her out as if for a ride. But you drown her in the well that's out there in the country." On the morning of the next day, the servant got up and told the king's daughter, "We're going to the country today." "Oh, very good," she said. They mounted a horse, she behind and he in front. They were very cheerful as they went along, but as they came closer to the well, the servant got very quiet, very quiet. She asked him, "What's wrong with you?" He said, "Nothing is wrong with me." Farther on she said, "Something has happened to you." He said, "No, nothing has happened to me." And they went on. And as they came to the well, she said, "Something has happened to you. You have to tell me." He said, "Look, your father told me to throw you into a well and drown you. But I don't have the heart." In those days one did what parents said to do. The King's daughter went to the well, stood on the horse, and threw herself in.

But a palm tree grew inside the well, and there she was in the middle of the palm tree. She spent one night there, the next day, and another night. The next day some gentlemen came by hunting. They were marquis, and their dogs barked at the well. One of them asked, "What's in the well?" The son of the count looked down and saw a very beautiful maiden. He asked the maiden, "How come you're here?" She said, "I'm in the palm tree." "How come? Who are you?" She said, "I'm the maiden of the palm tree." She said she came from the palm tree. Well, they made something to lift her out. One of the marquis took her home and married her. But a war broke out right after they were married, and her husband had to go to war.

She went out into the countryside and saw a soldier coming. She asked him, "Where are you coming from?" He said, "I'm fleeing from the war. And you?" She said, "I'm going to the edge of the sea." So he said, "Look, let's do this. I'll put on your clothes and you put on mine." And they went off to the edge of the sea. When they reached it, he tried to do some bad things. And she didn't want to. She said, "If you want to do this, you have to bring me the foam that comes on a wave." He said yes. He stooped down, and then she gave him a kick, and he fell into the sea and she came home dressed as a soldier.

Then they all came together in her father's castle. Joining them was her husband, discharged from the army, and the one who took her to the well. They were there having a little party, and the king said, "Let's tell some tales." They said yes. The king said, "Let the soldier tell me stories. Soldiers always know stories." The woman dressed as soldier said, "Come on! I don't know any stories." The king insisted, "Yes, soldiers always know stories." She said, "Okay, I'm going to tell you one." And now she repeated what we've been saying. She began, "One time there was a king who had a daughter, and she fell ill. I compare the king to this gentleman." She pointed to her father. "She fell ill, and he told the servant to take her out one day to the well and drown her. It was as if he were this man." She pointed to the servant. "The next day, the servant went forth and became very quiet before they came to the well. And she asked him what was wrong with him. He said, 'Nothing is wrong with me.' And she kept asking him. It wasn't until they came to the well that he said, 'Look, your father told me I have to throw you into the well and drown you. But I don't have the heart.' She said, 'One does what parents say to do,' and threw herself in. She spent two nights and one day there. The next day some marquis came hunting, as if one were this man" She pointed to her husband. "And after they were married, her husband had to go to war. And she went out and she saw a soldier come, as if he were this other man." It was the one she threw into the sea. "He said, 'Let's change clothes. I'll put on yours and you put on mine.' So after changing their clothes, they went to the edge of the sea, and he wanted to do some things that weren't right. Do you know what I mean? And she said she wouldn't do them. When a wave came from the sea, a spiral of foam appeared on the wave, and she said to him, 'If you want to do this, you'll have to bring me that spiral of foam.' And then, as he went to fetch it, she kicked him, knocking him into the water, and then she came home."

After she said all of this, her husband declared, "Listen, soldier, do you know anything about my wife?" She said, "No, sir!" Her husband insisted, "You have to tell me where my wife is." She said, "You'd know her if you saw her?" He said, "Yes, sir." She said, "Wait a minute." She went into a room and took off her clothes, then dressed as she was before. And as she came out, her husband said, "That's my wife!" She said, "And that's the soldier." And that's it, and they lived happily. Right?

José's story presents a scenario for an innocent but virtuous maiden that has some of the characteristics of the ones presented by Narcisa and Florencia, along with some interesting differences. Like the feminine narrators, José describes the heroine as a victim of injustice in the hands of men, banished from her family, defending her marital chastity, and then assuming the guise of a man in order to restore her moral reputation. The similarities illustrate that men and women share an awareness of the difficult position of women who face male sexual predation. The affirmation of the common plight of a maiden is the first step in the storytelling dialogue, which mediates the fear in gender relations. José's tale also has some interesting differences, which exemplify how men and women view the position of women in contrasting ways according to their gender concerns. José's story cuts down the degree of male sexual predation, presents a critical picture of a maiden's father, reduces but does not eliminate a concern over women's moral reputation among men, changes the circumstances under which the improper attempted seduction takes place, and reduces the costs to women.

The first attempted seduction of the maiden by a safe-appearing but dangerous man is replaced in José tale by a father's cruel punishment of his sickly daughter. The father's punishment has ironic results, illustrating that a father's actions may not be what they seem at first glance. Ostensibly, the father wants his daughter taken to the countryside and drowned in a well because she does not recover from a mysterious illness. No father actually would order his daughter drowned, but many fathers might wish exceptionally passive daughters to enter courtships, marry, and become established in their husband's household. The sickly daughter might represent an unmarriageable maiden who cannot work and is a burden as well as a responsibility for her father. In terms of honor and shame, a father wants his maiden daughter married so he can transfer part of the responsibility for maintaining her feminine and, by extension, family honor to her husband. The father's punishment thus could be a metaphor for a father's desperation to marry off a maiden daughter slow to enter a courtship. He takes action that ultimately results in his daughter's marriage because she is rescued and marries a marquis who finds her sitting in a palm tree inside the well. The cruel father of a maiden is also a theme running through many stories told by Cáceres men, who tend to project very negative images of fathers-in-law in their tales of courtship and marriage. José appears to have incorporated this theme into his story in order to persuade women to understand the position of men when courting women. Many men describe in other stories and in accounts of their own courtships how a man must prove himself to win the trust (*confianza*) of a courted maiden's parents, who often appear hostile toward the men who come courting their daughters.

Fear in gender relations probably makes it difficult for Narcisa and José to fully understand the other's position. The two narrators treat very differently the circumstances and the cost of sexual predation to women when dealing with more parallel situations in their stories. Narcisa, like Florencia, describes the attempted seductions taking place when their heroines were in the right place at the right time to place the responsibility squarely on the sexual predators. Narcisa's heroine was following her father's orders, watering the flowers in his garden, when the priest pursued her, much as Florencia's heroine was in the convent to which her parents had sent her for an education. José describes the heroine facing a predator when she is in the wrong place at the wrong time and thus places some of the blame of the attempted seduction on the victim. His heroine mysteriously wanders off to the countryside, meets a soldier, changes clothes with him, goes with him to the edge of the sea, where he makes illicit advances. Unlike Narcisa's heroine, José's protagonist does not wander into the countryside because she finds herself hated by her in-laws; rather, he makes her responsible for her unconventional and risky behavior, which a man might consider tempting. Moreover, José reduces the cost to women for male sexual predation because his story does not mention the death of the heroine's child.

The accounts of the attempted seductions in the masculine and feminine variants of "The Innocent Slandered Maiden" probably run parallel to the ways women and men describe the moral reputations of maidens with a history of broken courtships. On the one hand, Florencia Herrero described in her anecdote a maiden willing to break her courtship because of the behavior of the man she was about to marry. She too was in the right place at the right time and she acted entirely in accord with the highest ideals of femininity. On the other hand, Florencio Ramos expressed

his suspicion about the premarital chastity of any maiden in a long courtship that ended before marriage. He is prepared to believe that a once
courted but never married maiden was in the wrong and had probably
surrendered her virginity before the courtship came to an end.

The masculine suspicions about the conduct of women make it very
hard for a woman, as a woman, to defend her moral reputation if any
question is raised about her premarital or marital chastity. The heroine in
José's story, like her counterparts in the tales by Narcisa and Florencia,
must assume the identity of a man to restore her reputation in the eyes of
men. José's heroine dresses as a soldier and tells the story of her life to her
father, the servant who took her to the well, her husband, and her seducer. Only dressed as a man can she make "other" men hear her and can
she extract confessions from the men who did her harm. Both men and
women concur, then, that in terms of morality the male voice is the ultimate arbiter.

### Other Stories about Sexual Predation

Male and female narrators from the Cáceres villages tell other popular
folktales that illustrate how they concur in the storytelling dialogue about
the vulnerability of women to male sexual predation and slander. One
circulating in Cáceres oral tradition is "The Wager on the Wife's Chastity" (AT 882), an account of a virtuous wife who defends her marital
chastity but temporarily loses her moral reputation because her husband
believes she has been unfaithful. "The Wager," like "The Innocent Slandered Maiden," has circulated widely throughout Spain, illustrating how
men and women have recognized and continue to recognize the vulnerable position of women in rural Spanish society. Zacaria Iglesia (from Piornal), Ulalia García Castaño (from Garganta la Olla), and Natividad Corrales (from Serradilla) told closely related versions of this story, which are
listed in the Appendix. Moreover, Curiel Merchán (1944: 220–222) collected a variant in southern Cáceres, Cortés Vázquez (1979: 1: 203–210)
found another in southern Salamanca, and Llano Roza de Ampudia recorded two versions in 1920 and 1921 from women in Asturias (1975:
228–233, 344).

"The Wager" tells of two men who make a bet that one can sleep with
the other's wife. To collect the bet, the husband's friend first tries to seduce the virtuous woman, and when he fails, he uses another woman to
discover a mark on an intimate part of the woman's body and steal some
of her finery. He produces the proof, wins the bet, and the grief-stricken
husband leaves his wife. The virtuous but wronged woman wanders
about the world and manages to bring the truth to light, reunite with her
husband, and bring the slanderer to justice.

The tale in its masculine and feminine variants is interesting for how it shows that men and women can concur greatly in their understanding of the plight of women. All versions describe the heroine's predicament in nearly identical ways; the heroine is entirely innocent and virtuous, and unlike her counterpart in José's "The Innocent Slandered Maiden," the wife in the "The Wager" is always in the right place at the right time when she becomes the victim of male sexual predation and slander. Whereas the depictions of the heroine's plight remain constant, narrators present different scenarios for what she can do to restore her moral reputation. Most narrators describe how the heroine as a woman cannot bring the slanderer to justice and must assume the identity of a powerful man. Zacaria, Ulalia, and Natividad tell how she puts on the clothes of a man, acquires a position of authority, and then extracts a confession from the man who took away her feminine honor and destroyed her marriage. But two women, one in southern Cáceres (Curiel Merchán 1944: 220–222) and another in southern Salamanca (Cortés Vázquez 1979: 1: 203–210), describe a different scenario in which the heroine, as a woman, brings the truth to light and restores her marriage. In the tale from Trujillo in southern Cáceres, the heroine learns that her husband is sentenced to die by decapitation for losing the wager. So she goes to a silversmith, has him make a suit of silver missing one sleeve, and then appears with the suit just before the executioner is about to chop off her husband's head. She accuses the slanderer of stealing the sleeve; he denies the accusation and protests that he has never laid eyes on the heroine before and doesn't know who she is. At that point the truth comes out and the winner changes places with the loser and loses his head. The tale from southern Salamanca has a similar ending except that the heroine accuses the slanderer of stealing her shoe.

The concluding episodes of the two feminine stories, where the heroine as a woman restores her feminine honor, present scenarios according to which women can help themselves by relying on their own internal resources. In both tales, the heroine is extremely smart and manages to trick the slanderer. Crucial to the plot of these stories, however, is the fact that the slanderer never laid eyes on the woman he claimed to have seduced to win the wager. The heroine never strayed far from her castle and never put herself in a place where she could have encountered a sexual predator. Taken together, then, all known versions of "The Wager" and "The Innocent Slandered Maiden" are folktales that make the point by dramatic example that women must be very careful to guard their chastity and feminine honor. Florencia and Narcisa, of course, told their versions of "The Innocent Slandered Maiden" to make the point that even being at the right place at the right time is not enough. The next chapter considers other steps taken by women to defend themselves against the sexual assertiveness of ungallant men.

CHAPTER FOUR

# Maidens and Thieves

WOMEN AND men enter the age of courtship sharing the widespread suspicion of anyone outside one's own nuclear family (Brandes 1975: 149–155; Gilmore 1987a: 29–52). Men fear other men who might seduce their women and rob them of their masculine honor (Pitt-Rivers 1966: 115–117; Gilmore 1987a: 144–149). They fear women's sexuality, a fear men express by attributing to women the destructive powers of menstrual magic (Pitt-Rivers 1966: 196–197) and by regarding women as seductresses whose power men cannot resist (Brandes 1980: 77). A woman fears the sexually predatory man against whom she must guard her chastity and feminine honor. The fears one gender has of the other are widespread in Mediterranean Europe and other cultures in which beliefs about masculinity and femininity sharply differ.[1]

Older Cáceres women tell their daughters and granddaughters many stories about maidens and thieves socializing the younger women to guard their modesty and avoid falling prey to male slander. They deliver messages of fear that tie young daughters close to their parents, who have the primary responsibility of guarding their feminine and the family honor. The older women deliver their stories in very dramatic language, carrying the message that women must learn that safe-appearing men may actually be dangerous sexual predators. Their stories present a metaphor of marriage that involves vulnerable maidens falling victim to vicious, predatory thieves, and inculcate a fear of men by describing defloration as a brutally violent experience. They place women's fear of men in the context of the general suspicion between neighboring families and villages by representing the thieves' families as cannibals.

Women from several of the Cáceres communities told a number of closely related stories about maidens and thieves (AT 956, 970). Most of the women who knew the tales said they learned them from their mothers and grandmothers, and many said they learned the stories as young, school-age children about to enter adolescence. Like many of the folktales in contemporary Cáceres oral tradition, the stories of maidens and thieves appear widely over time and space in Spain. The general popularity of the stories is testimony that they address widely held concerns of women of past as well as present generations despite the regional diversity and temporal changes in Spanish culture. I collected variants from storytellers in Piornal, Navaconcejo, Ahigal, and Serradilla, and the tales are circulated in Extremadura, adjacent areas, and elsewhere in Spain. Curiel Merchán collected two variants in southern Cáceres (1944: 118–120), Larrea Palacín collected another in Andalusia (1959: 79–82), Cortés Vázquez published others from Salamanca (1979: 1:277–279) and Zamora (1976). A. Espinosa (1923: 88–91) includes several versions he collected from unknown narrators in Santander and Toledo during his expedition to Spain in the early 1920s.

## Defloration as Violence

Filomena Arivas Miguel, who currently lives in Navaconejo, told one of the more complete stories of maidens and thieves presenting a woman's defloration as brutal and violent. She told her tale from the perspective of a mature married woman who lives with her husband, with whom she has three daughters. She was fifty-four years old when she told me her tale, and she had been married for thirty-two years. Filomena learned the following story from her mother, also a Piornalega, who currently lives with Filomena and her husband. Filomena's tale resembles a story Curiel Merchán collected from a woman in Trujillo (1944: 271–272).

"THE MAIDENS AND THE THIEVES," BY FILOMENA ARIVAS MIGUEL

Once there was a couple who had three daughters, and the father and mother were going on a trip. The father told his daughters, "Don't open the door for anyone who isn't your uncle the priest." Then someone knocked, and the girls went to the door, and one of them said, "No, we won't open. My father told us not to talk to anyone who isn't my uncle the priest." And then the man came back and knocked again and said, "Open up for me, I'm your uncle the priest." And they opened the door for him. They were having supper and everything was fine. Then, when they got ready for bed, he asked, "Where should I stay?" One of the girls said, "You stay here in this room." He said, "No, I'm going to stay here in the kitchen. I'll stay here in this little corner." And there he stayed.

One of the three maidens, the youngest, was very smart. Around one in the morning, or thereabouts, she got up. She went to see if the man was asleep. And she looked through the keyhole and saw what he was doing. He was melting a little wax from a candle. And then he went upstairs to the bedrooms and put a little wax onto the eyes of the older ones. He went where the youngest was, but she didn't let him stick her eyes shut. And he said, "We'll leave this one. She's nothing. We'll leave her alone." It turned out he was a thief who was going to rob the house. He went to the window and began calling the thieves who were in league with him. He began blowing a trumpet. Then, while he was standing at the window calling the others, the little one got up, grabbed him by his feet, and threw him out the window. And then she woke her sisters up and one of them said, "We couldn't open our eyes."

And then the man came back and said, "Open the door for me. Hurry. I have to get my clothes." She said no. He said, "Well, give me the knives I left there." And she said, "No, I won't give them to you." He said, "Open the door for me. I won't do anything to you. Open up for me. Give me the knives." She said, "Well, take your knives." She opened the door a little for him and he reached inside the house. She gave him the knives. She said, "Put your hand through this crack." And when he put his hand through the crack, she cut off three of his fingers. And she stabbed him and then she threw the knives to him through the window. Then the parents came home, and the older sisters started to tell them what had happened. Of course, they had been asleep and their eyes were stuck shut. The youngest told the parents everything.

After the passing of time, the man who was the thief became a storekeeper, a merchant. He went about selling his wares. And someone told him there was a chance to make a sale. A woman wanted to buy from him. The woman told him there were various things that she wanted, and he said, "It'll be this much." And then he said, "Look, I'd like to marry your youngest daughter." The woman said, "As you wish." "It really is what I want most," said the merchant. And the daughter said one day, "Mother, I think he's the man whose three fingers I cut off." The mother said, "Oh, no, daughter. How could he be? Don't you see his hand is fine?" The daughter insisted, "Mother, I think he's the one whose fingers I cut off." In the end, the mother made her marry him because he was so wealthy and because they used to arrange courtships in those days.

The merchant said to her, "Come along." Halfway down the road she asked him, "What about your hand? You never seem to take your glove off." He said, "Yes, woman. I'll take it off it so you'll see. Look where you cut off my three fingers. There they used to be." She said, "Ah ha, it's just as I told my mother." They came to the town where they were going to live, and he told her, "Get yourself ready. Hurry up. Go upstairs. Get yourself ready. Take off all of your clothes. I'm going to kill you with one of these knives, with the knife you used to cut off my fingers. I'm going to stab you just as you stabbed me and cut off my fingers." Then he went away.

Her mother had told her she would put two doves called Pimpa and Pompa on the roof of each house. And so when the maiden went upstairs to take off her clothes she spoke to one of the doves: "Pimpa, isn't Pompa coming?" "No, he neither comes nor appears," said Pimpa. "What shall I do on these roads so sad and lonely?" asked the maiden. Then her husband called out, "Mariquita, are you getting ready or not?" "Yes, I'm getting ready. I'm taking off the beautiful pendants my mother gave me when I married you." Then she asked, "Pimpa, isn't Pompa coming?" "No, he neither comes nor appears." "What shall I do in this countryside so sad and lonely?" "Mariquita, are you getting ready or not?" "Yes. I'm getting ready right now. I'm taking off the beautiful petticoats my mother gave me when I married you." And she said, "Pimpa, isn't Pompa coming?" The dove answered her, "Yes, he's coming. Now he appears." At that moment her parents came, and one of them asked her husband what she was doing. He said, "We're going to the bullfight. I sent her to take off her clothes and put on fresh ones." Then her parents went home.

And the maiden and her husband walked and walked and came to a well for drinking water. She said to her husband, "Give me a little water." Her husband gave her the water and said to her, "Now you give some to me." She said, "Come on! Who ever heard of a woman who has to give water to a man? You go get a drink for yourself. Get down a little and drink." So he placed himself to drink from the well. She grabbed him, threw him down into the well and there he drowned. And then her mother said, "But daughter! What have you done?" The maiden replied, "Don't worry. He was the one whose fingers I cut off, and he was sharpening his knives to kill me when you arrived." And then she went home very happy with her parents and did not worry about anything. And her husband stayed there in the well. And she came home and they lived happily.

Filomena begins her tale describing in the language of a story a woman's fear of a sexual predator by telling of maidens left in a vulnerable position because they are without parental protection. The maidens' parents have gone away on a trip. Maidens require the actual presence of their parents rather than just parental advice to protect them from men who might do them harm. Filomena makes clear that parental advice alone fails to provide adequate protection for the daughters left alone by their parents by illustrating how easily a clever thief can take advantage of the innocence of young maidens. She tells how the maidens innocently tell the thief that they are under strict orders not to open their door for anyone who is not their uncle the priest, and then describes how the thief simply returns, claims that identity, and gains entry to the house.

Attempting to rob a house in a story can be a metaphor standing for many things, but it has a specific meaning in the context of gender relations. To anyone familiar with the norms of speech in courtship, stories about thieves attempting to rob the house of maidens left alone by their parents signify the violation of a maiden by a sexually assertive and predatory man. Entrance to a house and access to a maiden daughter are symbolically connected by the use of a common verbal noun for entrance and access (*entrada*) in the ritualized speech of a man formally initiating a courtship. The reader may recall that a suitor normally goes to the home of the woman's parents to ask for permission to enter the house of his sweetheart (*pedir la entrada en casa de la novia*). The young man asks the maiden's father for access to his daughter with the same word (*entrada*) used when asking for permission to enter his house. Thieves in the stories thus represent men attempting to gain unsanctioned or illicit entry to houses and maidens.

The story by Filomena represents predatory men as thieves who assume the identity of priests and relatives. Thieves in Cáceres stories live in caves in the forest and thus stand for dangerous, predatory men who are outside of the nuclear family as well as the village and thus outside of the moral order. They could represent sexually assertive men unregulated by the ideals of gallantry. Their thinly disguised identity as priests and relatives illustrates the general tendency to regard as truly safe—that is, regulated by the ideals of gallantry—only those men who are members of a maiden's own nuclear family (see Brandes 1975: 151). The long and elaborate courtship practices have the ostensible purpose of turning distrust and fear into confidence.

The heroine is the youngest of three maidens in many variants (see the stories by Julia Perez listed in the Appendix and those by Julia Perez, María Fernández, and José Díaz considered below). She suspects the priest who is their uncle is really a thief, whereas her older sisters are more willing to accept appearances as reality. She refuses to let the intruder cover her eyes with wax and she is the one who disfigures the thief by cutting off his fingers when he tries to reenter the house. The youngest child as heroine or hero appears in many stories told by women and men in Spanish and European oral tradition (Bettelheim 1977: 106; Lüthi 1984: 127). The sexual latency of young maidens may be one of the reasons the youngest is the heroine in the stories about maidens and thieves. The tales warn young women about sexually predatory men, and younger maidens are probably more likely to heed the warnings of their elders than are older maidens, who are more ready for sex and marriage.

The maiden's disfigurement of the thief's hand is undoubtedly a reference to castration and appears in a number of maiden-and-thieves stories by women in Cáceres oral tradition. The women appear to warn men that castration is poetic justice for the man who attempts to violate an innocent maiden. Ironically, the disfigurement of the thief's hand becomes the basis for the maiden's recognition of the true identity of the thief, who reappears as a merchant and a man of good appearances who becomes her husband later on in the story. Disfigurement or castration is consequently a symbol of women's fear of men's sexuality, a symbol present throughout the story. It is interesting that the maiden's mother approves of and even encourages the marriage of her daughter with the thief-turned-merchant, much as actual parents sometimes encourage their daughters to enter courtships with men of whom they approve. The maiden in the story, like some actual women unready for sex and marriage, is unsure and wavers. She tells her mother that she suspects the suitor to be the man whose fingers she cut off when he tried to enter and rob their house. The sexual symbolism becomes more explicit as Filomena's story builds to a climax when the thief sends the maiden upstairs to remove her clothes so that he can stab her with the same knife she used to disfigure his hand. The maiden removes one article of clothing at a time, telling the doves of her plight and noting that each article was a gift from her mother. Perhaps the removal of the articles of clothing represents the casting away of the maiden's identity as daughter at the precise time she needs her mother's protection the most. Defloration as violence and the knife as phallus become particularly apparent if one considers the seemingly incredible response of her parents when they come to the aid of their daughter after doves inform them of her situation. They simply go away when their son-in-law tells them that their daughter is changing her clothes to go to the bullfight. The transparency of the knife as symbol of the phallus is clear when the maiden does not offer her parents a counter-explanation of why she has removed her clothes and allows them to return home without helping her: there is no legitimate defense for a girl against defloration by her husband, as fearful as he may be. Filomena's tale deals with one of the contradictory themes in gender relations that must be mediated if a maiden is to make the transition from courtship to marriage. A young maiden, socialized to fear men and her own defloration, is also expected to marry and consummate her marriage on her wedding night. Rural Cáceres is not a culture that permits trial marriages.

Filomena ends her story by describing a scenario for the maiden whose fear of men outweighs her desire to give her marriage a chance. The maiden takes matters into her own hands and kills her husband by drowning him in a well. She clearly acts on a fear of men learned from her parents and returns home without making the transition from courtship to marriage. It is interesting that Filomena describes the maiden refusing to carry out a reciprocal exchange of favors with her husband just before killing him. Most narrators and other informants describe their marriages as mutual interdependence between a man and a woman who cooperate in terms of the rules of the sexual division of labor. The maiden in Filomena's story ends her marriage by refusing to engage in the reciprocal exchange that occurs as husbands and wives regularly cooperate in a marriage. She asks for water, he serves her; he asks for water and she refuses to serve him. Refusing to serve her husband water is perhaps symbolic of a woman refusing to serve her husband food, which would cause a serious crises in any marriage in the Cáceres villages.

Julia Perez, another Piornalega who lives in Navaconcejo, told a version of this story that handles the contradiction differently. Her tale describes a heroine who apparently fears her defloration less and wants to make her marriage work more than her counterpart in the story by Filomena. Julia could not remember from whom she heard her story, but she did recall that she learned it as a young girl. Like Filomena, Julia told this story from the perspective of a mature married woman; she was fifty-one when I recorded her version.

### "THE MAIDENS AND THE THIEVES," BY JULIA PEREZ

This is about some people who had two daughters. The parents were going to the fair, and they told their daughters not to open the door for anyone who came to their house. Then at night their uncle the priest came and said, "Open for me, I'm your uncle the priest." "Oh, no, sir, my father and my mother have told us not to open the door for anyone." "Come on! They won't let you open the door for your uncle the priest?" "No, sir. My father and my mother have told me not to open the door." "Aren't you ashamed, an uncle who is a priest?" The older daughter was ashamed, and so they opened the door. They went upstairs and asked him what he wanted for supper. He said a couple of eggs would be enough for him. They were eating supper, and he gave each one an orange to eat. The oranges contained a sleeping potion. The older girl ate hers, but the younger one threw hers under a bench. They got ready to go to bed and told him, of course, he would sleep in a bed. He said no, he'd just sleep in the kitchen. One of the maidens asked him if she should give him a little receptacle in case he had to urinate. He said, "No, no. I'll go out to the balcony." They went to bed, and the older maiden went to sleep at once because she had eaten the orange. The younger one was awake with her eyes open. When she heard the least little noise, she got up and peered through the keyhole and saw the priest melting tar. Then he came in to close their eyes. He closed the eyes of the older one because she was asleep. But as he tried to close the eyes of the younger one, she turned and wouldn't let him close hers because she was awake. After a little while, when it seemed right to her, she got up again and saw he was sharpening knives. Instead of lying in the bed, she got dressed under the bed. Her father had a pistol for when someone might try to kill her. She went into the room after him, he ran out, and she went after him down the stairs firing the gun. As he was leaving, she closed the door and caught his finger. She grabbed his finger, and he cried, "Let it go, let go of my finger. You're biting me." She bit him. And he went on his way.

Then their parents came home, and she told them what had happened. They said they would never leave home again after what happened the one time they went away. Then, after time passed, the same man came looking for a bride again. He wore gloves. The younger girl recognized him when he gave his hand to her, and said she didn't want to be his bride. He was the one whose finger she had cut off. But he said no, he was born wearing gloves; he couldn't remove them. The maiden told her mother he was a thief, but her mother said he was a man of good appearances, and he became her sweetheart.

After the passage of time, they arranged to get married. The maiden said she would marry him, but he had to buy her a big, beautiful caramel doll that looked like her. The night they were married they got ready to go to bed. He stayed up writing a letter, and she, instead of lying down in the bed, laid the doll down and went under the bed. When he came to lie down, he put a knife under his pillow and asked, "Do you remember when I went to your house and your sister wanted to open the door for me but you didn't?" She moved the bed a little from below so the doll would move and he would see it saying yes. He said, "Don't answer me with your head. Tell me with your mouth. Do you remember when I gave you an orange with sleeping potion and your sister ate it and you didn't?" "Yes," nodded the doll. "Don't answer me with your head. Tell me with your mouth. Do you remember when I went to kill you and you came after me shooting and there was a scuffle?" "Yes," nodded the doll. "Don't tell me with your head. Tell me with your mouth." And when he finished, he took out a knife from underneath the pillow and—plum!—he stabbed her. And when he stabbed her, he dislodged a piece of caramel, which popped into his mouth. He cried, "Oh, how sweet is Blancaflor's blood! If I had known, I wouldn't have killed you." He said it again in a louder voice: "Oh, how sweet is Blancaflor's blood! If I had known, I wouldn't have killed you." He looked at himself in the mirror and prepared to kill himself. And the maiden came out from under the bed and said, "You didn't kill me, man. I'm here. Now I'm going. You tell it all to my parents because it's true what they said." And they ate rabbits and partridges and to us, who were there, they tossed the bones at our noses.

Although Julia, like Filomena, describes defloration as violent, she uses softer imagery and describes the husband and wife showing some feeling for each other. A knife is still a phallus, but the husband uses it to stab a caramel doll in the likeness of the maiden rather than to stab the maiden herself. The husband loses his desire for vengeance when he exclaims how sweet is the blood of his bride after a piece of the caramel pops into his mouth. The maiden shows some human compassion for her husband as she crawls out from under the bed and prevents her husband from killing himself in repentant grief. Julia leaves the listener with questions about the maiden's next course of action. She announces she's going and threatens to tell her parents about her husband's true identity, but she doesn't kill him. Julia's tale suggests that a maiden can make the transition from courtship to marriage if she and her husband can manage to see each other as humans with feelings.

## Thieves as Cannibals

Courtship takes place in a climate of fear not only between women and men but also between nuclear families. The distrust between families and a male competitive worldview are themes in a number of accounts of small village life from Andalusia (Gilmore 1987a: 29–52) to southern

Avila (Brandes 1975: 149–155). I have no reason to believe that distrust, fear, and male competition are any more or less prevalent in Cáceres than in other parts of Spain. Stories about maidens and cannibalistic thieves express women's fear of men in the context of the general distrust between families. These tales, like the others preceding them, define the barriers that courting couples must transcend if they are to create an illusion of love and reach accommodation in married life.

María Fernandez, a married woman of forty-five who lives in Piornal, told a version of maidens and cannibalistic thieves that expresses women's fears of sexually predatory men extended to include their families. The fears expressed in María's tale are probably widespread in Spanish villages because they show up in parallel folktales collected by Larrea Palacín from a twelve-year-old girl in Cádiz (1959: 79–82) and by Cortés Vázquez from a woman in her sixties in Hinoja de Duero in northwestern Salamanca (1979: 1: 277–279). Moreover, María's tale is very similar to a second story of maidens and thieves told by Julia Perez, which is listed in the Appendix.

### "THE MAIDENS AND THE THIEVES," BY MARÍA FERNÁNDEZ

Once there was a married couple who had three daughters. They left the girls alone in the house and told them, "Please don't open the door if someone comes who isn't your uncle the priest." Someone heard what they said and seized an untimely moment at night to come knocking at the door. "Open the door for me, I'm your uncle the priest." The man brought three apples and he gave them to the girls. The youngest didn't eat hers and didn't go to sleep. The others slept because they ate theirs. And the man wasn't a priest, he was a thief. The man said, "You have to leave the door open for me. I have the habit of going out at night to urinate in the street." They left the door unbolted. Later, when the youngest was on her way to bed, she looked through the crevices in the door and saw knives, pistols, and ropes on the table. She said, "He isn't our uncle the priest. He's a thief who has come to rob us." And when the man went downstairs to urinate in the street, she barred the door. The man cried, "Open the door for me." "No, we won't open the door for you. You're a thief." As he was climbing onto the balcony, she cut his hand.

Then, after a lot of time passed, he came by again wearing gloves. And the girls' mother said, "Let's buy something from this man for your trousseaus, sheets or something." But the youngest protested, "No, dear mother, because that's the man whose hand I cut." After a lot of time passed, he came by again and took away the maiden who cut his hand. Maybe he was going to marry her, but I don't know for sure.

As they were going along the road, she asked, "Haven't we arrived? Haven't we come to where we're going?" He said, "No, we still have a ways to go. Look at my hand you cut. This is going to be the death of you." They finally reached the hut where the thieves lived, and there was an old woman who took care of them. The maiden's husband went away and told the old woman to take care of his wife. "You tell her, 'Come, I see a louse.' And you kill her. Prepare her for me to eat." But instead the maiden said to the old woman, "Sit down; let me look for your lice first. And then you look for mine." The maiden killed the old woman. And she readied a caldron to cook her for when the thieves came home to eat in the middle of the day. Then three or four thieves appeared together; they came to eat. The maiden had cut off the old woman's head and filled her bed with some clothes so it would look bulky, as if the woman were sleeping in bed. And the maiden fled. When the thieves came to eat, one of them said, "The meat is tough, isn't it?" Another said, "Why wouldn't it be tough? It took a lot of work to open her, chop her up, and cook her." Another said, "Well, where is grandmother?" They got up and saw her head in the bed and said, "Let's leave her for a little while, let her rest. She's very tired." They left her for a little while. Later they uncovered the head and saw her head was there alone. They went looking for the maiden.

She came to two or three shepherd's huts. The thieves had taken three horses—one was air, one was wind, and the other was thought. The maiden came to one of the huts and said, "If some men come here looking for me, say I passed by a long time ago. Instead of taking this road, say I took the other one." That's what the shepherd did. The maiden came to another hut and said the same thing: "If some men come here looking for me, say I passed by long ago and took a different road." The men came looking for her and asked, "Have you seen a young girl pass by here?" "Yes. She passed by a long time ago." "What road did she take?" Instead of saying the right one, the shepherd said she took the left one. And so the maiden came home without anything happening and there isn't anything else.

María's tale begins much as the tales discussed earlier, which give voice to women's fear of sexually predatory men represented as thieves. Once again parents leave their maiden daughters alone in the house with instructions not to open for anyone other than their uncle the priest; a thief claiming to be a priest comes knocking on the door, and the older maidens let him in. Using biblical sexual symbolism, the thief offers apples to the maidens, representing his attempt to seduce them. The older maidens accept the apples perhaps because older maidens are more likely to give in to sexual temptation. But the youngest maiden refuses to eat her apple, foils the thief's attempted robbery, and disfigures his hand. The thief reappears as a merchant selling attractive garments and becomes the maiden's husband, with the approval of her mother. It is interesting that the mother ironically proposes to buy items for her maiden daughter's trousseau (*ajuar*) from the same man who attempted to rob her house earlier.

The tale diverges from the preceding stories when the maiden accompanies her husband to his home in the wilderness. At this point in the plot, women's fear of sexually predatory men becomes extended to all the members of his family, including his grandmother. The maiden's trip to the home of her husband expresses a feminine view of the horrors of patrilocal postmarital residence, where a maiden goes to live with her husband's family in the same or in a different village. Patrilocality is relatively rare; most couples marry endogamously and establish an independent household immediately upon marriage. When young couples live with one of their parental families during their early marital years, they more often live with the family of the wife (see Table 1 in Chapter 2). Spatial dislocation is very great for the heroine, whose journey to her husband's home seems to take forever. The maiden finally arrives to find an old woman whose appearance is deceptive because the old woman acts kindly but actually intends to do the maiden harm, acting on instructions from her grandson, the maiden's husband. He tells her to offer to remove the maiden's lice or comb the maiden's hair, acts of ostensible kindness carried out with the sinister intention of killing and eating the girl. The old woman represents a bride's mother-in-law, whose appearance of kindness cannot be trusted. The mention of combing or removing lice from the maiden's hair might refer to jealousy between a mother and daughter-in-law over the younger woman's youth and beauty. The husband's instructions to the old woman to kill and cook his wife represent his strong loyalty to his mother and his weak loyalty to his bride. Cooking and eating probably have some sexual symbolism and they most assuredly stand for mistreatment of a daughter-in-law. The wise maiden sees through the appearance of kindness, kills the old woman, and ironically feeds her to the thieves. She flees, just as a patrilocally living bride might wish to flee from her husband's family. Once again the maiden's fears outweigh her desire to make her marriage work, and she escapes from her husband's family and returns home. Julia Perez's second maiden-and-thieves story (listed in the Appendix) ends on an even more hopeless note: the maiden drowns her husband in a well.

The cautionary tales older women tell of safe-appearing but dangerous men who brutally deflower innocent maidens and live as cannibals in the forest appear to get through to some modern young women who are ready to begin a courtship, despite the changing sexual mores following the collapse of the traditional agrarian economy. I found maidens ready to court who learned and internalized the messages of tales told by older women, messages that warned their daughters and granddaughters to be wary of men who come courting. Isabel García, an eighteen-year-old maiden from Ahigal, told a chilling tale she learned from her grandmother, which contains the message that young maidens should heed parental advice about the men who say they want to marry them. The story, listed in the Appendix as "The Poor Girl Seduced by Her Rich Sweetheart," tells of a maiden from a modest family courted by a wealthy young man who jokingly proposes marriage. The maiden's father tries to persuade his daughter against the marriage because the young man's parents will eventually hold her inferior social status against her. The maiden ignores the advice and elopes with her rich suitor, only to be raped in the woods by him and his cousin.

## A Masculine Variant

Men are well aware of women's fears of them because many have heard stories of maidens and thieves told by women. Men tell a number of stories intended to soften the polarization in gender relations by humanizing the same characters women use to personify their fears of men. José Díaz Sanchez, the narrator from Serradilla whose version of "The Innocent Slandered Maiden" was discussed in Chapter 3, told a variant of the maiden-and-thieves story that has much in common with that told by María Fernandez. I did not find a masculine variant of the maiden-and-thieves story from the same villages as that of the feminine narrators, although I suspect that many men know a version of this story. It is ideal to compare masculine and feminine versions of the same story told by narrators from the same storytelling community because each village has a slightly different way of telling common tales. In the absence of these, however, the examination of parallel stories from different villages can illustrate some of the ways men and women deal with the same themes.

José's tale is like those of María Fernández (discussed above) and Julia Perez (listed in the Appendix), because it has three maidens, the youngest of whom is the most courageous and heroic. It has a thief transporting a maiden far away to his cave in the forest, where she confronts life with cannibals. The heroine flees from her husband and returns home like her counterparts in the stories by women. José, however, masculinizes his tale by narrating the action from the point of view of both thief and maiden. His style of narration humanizes the very character women use to personify their fears of the sexual predator.

"THE MAIDENS AND THE THIEVES," BY JOSÉ DÍAZ SANCHEZ
    Once there was a band of thieves. And aren't thieves determined to rob? They always rob. They were in the countryside and didn't have one woman living with them. Not one. So the captain said to his companions, "We ought to get married. I'm going to that town over there to see if I can find a bride and get married, because we have to have a woman here. We're lonely, aren't we?" "Yes, man, yes," the thieves said. "That's a fine idea." The captain went to the town and fell in love with a maiden. They were married in town. Afterward he

said, "You have to come with me to my country." "Oh fine, I'll go," she said. "Do you have family there?" "Yes," said the captain. "I have family there and that's where they're from." Well, then, I'd be delighted," replied his wife.

He put her on a horse and took her away to the forest, where they lived in a cabin. All of his companions came running out of the cabin as they arrived. One of the thieves said, "Hey! Our captain is coming. He's bringing a woman here who—" The captain said, "Take it easy. Yes, a woman has come here." He dismounted and said, "Someone has to make something to eat." "Oh, well, yes," his wife said. "And you live in this place? This is a forest. There isn't anyone here." "Yes, we live here," said the captain, and he got up and took out some dead bodies. Their throats were cut. He said, "You have to cook these. You have to put them in hot water, skin them, and make supper for tonight." "Oh, no, no. I won't do that," she protested. He said, "If you don't, I'll kill you." She said, "Kill me, but I won't do it." He killed the maiden and said, "I have to go back because there are three sisters."

He went back alone to the town. The maiden's father and her other sisters said as he came, "You're here!" "Yes," he said. "Well, how is my sister?" "Your sister is just fine. She asked if you wanted to be with her. And after a certain amount of time, you can come back here and she'll stay there," said the captain. "Oh, yes, yes. I'll go where my sister is." He mounted his horse, and she got on behind him, and he took her away. Pin pan, pin pan.[2] She asked, "Well, where is your town?" He said, "Not far, it's very close." Pin pan, pin pan. "Where is your town?" He said, "It's over there very close by. We're almost there." They went on and finally arrived. "Wow! Hurray for our captain!" said the thieves. "He's coming with another woman. She's our captain's woman and—" She asked, "Where is my sister?" "I'll bring you to your sister right now," said the captain. He showed her the body of her sister and said, "Here are two others. You have to skin them and make supper for me tonight. They're to eat." "Oh, no, no, no. I won't! I won't do this!" "If you don't, the same thing will happen to you that happened to her. You do what you want. But if you don't, the same thing will happen to you that happened to her." She said, "Kill me, but I won't do it." So he killed her too.

He went back to town for the youngest. "Why did you come back here again?" she asked. "Your sisters told me to take you there, and when you're tired of being there, the two of you will come back here in love and harmony. Your sister will stay there with us, but the two of you will come back here." "Good, I'll go." As they went on and on and on and on, she asked, "Where is your town?" "Oh, it's farther inside the forest. We're just about to get there." So they arrived, and his companions came out to greet them: "Wow! Here comes our captain with the woman." He said, "Sh. Quiet! Eh!" And he dismounted from his horse. They all were very nice to her because she was the captain's wife. The captain said, "Is there anything here to make for supper?" "Oh, yes, yes," she said, and then added, "My sisters, where are they?" He said,

"Your sisters will come out right now." He took out the two heads of her sisters. "Look! You have to cook these for tonight. Skin them and cook them." "Bring them here. I'll cook them and I'll skin them and we'll eat them for supper tonight," she said. "Ala!³ That's more like it! Skin them." She put them into hot water, skinned them, and made supper. When they were eating he said, "She's the one who should be my wife here in the farmhouse and watch over all of this and all that we do. She is the one in charge here. And that's how it'll be. The captain gave the woman the keys to everything in the farmhouse.

And they went to rob because that was their profession. They were gone for two or three weeks or a month and then they brought money and went away again. The captain said, "We'll come back in two or three weeks or a month. God knows how long it will be before we come back." She said, "Fine," And they went away. Then she heard a voice: "Ohhh. Ohhh, my God." She went to the back of the house, where the voice was coming from. "Who is it?" The thieves had locked a man inside a room and hadn't given him anything to eat or drink. The poor thing was twisted and could barely speak. He was in the agony of death. And because she had the keys to everything in the farmhouse, the woman went about opening everything including the room where he was. She asked, "What happened to you?" "I'm in very bad shape." The man was very ill, and she took care of him. She fed him all he wanted because she had everything anyone would want to eat, and she nursed him for fourteen or fifteen days. The man got well. She said, "Let's get out of here because they're about to come back. They're as likely to come back in two days as three, but they're bound to come back soon. We have to get out of here." "Ah yes," he said, "let's go."

They got out of there—tran, tran, tran, tran.⁴ And as they were going through the forest, they heard the hoofbeats of horses coming nearer. They climbed a tree, she and the sick one. They were up in the tree and heard the thieves say, "We have to spend the night underneath this tree." The thieves camped and made a fire, and that night they cooked and ate their meal. After they finished eating, one said, "Give me a glass of water." A companion gave it to him, and after he finished drinking, he said, "This glass of water is for the health of our captain's wife. His wife is . . ." And just as he was about to say she was up in the tree, the captain slapped him. He said, "Don't mention my wife for either a good reason or a bad one." So the companion kept quiet.

Well, a new day dawned and they went to their farmhouse. They arrived, and the farmhouse was empty. They didn't see the woman or the one who was in the room. No one was there. "I shit on God," said the captain. "If I find her, I'll kill her, I'll skin her, I'll do this and that to her." And he who had asked for the glass of water the night before said, "Captain, last night when I asked for the glass of water to drink, I was about to say, 'This glass of water is for the health of our captain's wife who is . . .'" He was going to say she was up in the tree. "And you slapped me. If you hadn't slapped me, I would have said it.

But you slapped me, and I had to be quiet." "I shit on God. If she did this to me, I'll grab her, I'll skin her, I'll . . ."

That's how it was. He said, "I have to do something." They had a very big dog that was part wolf. He said, "We have to kill this dog. The hide will be flayed, and I'm going to put myself inside of it. Put in a whistle for me. Put in a knife for me. Put everything I'll need inside. Put a collar with a chain on this dog. Lead it by the hand and take it to her town. She's going to buy it when she sees it. When they buy it from you, they'll have to give you a place to spend the night. You'll have to stay there."

So it was that they went about the town. They went down her street, and she was standing on the balcony. She, who had come with the other one, was standing on the balcony. And because she was the only daughter left, she asked her father, "Won't you buy me this dog? I like it." "Yes, I'll buy it for you," her father replied. He went downstairs and said, "Sell me that dog. How much is it?" "This much." The one who was with the dog said, "Take it. But you have to give us lodging for tonight, and we'll go on our way tomorrow." "Well, sure." "Father," said the maiden, "this is the thief who killed my two sisters and now he comes for me too. Tonight you warn the Civil Guard and put them here in the house." She slept that night with four lights on, and she put the dog in the room where she slept. The captain took out his hand from beneath the animal skin and, psst, he put out a light. After a while, he removed his hand and, psst, he put out another light. Then she moved and turned over in bed. But it was all set up. His hand came out and psst, he put out another light. She moved. There was just one light left. When he stuck out his had to put out the last one, she said, "All right! Stop! You've put out enough lights, eh." They discovered that the captain was inside the hide. They grabbed him and opened him and unstitched him and took off the hide. And they took the whistle. Blowing the whistle was a signal for his companions to come, because he had arranged for them to kill the maiden and everyone else in the house. They blew the whistle, and the others came. But as the thieves came, the guards were there, and bam, bam, until they cleaned them all up. Soon she married the man she had brought from the forest, the one whom she was hiding and who was near death. She married him, and they lived happily. And they threw a bone at my nose. I came back with this bump.

José's story presents a more human picture of the thief in his relationship to innocent and vulnerable maidens than do the tales by María Fernandez (discussed earlier) and Julia Perez (listed in the Appendix). His tale retains some of the terrifying imagery found in the stories by women to acknowledge rather than deny that men can appear very threatening to women. Acknowledging women's fears of men is probably a necessary step in the dialogue through storytelling to soften the polarity and reduce the level of fear in gender relations.

The narration of the story begins from the point of view of the captain of the thieves. José makes the captain look human by saying that he needs to have a woman because he is lonely. The captain is not a sexual predator because he does none of the things his counterparts in the feminine stories do to vulnerable maidens suggesting sexual predation. He does not enter their houses with the pretext of robbing them, he does not feed them apples, and he carries no phallic knives. Instead he comes to town looking for a bride, falls in love, and marries a maiden. When he takes his bride to his cabin in the forest to live with his family, he displays gallantry and makes sure his companions keep their distance.

José retains the image of thieves as cannibals to acknowledge that brides probably have a lot to deal with when adjusting to their in-laws. Absent from José's tale, however, is the grandmother who appears kind but actually has very sinister intentions toward the bride in the stories by women. María Fernández raised questions about the thief-turned-husband's conjugal loyalties by describing him telling the grandmother to kill his bride. The nice-appearing but actually sinister grandmother and the husband's instructions that she kill his bride are important elements in the feminine stories. They express the feminine view that brides face hostile mothers-in-law and that men have conflicted filial and conjugal loyalties. Conflict between mother and daughter-in-law is an important concern for women and is expressed in a number of stories discussed in later chapters. Mother-and-son ties remains close in actual family relations, and some mothers complain about their their sons' treatment by their daughters-in-law (see Brandes 1975: 119). By removing the grandmother entirely and by depicting the captain as telling the members of his band to treat his bride with respect, José represents the captain as having clear loyalties to his wife, particularly after the third one agrees to his demand that she skin and cook her sisters.

The captain is cruel: he murders his first two brides when they refuse to obey his unreasonable request to skin and cook the dead bodies of murder victims for supper. The captain as a brutal murderer is a way of acknowledging the fears women have about men. Moreover, men socialized according to the ideals of manliness learn to present themselves with an aura of danger, and the captain as a thief capable of murder fits that manly image. The captain's return for his murdered bride's sisters and his repeated request that each flay and cook the bodies of murder victims, including their own sister, have a number of possible meanings. The captain's return with a series of women is an expression of manliness, making the captain a little like a Don Juán in the eyes of the other thieves. After all, he manages to return with three different women, and every time he appears with another woman, the men express their awe and admiration. Upon arriving with the second sister, they say, "Wow! Hurray for our captain!" (¡Jo! ¡*Viva nuestro capitán*!) The three sisters could easily represent three aspects of the same woman, and the succession of sisters may stand for the changes a woman goes through as she makes her transition from daughter to wife. The succession of maiden sisters may represent the gradual weakening of a woman's familial loyalties represented by the willingness of the third sister to skin and cook her two older sisters. José further humanizes his captain by describing how he trusts the youngest maiden sister, giving her the keys to the farmhouse, much as many men trust the woman who transfers her filial loyalties to her husband. The maiden betrays the captain's trust, however, perhaps representing how men fear that if they trust their wives entirely they may find themselves betrayed. The captain is blinded by his trust because, in his effort to protect his bride's honor, he slaps the thief in his band who is about to tell him that his wife is hiding in the tree above them. The spatial symbolism of the woman above and the thieves below is an ironic detail representative of the polarization in Christian culture between the divine above the earth and the demonic below the earth. Placing the woman in the tree above the thieves is a metonymical association of the captain's wife with the divine and the thieves with the demonic. José uses this poetic device with irony because the bride is above the thieves at the very time that she is betraying her husband with another man.

When the captain discovers the treachery, he exclaims, "I shit on God," a common blasphemous expression used by men to express astonishment, fear, surprise, and any other very strong emotion. This expression, which appears in many masculine stories and is common in masculine speech, is a linguistic marker of agrarian working-class identity. It is another example of the general tendency to regard appearances as different from reality. "I shit on God" is an expression that makes a man appear to be blasphemous, but in fact a number of narrators, women as well as men, tell the tale of "The Two Ploughmen" (listed in the Appendix), which makes the point that a man who uses blasphemy is actually more pure in his heart than a man whose speech is free from blasphemous expressions. I shall discuss masculine and feminine blasphemous expressions more fully in Chapter 10, where I present a tale by a narrator who liberally uses them in his stories.

The captain swears vengeance and returns to the maiden's town hidden inside a dog. The detail of thieves hidden in animal hides is common in maiden-and-thieves tales circulating in Spanish oral tradition. José's particular portrayal of the captain's return to avenge his betrayal expresses a masculine view of women as having conflicted rather than clear loyalties. After fleeing with a moribund man, the maiden displays a mysterious attraction to her thief-husband. She tells her father that she wants the dog in which her husband is hiding, and she places the dog in her own bedroom. Although the maiden acts to set a trap for the captain, she does it in a curious way, giving the impression that she likes to play with danger, much as maidens like to flirt with the Don Juans of their village.

José's tale concludes with a happy marriage, which does not appear in many of the maiden-and-thieves stories told by Cáceres women. Most feminine variants depict heroines acting on their fear of men and returning to their parents. José's final episodes give clear voice to the often-expressed masculine view of a woman's love as nurturance. The heroic maiden nurtures a man who becomes her husband; she feeds her future husband "all he wanted and nursed him for fourteen or fifteen days" and brings him back to health from the agony of near death. Women as nurturer of men is a theme noted by many observers of rural village life in this part of Spain (see Brandes 1975: 117–118). It is men's dependence on women that probably made the captain go to town and look for a bride in the first place.

So far the stories by women have described in the storytelling dialogue the vulnerability of maidens and married women to male sexual predation and slander, given voice to women's fears of male sexuality, and expressed women's fear of men's families. Men have retold the same stories affirming the vulnerable position of maidens and married women, an affirmation that is the first step in mediating the fear and the difference in gender relations. Men also see the plight of women from a different point of view, however, and lay a great deal of responsibility on women to maintain their chastity and feminine honor in the eyes of men. They attempt to mediate some of the fear in gender relations by humanizing the characters women use to personify their fear of men's sexuality. But the retelling of "The Innocent Slandered Maiden," "The Wager on the Wife's Chastity," and "The Maidens and the Thieves" leaves many issues unresolved, and so it is necessary to turn to other stories that women and men tell about courtship and marriage.

# CHAPTER FIVE

# "Snow White"

THE TIES between a mother and daughter remain strong throughout the life course in many parts of rural Spain. Young girls help their mothers by performing household tasks and taking care of children (Brandes 1975: 116). The relationship changes little after a daughter's marriage because many married women continue to care and worry about their elderly parents (Pitt-Rivers 1966: 102; Brandes 1975: 120).[1] By contrast, a man's ties to his mother are more ambivalent and discontinuous. Brandes (1975: 119–120) observed that Becedas men in southern Avila have close emotional ties with their nurturing mothers; they resent their mother's possessiveness and are fearful of hurting them at the same time. So when sons marry, they often break from their mother and find a replacement in their wife. To a greater or lesser degree, Becedas men seem like their Andalusian brothers, who develop a manly identity by rejecting the feminine in themselves while separating from their mothers (Gilmore 1987a: 126–153) and express fear of the power of women (Brandes 1980: 77). The contrast between a man's and a woman's relationship with the mother creates a gender difference requiring mediation in courtship. Cáceres men break with their parents and expect their wife to do the same, an expectation that conflicts with a woman's strong maternal loyalty.

This chapter looks at the storytelling dialogue as it deals with the masculine and feminine perspectives of a woman's relationship with her mother. I reconstruct the contours of that dialogue by examining how women and men tell the "Snow White" story differently. The tale is about a maiden's separation from her mother, her fight to develop a separate feminine identity, and her transition from daughter to wife. The story communicates the contrasting perspectives of men and women, mediates the fear that comes with difference, and describes men's attempts to persuade women to break from parents and make a complete transfer of loyalties at marriage.

## Mothers and Daughters

The "Snow White" story becomes more meaningful if one considers the ways mothers and daughters actually depend on each other in the Cáceres villages. A number of women explained why they need their mother throughout the life course. Florencia Herrero of Garganta la Olla illustrated with the case of her own mother, who married patrilocally into Garganta la Olla from another region in Cáceres. Florencia was the oldest of five children and had to stay home because her mother had no one else to help her with the children. Florencia put it this way: "I couldn't go to school very much because my mother was not from this town. She was from a province in Cáceres, but up there in las Hurdes. And then, of course, she didn't have anyone. Upon having very small children, I had to be the nursemaid from the time I was very small." Many other women described how they needed their mothers to help with child care in times of particular need. Petra, also of Garganta, had great difficulty when her husband, Guillermo, spent five years in prison during and after the Spanish Civil War for being a socialist. She did not have her mother to help care for her two children as she tried to earn a living selling tobacco in villages and towns within walking distance of Garganta. Her mother died before Petra's marriage to Guillermo, and so Petra had to leave her two young children alone to make their meals by themselves as she went off before dawn to sell the tobacco. She said, "I went to sell in Jaraíz and Plasencia. I bought tobacco and I took it to sell in Plasencia. Sometimes I took a load on my head and another under my arm. And there were times when I walked from here to Plasencia with tobacco. My children stayed alone in the house, and I taught them to cook for themselves. They measured out olive oil with a spoon. I told them, 'Son, this oil is for your dinner.' In that way they got used to being in the house, but I went without peace of mind. . . . I told a neighbor, 'Look out for the children. When they get up in the morning, watch them for me. Don't let them burn themselves. When you see that they make a fire [to cook their food], go in to see how they are.' "

Under more ordinary circumstances, women place their children in the care of their mother while they work with their husband in the fields. Women in all the Cáceres communities help plant and harvest crops in addition to caring for children, mending clothes, baking bread, preparing sausages (*morcillas*) during the winter butchering (*matanza*), making cheese, fetching water from the fountains when houses lacked running water, and preparing meals. Women with very young and dependent children, however, have restricted mobility and often must turn to their parents, particularly their mother, for help if they want to work away from the home. The case of María Victoria (from Serradilla), the wife of the narrator Juán Julian Recuero, illustrates how women help in the fields during much of their lifetime. But it also exemplifies how women with young children must retreat from work in the fields unless they can get help from their parents (particularly their mother) for child care. María recalled how, as a young girl, she helped her father thresh wheat, prepare meals for the workers on the harvest teams, gather olives and acorns knocked to the ground by men, and hoe the plots of chick-peas alongside men in Serradilla. After her marriage and the birth of her children, however, she said, "I had the children and I couldn't do anything except things in the house, take care of the children." Shortly afterward, the Spanish Civil War broke out and her husband was called to serve in Franco's army. She, like Petra, earned her living by selling produce. At that time she relied heavily on her parents for child care. Afterward, when the children were grown and her husband, Juán, had returned from the war, she resumed farm labor with him, raising potatoes and other crops. Normally her husband prepared the ground for planting potatoes, and María Victoria followed along inserting potatoes in the furrows; then Juan ploughed earth over the planted rows. The two worked together harvesting the crop, and María sold the potatoes door to door throughout the community. She remarked that Juán was an excellent worker in the fields, but she had the better head for commerce.

Women married to pastoralists and living an isolated life in the countryside are dependent on their mother for help in child care for longer periods of time. Florencia Real Cobos (whose version of "Beauty and the Beast" is listed in the Appendix) is a case in point; she relied on her mother to care for her son during his years of schooling. Florencia is from Serradilla, but her situation is like that of many wives of pastoralists living in isolated areas outside of Piornal, Navaconcejo, Cabezuela, and Garganta la Olla. She described her life and her dependence on her mother for help in child care this way:

> We got married and we went to the country. I lived in a hut [*choza*] in the country. A *choza* is a place where one made three beds, all in the same place. One for the children, the other for us, and another if someone comes to visit. And there one cooks and there one eats. . . . It was a bedroom, a dining room, a kitchen, and everything. It was one place for everything. . . . There was no running water, there was nothing of anything. One had to fetch water with pitchers and one had to wash in the streams and kneel to wash. . . . The job of Lucio [Florencia's husband] was to look after the livestock, and I attended to the house and made the cheese, washed the dishes. . . . I had very small children and I couldn't come to town . . . lest they suffer cold or something. Lucio went to town, and I had to stay with the livestock, taking care of them. . . . I wanted my boy to come to town so he would have friends. . . . I let him come, and until he was thirteen, he regularly went to school, living here in the town with my mother.

Women in the Cáceres villages are very protective of their mother. Florencia Herrero (of Garganta la Olla) recalled how she spoke on behalf of her mother when the time came to make a division of the family property.

My father had two houses and he had some plots of land. And my father had some money, which in those times was forty-five thousand pesetas, in the savings bank. When he no longer had the use of his reason [he had suffered a stroke], when he was so ill, we called a notary because he had not made a will. Then he left all three children equal parts. My father had no favoritism whatsoever. And he being so ill, we sent for my mother's brother, who lived in Madrigal, my mother's brother who was "little father," as we say here. He came and we called the notary. And my father was as if unconscious. That is to say, he was not able to make a will. But he understood. He did not speak, but he understood. Then the notary questioned him and said "Of the capital that you have, do you leave equal parts to your children?" My father said yes with his head. There were two witnesses. There was no favoritism. Then I told the notary, "I want the property to remain with my mother for the rest of her days and then have it come to us afterward."

*Feminine Versions of "Snow White"*

Although, or perhaps because, mothers and daughters retain a lifelong closeness, they also undergo a struggle for a separate identity, a struggle sometimes characterized by competition. A common theme in many "Snow White" (AT 709) stories is the narcissistic struggle between a girl and her mother. The narcissism of the mother is apparent when she consults the magic mirror to discover who is the most beautiful woman in the world. The mother's narcissism is the driving force in the plot because it causes Snow White's expulsion from home and brings about her enchantment. The struggle between Snow White and her mother is a metaphor for the efforts of a young girl to gain independence. Bettelheim (1977: 202–204) interprets that struggle as a dynamic process involving the mother as well as the daughter. Using the Grimms' fairy tale as an example, he suggests that the woman consulting the magic mirror represents both the narcissistic mother who feels threatened by her daughter's maturation and the daughter who projects her own jealousy of her mother's prerogatives onto the mother, symbolically recast as a wicked and narcissistic stepmother. The feelings raised in this struggle are very threatening to mothers and daughters because of their interdependent relationship, and consequently many versions of "Snow White" present split images of the good natural mother and the bad stepmother.

The splitting of parental images is common in fantasy because it is a relatively nonthreatening way for a child to express ambivalence toward a parent. The origin of a child's ambivalence and the splitting of parental images are complex and depend on the gender of the child. Although all children may develop ambivalence toward the mother, who sometimes scolds and sometimes nurtures her child, girls and boys also split maternal images in fantasy for different reasons related to their contrasting early childhood experiences in families in which the mother is the primary parent. Chodorow (1978: 126–127) notes that girls continue to regard the mother as a love object during much of their childhood and may split maternal images in fantasy as a defensive reaction while struggling for autonomy and an independent feminine identity. Spiro (1982: 113–124) argues that boys develop ambivalence and split maternal representations as a defensive reaction to the seductive mother who arouses strong and frightening feelings in her son and to the mother who rejects her son's efforts to monopolize her affections. Bettelheim, explaining the widespread appearance of split parental images in European fairy tales, notes that a child's anger toward a parent is extremely threatening and the creation of two parental images allows the child to keep "the good image uncontaminated" and feel angry toward the false parent without feeling guilty (1977: 67–69). In the fairy-tale versions of "Snow White," the split maternal images generally consist of the good natural mother and the wicked and evil stepmother who attempts to enchant the heroine while living with the dwarfs in the forest (199–215).

Spanish narrators keep the good image of the mother uncontaminated to varying degrees. In some stories, the heroine's natural mother is not symbolically recast and appears as an evil and narcissistic woman who throws her daughter out of the house, consults with the magic mirror over her own beauty, and tries to kill her daughter when the mirror tells her that the most beautiful woman is Snow White, who lives in the forest with dwarfs. A. Espinosa collected a variant from an unknown narrator in Jaraíz de la Vera, a community close to Garganta la Olla, which presents a startling picture of a natural mother jealous of her own daughter's beauty (1924: 230–231). He collected a similar tale in Toledo (1924: 227–230), and both Spanish stories resemble the original version of "Snow White" (*Sneewittchen*) in the Grimms' collection. The Grimms modified the story by recasting the natural mother as a stepmother in later published editions of their works (Ellis 1983: 74–77).

Other Spanish narrators (Llano Roza de Ampudia 1975: 113–115), including all of the storytellers from Cáceres, split their images of the mother by creating the good natural mother and the bad stepmother who is jealous of Snow White's beauty. Many Cáceres men and women use a food metaphor to distinguish the good mother, who gives a child bread and honey (*pan y miel*), from the bad mother, who gives bread and bile (*pan e hiel*), in the beginning of "Snow White" and other stories. Women and men, however, present very different maternal images in their versions of "Snow White," probably because of their different relationships with their own mother. Women generally guard more carefully their image of the mother by multiple recastings of maternal images and make other alterations to the plots to capture the complex and continuous relationship between a mother and her daughter. Domitila Prieto Perez of Piornal told a version of this story that illustrates how a Cáceres woman presents a complex image of the mother that actually expresses the complicated interdependence between mothers and daughters in her village. Domitila told her tale from the perspective of a sixty-seven-year-old married woman with seven grown children.

### "Snow White," by Domitila Prieto Perez

Once there was a man who was married for a number of years and didn't have any children. One day the man's wife was standing at a window and it was snowing. She was sewing and she pricked herself in the finger. She bled and she looked at the snow and said, "When shall I have a daughter as white as the snow and as red as blood?" And God gave her a daughter like the one she asked for. She was as red as blood and as white as snow.

Some years passed and the mother died. The father took the girl to another woman's house so the girl would be better cared for. The woman was a widow and she loved the girl a lot and gave her the best care she could give and all the best things. When her father came, the girl said, "Father, you have to marry this woman. She gives me bread and honey." Her father said, "Hush, daughter, someday she'll give you bread and bile." They went on and on, and it turned out that the man married the widow.

After they were married, things changed for the girl. And now the girl began to eat bile. The girl told her father, and he let it go on. But then he threw the woman out of the house, and the girl went with her stepmother. She had to go with the woman. One day the girl went out into the forest. There was a lot of snow and she got lost, and then she came to a cabin. Seven little dwarfs, who were in the cabin, came out and saw the girl. They picked her up and put her in their cabin. The seven little dwarfs worked and cut wood, and the girl was very happy there. They treated her well. The girl fixed dinner because she was very smart and she cleaned their house and did everything for them. And the girl was very beautiful. Then the seven little dwarfs said to her, "You stay here. Don't go away from here. Don't go out for a walk. There are a lot of bad people around here who can hurt you."

Well, there were enemies, two rivals. "I don't want her to be more beautiful than I." And she didn't want the other to be more beautiful than she. That's the way it was then and that's the way it is now. And the beautiful and high and mighty woman looked at herself in the mirror and said, "You are a marvelous mirror. Is there another face in the world more beautiful than mine?" The mirror replied, "Yes. She lives in the forest. They call her Snow White, and the little dwarfs watch over her." The woman got angry. She grabbed the mirror and threw it and broke it into one hundred pieces. She looked for a witch and told her, "You're going to go to the forest and look for that young woman and kill her." And that's what she did.

The witch went three times. The first time she went selling apples. "Who'll buy an apple?" And she called to the girl and the girl appeared at the window. "Look, look, I bring very good apples. Come downstairs and buy them from me." The girl said, "No. My little dwarfs told me not to go out of the house." "Eh! That's a lie. Come downstairs." She came downstairs. "Take an apple," the witch said. The girl didn't want to eat it, but the witch insisted: "Yes, you're going to eat it. I'm also going to eat it. Let's cut one in half. You're going to eat one half, and I am going to eat the other half." But one half had poison, and the witch ate the half without poison. The child ate half of the apple and died. The dwarfs returned home and found her dead. "What happened here?" They went to the girl and made her vomit up the apple. And the girl was saved.

The witch went the next day and told the high and mighty woman, "Ay, now I killed her." The lofty one was very happy. But then she looked at the mirror again and asked, "Mirror, marvelous mirror, is there a face more beautiful?" "Yes. She lives in the forest and is called Snow White and the little dwarfs watch over her." She looked for the witch again and told her, "This is what happened. She's in the forest." And the mirror told her she had to look for her. The witch went again and this time she went selling combs. And the girl appeared again at the window, and the witch did the same thing. "Look, I bring combs. Come. I'm going to put a beautiful one in your hair." "No, no, no. The dwarfs told me not to go downstairs." "Come downstairs, come downstairs," said the witch. She came downstairs to try on the comb, and the witch stuck it into her brain and killed her. The dwarfs came home and found her dead once more. They cried a lot because they thought they had lost her; they didn't believe she could be saved. They made a coffin and took her to be buried. As they carred her along the road, they fell with the coffin. The coffin broke open and the girl fell out, recovering again. The dwarfs took her away, and she lived well with them.

A prince passed through the forest when Snow White was with the dwarfs. He approached the house and asked if they had any water for his horse. But he was looking around and was distracted. The dwarfs were very helpful to him and told him he could rest his horse there a little, if he wanted. The prince was very happy and he accepted. Then he asked, "Are you the only ones here?" "No. We have someone else here. We have a little girl, Snow White." "Have her come out!" "We don't want her to come out because a lot of things have happened to her." The prince wanted her to come out, of course, and she appeared. He fell in love with her and married her. And the prince took the dwarfs with him and asked for her father. He took them all with him until the dwarfs and her father died.

Domitila presents a very protected image of the mother by multiple recastings and by tempering the image of the stepmother. Domitila has recast the mother three times, first as the initially caring and then heartless widow whom Snow White's father marries, second as the vaguely identified haughty woman who consults the magic mirror about her own beauty, and third as the witch whom the haughty woman sends to kill Snow White living in the forest. In a number of versions, Snow White leaves home because her stepmother gets rid of her, but in Domitila's tale the stepmother never forces Snow White to leave. Instead, the father throws the widow out of the house because Snow White complains that her stepmother mistreats her. The heroine goes with her stepmother because she, not he, is the one who cares for her. Even when fraught with conflict the mother-daughter bond is strong, and the the heroine simply wanders off into the forest and gets lost because there is a lot of snow. The woman who consults the magic mirror is not the stepmother but an unnamed rival who is like many jealous women the narrator knows in her own village of Piornal.

Other Cáceres narrators split the images of mothers and moderate the bad image of the stepmother in different ways. María Marco, a married woman in her early sixties, described the stepmother as jealous of Snow White's beauty but not for her own sake. The stepmother has daughters of her own and consults the magic mirror to find out if they, not she, are the most beautiful women in the world. María's tale, which she learned from her mother, is listed in the Appendix. Evarista Moreno, a thirty-three-year-old married woman from Cabezuela, describes the stepmother in a struggle with her stepdaughter, but the issue is not narcissism; instead it is the girl's failure to carry out domestic chores properly. The stepdaughter runs into problems when an eagle grabs the intestines her stepmother has sent her to wash in the river. (The reader can find the full text of Evarista's tale later in this chapter.) Clearly female Cáceres storytellers recognize the inevitability of conflict between mothers and daughters, but often they try to soften this conflict by removing jealousy as its cause.

Snow White's life with the dwarfs could represent maidens separating from their mothers when they become involved with peers. Maidens at the age of courtship actually develop intense peer-group relationships when they, like Domitila, join work teams to harvest paprika, tobacco, cherries, and raspberries. In Garganta la Olla, groups of maidens join the Italianas, a dance group that performs during the festival of Santa Isabel, the female patron saint of the village.[2] In the context of rural Cáceres society, dwarfs who live in the forest also stand for agrarian working-class men who work in fields outside of the villages. The small size of dwarfs represents the low social status of working-class men. The dwarfs in "Snow White" share some characteristics with the Big Heads, who walk next to much taller Giants in parades in many parts of Spain. Brandes (1980: 17–36) suggests that the relatively small stature of the Big

Heads associates them with, among other things, the nonelite members of stratified communities. Giants, on the other hand, represent agents of social control, including the landed aristocracy. Giants and Big Heads perform in Domitila's community of Piornal and in other northern and central Cáceres communities.

Big Heads in parades of southern Spain (Brandes 1980: 32–34) and dwarfs in the story of "Snow White" sometimes have phallic symbolism (Bettelheim 1977: 210). The heroine's refuge with dwarfs in the forest could consequently stand for a maiden conquering some of her fears of the men she has learned to regard as safe-appearing but dangerous sexual predators. In the maiden-and-thieves stories discussed earlier, sexual predators appeared as thieves who have something in common with dwarfs because both live in the forest. The dwarfs in the feminine variants of "Snow White," however, are benign because they protect and love the protagonist. When added to the picture of thieves in stories discussed in the preceding chapter, they reveal women's more complex view of men. Now the forest has men who are good as well as bad.

The attempts by the stepmother to kill Snow White by giving her poisoned food, combs, shoes, or necklaces represent, according to Bettelheim (1977: 212), the "parent who temporarily succeeds in maintaining his dominance by arresting his child's development." Snow White's acceptance of the safe-appearing but dangerous gifts from her mother could be the daughter's inclination to regress to earlier stages of development by continuing to accept what her mother offers her rather than asserting herself. Bettelheim further suggests that Snow White's enchantment is her death as a child, and her deathlike state represents the inertness or latency of a young maiden unready for sex and marriage (213–214). The items the stepmother or her agents use to place the protagonist in her state of enchantment have obvious connections with a young woman's efforts to establish a separate identity. Domitila, like other Cáceres women, describes Snow White enchanted by accepting items connected with a woman's femininity. She describes the stepmother sending a witch to Snow White with a poisoned comb, and other narrators mention similar items representing a woman's identity. María Marcos, for example, includes a poisoned comb, and Evarista Moreno mentions poisoned shoes. Domitila and the other feminine narrators also include poisoned fruit, which represents maternal nurturance because of woman's role in nurturing all her children with food. The fruit is poisoned, however, symbolizing the dangers for girls of remaining dependent on their mothers too long. Snow White's repeated enchantments postpone her marriage and convey the message that women need time to make the transition from daughters to wives. This message certainly rings true in the context of Spanish courtship and ideals of femininity, in which a woman is expected to marry long after puberty and guard her premarital virginity until marriage. Domitila closes her tale with the mother dropping out of the story, representing how a maiden may cease to struggle with her mother once she has developed more autonomy and a stronger sense of her own separate feminine identity. Domitila's heroine marries a prince and is reunited with her father and the dwarfs; perhaps she represents a maiden who has achieved some independence from her mother, developed heterosexual affection for her father, and is ready to transfer that affection to her husband.

## "Snow White" by the Gender of the Storyteller

Evarista Moreno, a thirty-three-year-old married woman, and Vito Flores, a seventy-four-year-old married man, both from Cabezuela, told closely related versions of "Snow White" that illustrate the contours of the storytelling dialogue between women and men. Despite the disparity in their ages, they told closely related story variants that express male and female relationships with the mother, mediate the fear between women and men by altering the images of men living in the forest, and express what they need and want from each other to make the transition from courtship to marriage. Evarista could not recall exactly where she learned her story, but she remembers hearing it told as a child and guesses that perhaps she learned it from a woman neighbor who told her many popular folktales. Vito remembered that he learned his version from his mother and grandmother, making his tale a masculinized version of a story originally heard from women. Their stories also illustrate how tales circulating in one community sometimes have distinctive features marking them off from variants of the same stories circulating in other communities. The versions of "Snow White" by Evarista and Vito differ from other variants I collected in northern and central Cáceres in that they describe the heroine guided by an eagle to the house of the dwarfs or thieves in the forest. The eagle guides Snow White much as a young girl might need guidance through the separation from her mother in preparation for marriage.

### "SNOW WHITE," BY EVARISTA MORENO

Once there was a king who had a daughter. Her stepmother sent the girl to wash tripe in the river. Then an eagle passed by and snatched the tripe, and the girl said, "Little eagle, give me my bit of tripe. If my stepmother finds out, she'll kill me." But the eagle said no and took the little bit of tripe away. Instead of going to her stepmother's house, she went to the house of the little dwarfs. They weren't there, and she went in the door. And their table was set. She ate out of the little dwarfs' plates, she drank out of their glasses, and she dove into their beds. And when the little dwarfs came home, one of them said, "Oh, my! Someone has eaten out of my plate." "From mine too." They started to search the entire house and they didn't find anything. They went up to the bedrooms and said, "Someone has slept in my bed." "In mine too." "In mine." "In mine." And they looked behind the door and there the girl was hiding. One of the dwarfs asked, "What are you doing here?" She said, "I'm here because a little eagle took a bit of tripe, and my stepmother will kill me if she finds out." The dwarfs said, "Don't go back to your stepmother. Stay here."

Then the stepmother passed through, selling apples. She appeared in the window saying, "Delicious apples. Delicious apples. Are you there, child?" The girl said yes. "Come downstairs and buy an apple. Look how good they are. Come downstairs." So then she came down and bought apples from her stepmother. She fell down after eating an apple. The little dwarfs came home and found her. They removed the apple and revived her.

Then the stepmother came again. "Ala! Fine combs. Ala! Fine combs. Girl, come downstairs and buy a comb. Look how good they are." "No, no. My brothers told me not to go away from here. I won't go downstairs. No." Well, her stepmother convinced her to come downstairs. Then her stepmother said, "Wait, I'll comb your hair." And as she went to comb the girl's hair, she stuck a pin into her head. The little dwarfs came home again and saw what happened to her. They removed the pin, and she revived.

The stepmother came again selling more things. But now the girl didn't want to come downstairs. The dwarfs had told her, "Don't go downstairs or this will happen to you again." But the stepmother came selling shoes. She said, "Ala! Fine shoes. Ala! Fine shoes. Come downstairs, child. Come down. I know you're there. Come downstairs." "No, no. My brothers told me not to go downstairs." But her stepmother insisted, "Come on. Come down. Look, they're very beautiful. They'll look very nice on you." She came downstairs and her stepmother said, "Come, we'll try it on you. Let's see how it fits." The girl put on the shoe and sat down. And when she put on the other one, she fell down dead. And then the dwarfs came home and looked at her and couldn't find anything wrong.

So then they buried her in a beautiful glass coffin without covering her or anything. They took it to a faraway place and there they left her. And then a hunter passed by. He saw what looked like a house and it shined. He came closer and closer, and he saw her. He said, "Oh, my! She's dead. No, she isn't dead. She isn't dead." He removed one of her shoes and she moved. He removed the other one, and she stood up. She was revived. Then she went back to the house of the little dwarfs. He was a prince and he married her. He saved and married her. *Colorín colorado*, this story is finished [*acabado*].

"SNOW WHITE," BY VITO FLORES

Once there was a man who was a widower, and a woman fell in love with him. She was a widow and had a daughter, and the widower also had a daughter. When he came home from the fields, his daughter said, "Father, Aunt Mariquita gives us bread and honey." The father jumped up and said, "My daughter, someday she'll give you bread and bile." Another time she said, "Father, Aunt Mariquita gives us bread and honey," and he said, "Someday she'll give you bread and bile." But the day came, and they were married. The stepmother loved her own daughter and threw the other one out of the house.

The stepdaughter, a maiden, went for a walk by the river. She got close to the water and one of her shoes fell in. It went floating down the river, floating and floating. And an eagle said, "You'll walk, you'll walk; at the house of the seven dwarfs you'll stop. You'll walk, you'll walk; at the house of the seven dwarfs you'll stop." After walking and walking she found a cave. The maiden went inside and saw that everything was in a mess. She cleaned everything up, put the tables in their places, put everything away. And the dwarfs came home. She saw they were bandits, and the bandits came to the cave and said, "I smell human flesh. I smell human flesh." The captain of the bandits said, "Listen, don't touch the girl who's hiding here. Don't touch her, eh! She has good intentions toward us." She was hiding behind the door. "Girl, come out. We won't do anything to you. You come out." She came out and, man, they loved her a lot.

She was there for at least three or four months. They began buying her golden finery and many, many gifts. After they dressed her very well, she asked permission to go see her father. They gave it to her. The girl went back home, and they didn't recognize her because of her finery and how well off she was. Her stepmother asked her, "Where have you been? You come home so beautiful!" She said, "I've been in a cave with some bandits." "But you come home so well dressed. What have you done?" She said, "Oh, I threw out everything they had there, and after they went away I stole all I could and bought this." She told her stepmother just the opposite of what really happened.

Her stepmother sent her own daughter, and of course she dirtied everything, threw out their dishes, and so on. They came home saying, "I smell human flesh." They gave her a good caning and threw her out half dead. She came home after they threw her out half dead, and her mother asked, "But, daughter, who hit you so much? Who did this to you?" "It was the bandits. They hit me. And then they threw me out." The eagle came back again after the bandits had thrown her out and said to the girl, "You'll walk, you'll walk; at the house of the seven dwarfs you'll stop." And the young, well-dressed woman went back to the house of the bandits. She married a bandit, and they lived happily and threw their bones at our noses.

## The Affirmation of Difference

Evarista describes the heroine breaking away from her mother much as women actually separate from parents in a continuous process. The heroine separates in gradual stages, and her relationship with her stepmother is continuous throughout much of the tale. Snow White separates from her stepmother when she follows the eagle to the dwarfs in the forest, but she does not become free of her stepmother's influence until very late in the tale when, after her third enchantment, she is saved by a prince. In many respects, Evarista's tale is like Domitila's narrative (discussed earlier) and María Marco's composite story of "Cinderella" and "Snow White" (listed in the Appendix). All three narrators represent the mother-daughter relationship as continuous and complex, and all three shield the mother by symbolic recasting and avoiding the depiction of the daughter and stepmother in a direct narcissistic struggle. The representation of the mother and daughter in a continuous relationship accords with the way Cáceres women described their actual relationships with their own mothers in the first part of this chapter. Marriage certainly changes the living arrangements and the patterns of cooperation in the organization of work for a mother and her daughter, but married women remain dependent on their mothers and care for their elderly parents once they are no longer able to care for themselves.

Vito's tale describes a much more discontinuous relationship between the heroine and her stepmother, which resembles the comparatively abrupt change for men at marriage when the wife replaces the mother. Vito describes the stepmother simply throwing her stepdaughter out of the house, and after the heroine reaches the home of the seven bandits, the stepmother does not reappear selling poisoned fruit or combs as she does in the tale by the three women. Vito's heroine returns to her stepmother, indicating some residual emotional ties after separation; however, she returns as a triumphant woman able to protect herself from her stepmother's meanness. She protects herself by turning the truth on its head to account for her fine appearance. She gains vengeance on her stepsister not only by returning home with beautiful clothes and finery but also by setting the stage for her stepsister's caning. Greater hostility in the mother-daughter relationship appears in other masculine versions of "Snow White." For example, in the story by Eugenio Real Vázquez of Serradilla, the mother, symbolically recast as the stepmother, is jealous of her beauty for her own sake. Eugenio (whose tale is listed in the Appendix) depicts a more direct narcissistic struggle between the heroine and her stepmother than any of the feminine narrators from this part of Spain. The discontinuous and hostile relationship between heroines and stepmothers in the stories by Vito and Eugenio are more like the actual relationship between a man and his mother. Boys generally develop hostility toward their mothers as they reject the feminine in themselves while developing a masculine identity (Chodorow 1978: 180–190; Gilmore 1987a: 126–153), they may feel hostile toward the mother for rejecting

their efforts to monopolize her affections (Spiro 1982: 113–114). Older
sons near the age of marriage resent their mother's possessiveness
(Brandes 1975: 119—120) and generally fear the power of women
(Brandes 1980: 77). It is important to emphasize that hostility toward the
mother is only one dimension of a man's relationship with his mother in
particular and women in general. I mention hostility at this point to explain why men tell the "Snow White" story differently from women by
projecting into their versions of this tale their own negative maternal images when describing the mother-daughter relationship. Men, like
women, develop split images of women and project the good mother in
other stories considered in later chapters.

## The Mediation of Fear

The different perspectives on relations with parents are affirmations of
difference that contribute to misunderstanding and fear between women
and men moving through courtship toward marriage. Men who fail to
understand the interdependence between mothers and daughters and who
expect their wives to break with parents are a problem for women. No
woman wants to have to choose between her suitor and her parents, and
mothers socialize their daughters to fear a man who takes his bride to live
far from her mother. Chapter 4 discusses stories older women tell their
daughters and granddaughters that describe cannibalistic thieves taking
their brides away from their parents to live in the forest. The stories give
voice to women's fear of men who threaten the ties that bind a mother
and her daughter.

The "Snow White" stories by Evarista and Vito carry the message that
maidens of the right age are ready to begin conquering their fears of men
learned earlier in socialization. Their heroines stand for maidens at a
more mature stage of development relative to the heroines in the stories
older women tell younger women in order to reinforce the norms of premarital chastity and bind daughters to their mothers. In contrast to the
heroines in the stories considered in Chapter 4, Snow White has lost her
natural and presumably nurturing mother and is in the throes of developing her independent feminine identity. As a consequence she is the
maiden more ready to conquer her fears of sex with men and enter a
courtship. The heroines in the maiden-and-thieves stories, by contrast,
were the youngest in a group of daughters and represent maidens more
closely attached to parents. Both "Snow White" stories mediate women's
fear of men by humanizing the characters who personify sexual predators. They rework the imagery of men who live in forests by making them
kind and loving figures who give the heroine refuge as she struggles with
her cruel and demanding stepmother. Evarista, like all women who tell

the "Snow White" story, presents the men in the forest as little dwarfs who lack all of the sinister imagery of the thieves in other stories, who threaten to take advantage of vulnerable maidens. They are like children and are capable of demonstrating loving human emotions. In Evarista's story, the heroine even calls them "my brothers," men who are truly trustworthy.

In the dialogue through storytelling, men and women tell stories to persuade others to action, and Vito's tale attempts to persuade women to trust and transfer their loyalties and affections to men even when they appear threatening. He, like other narrators, plays with appearances and reality by describing his heroine finding refuge with thieves, who on the surface appear like some of the sinister characters in the stories older women tell younger women to reinforce the norms of premarital chastity and bind a daughter to her mother. Vito's thieves are like the cannibals who threatened to eat the innocent maidens in the stories considered in Chapter 4; they come home declaring that they smell human flesh. Vito plays with appearances and reality to present a picture of men diametrically opposed to that found in stories of maidens and thieves told by women. Whereas women sometimes make men safe appearing but actually dangerous, Vito makes men dangerous appearing but actually safe. The thieves who give the heroine refuge are humanized because they treat Snow White very kindly, giving her many gifts and a lot of finery. But they are still strong and potentially dangerous in a way that the dwarfs in the women's stories are not.

It is impossible to determine how Vito changed the story from its original form as told by his mother and grandmother. The two women died many years ago, and Vito learned the tale as a young boy over sixty years before he told it to me. Comparison of the feminine and masculine variants of the "Snow White" story support the conclusion that the transformation of dwarfs into thieves is a masculine change. All the women storytellers I knew told "Snow White" with the heroine finding refuge with dwarfs. A. Espinosa collected a variant in which thieves replace dwarfs from a narrator who came from the Cáceres community of Jaraíz de la Vera, but he did not report the narrator's gender (1924: 230–231). In addition to Vito, Julio Lopez Curiel, a narrator from Garganta la Olla, told a highly masculinized version of "Snow White" in which the heroine finds refuge with thieves in the forest. Julio's story (listed in the Appendix) uses a style of narration that makes the thieves principal protagonists who care for and are loving toward Snow White, who is actually the sister of the thieves' captain. Kind thieves occasionally appear in the "Snow White" stories told by women (Llano Roza de Ampudia 1975: 113–115), but the feminine narrators live outside of Cáceres and the surrounding area.

*Some Unresolved Issues between Women and Men*

Women and men conclude their "Snow White" stories differently indicating that the telling and retelling of this tale does not resolve all of the discordant themes in Cáceres gender relations. Whereas women and men both end their stories with their heroines marrying and presumably making the transition from daughters to wives, they describe Snow White's marriage very differently. Women generally conclude their tales with the heroine marrying a man of high social status; he is a prince or a hunter, an aristocratic man who enters the forest for recreation rather than work. Vito and other Cáceres men end their stories with Snow White marrying one of the men who gives her refuge in the forest. In the storytelling dialogue, men attempt to persuade women to lay aside their fear of men and transfer their affection and loyalty from their parents to men like themselves. The men who give Snow White refuge in the forest are very much like the agrarian working-class men of the Cáceres villages. Eugenio makes the similarity between dwarfs and men of the agrarian working class clear by describing the dwarfs fetching firewood, caring for an orchard, and hoeing a garden, tasks men regularly perform in his community of Serradilla. Eugenio adds a second wish: that women of the landed aristocracy in the agrotown of Serradilla marry men of the agrarian working class, a wish he expresses by making his heroine a princess. Marriages between women of the landed aristocracy and men of the working class in Serradilla are extremely rare, but Eugenio's wish is understandable in a community where many men are rejected as unsuitable husbands because they are poor.

Marriage to a prince or a hunter in the stories by women may express the wish of humble maidens to make a marriage with high-status men in a culture in which the wealth of a suitor is an important consideration in a marriage. But the women, who end their stories with Snow White marrying someone who is not symbolically associated with the men of the agrarian working class of their villages, are also delivering the message that maidens in the midst of separating from their mothers are not ready to fully conquer their fear of men. Snow White represents the maiden who is still emerging from her parental family and is not ready to bond with a man in heterosexual love. Evarista concludes her tale by telling how a hunter saved Snow White by removing her from enchantment and marrying her. Perhaps she is saying that a maiden needs the help of romantic love to make the transition from daughter to wife.

# CHAPTER SIX

# "Cinderella"

ROMANTIC LOVE is an important part of courtship: it helps a man and a woman transcend their fears and differences. In Cáceres, as in other parts of Spain (Pitt-Rivers 1966: 94), a man is expected to make a woman fall in love by paying her compliments and showing her gallantry. The aura of romantic love is called illusion (*ilusión*), a word that connotes the feelings of euphoria and well-being when someone believes he or she is the most wonderful person in the world in the eyes of another. Women and men in Cáceres tell the story of "Cinderella," a very popular folktale in Spanish oral tradition, to share what romantic love means to them.

In the stories told by women, Cinderella alternates between states of beauty and ugliness. Lüthi (1984: 13, 28, 37) suggests that beauty stands for visible perfection and represents the divine in many popular European fairy tales. Following Lüthi's line of reasoning, Cinderella in her beautiful form is the woman glowing in the aura of romantic love who believes she is the most wonderful person in the world in the eyes of the man who courts her. Cinderella's switch from beautiful to ugly stands for the struggles of a woman in courtship as she attempts to conquer her fear of men, temper her sexual anxieties, and contend with men's idealization of women. A maiden hearing the compliments of a young man has already been told by her mother and grandmother not to trust the appearances of young men who attempt to make her fall in love. She has acquired sexual anxieties because she has learned that her defloration may be a brutally violent experience. A woman still struggling with her own identity may resist accepting the compliments of a young man who conveys through his conception of romantic love an idealized image of women based on his own needs.

## Cinderella and Her Stepsisters

One type of "Cinderella" (AT 510) story circulating in Cáceres and Spanish oral tradition begins with the death of the heroine's natural mother and her replacement by a cruel stepmother who favors her own daughters.[1] The stepmother treats the heroine poorly by giving her the worst household tasks and dressing her own daughters well for a ball to attract the attention of a prince. Bettelheim, who interprets written fairy-tale versions of this tale from other parts of Europe, suggests that sibling rivalry is a major theme in all variants of the story. Cinderella represents the child who feels "hopelessly outclassed by his brothers and sisters" (1977: 237). The child's siblings, however, are only incidentally the source of the heroine's misery because actually Cinderella represents any child who no longer feels loved by parents once he or she has entered the stage of Oedipal entanglements. The heroine's debased position, a feature of all "Cinderella" tales, expresses the guilt of a child who wishes to replace the same-sex parent as the object of the other parent's love (1977: 238–245).

Freud considered Oedipal themes at the root dreams (Freud 1978); the same themes appear in many European fairy tales (Bettelheim 1977) and the myths of many other societies (Fischer 1966) because they are a universal part of the human condition (Spiro 1982: 144–180). Siblings and Oedipal rivalry are common to men as well as women, but more women tell this type of "Cinderella" story in Cáceres and other regions in Spain. Five women and only one man told the tale of Cinderella and her stepsisters in the Cáceres villages. The lone masculine version is really a story fragment and contains too few details to reveal how men might masculinize this type of "Cinderella" story. (All Cáceres tales that I collected either appear in this chapter or are listed in the Appendix.) Women more than men appear to tell the "Cinderella" story in other provinces as well; Cortés Vázquez collected the tales from women but no men in Salamanca (1979: 2: 118–123), and Llano Roza de Ampudia reports more feminine than masculine variants from Asturias (1975: 118–125). Other folklorists who collected this story do not report the gender of the storytellers (A. Espinosa 1924: 212–220; Cabal 1924: 30–40).

Cáceres women more than men apparently tell this type of "Cinderella" story to one another to share their experiences in working through their ambivalence in courtship. Ulalia García Castaño, a seventy-eight-year-old widow from Garganta la Olla, told a representative version of "Cinderella" alternating between the heroine appearing beautiful and ugly. Ulalia said she learned her story while working as an adolescent maiden in the paprika harvesting groups in the Tietar River valley below Garganta. Ulalia describes Cinderella alternating between revealing her inner beauty, represented by the star on her forehead, and appearing ugly when dressed in a pelican suit. The pelican suit is a feature of "Cinderella" tales told by a number of contemporary women in Cáceres and may be a regional way that storytellers have chosen to represent the heroine in her ugly form. Several women in Garganta la Olla told of Cinderella dressed as a pelican, and Curiel Merchán (1944: 358–361) collected a similar tale from a woman in Navalvillar de Ibor in southern Cáceres. A. Espinosa collected a variant much like the Garganta stories from an unknown narrator from Jaraíz de la Vera (1924: 204–209). The pelican suit may represent a woman with a goiter, a physical deformity of women with iodine deficiency, which is common in some areas of Spain. The pelican as a symbol of Cinderella in her ugly state does not appear in tales collected in other regions (Cortés Vázquez 1979: 2: 118–123; Llano Roza de Ampudia 1975: 118–125; A. Espinosa 1924: 212–220; Cabal 1924: 30–40), even though women have iodine deficiency and goiter outside of Cáceres (R. Fernandez 1986).

### "Cinderella," by Ulalia García Castaño

Once there was a girl who went to school, and her teacher was a widow who had two daughters. The girl said, "Father, every day the teacher gives me bread and honey." Her father replied, "Hush, my daughter. One day she's going to give you bread and bile." The father said that because he intended to marry the teacher. Again the girl said, "Listen father, every day she gives me bread and honey." He said, "Hush, my daughter. One day she'll give you bread and bile." Well, they got married.

And the son of the king couldn't find a bride. So the king issued a proclamation saying they were holding a dance with free admission for all who wanted to go. It turned out the girl had a star on her forehead, but she always kept it covered. When they held the dance, the teacher's daughters went dressed as queens, but they were ugly. The girl also went to the ball and she too was very well dressed. When she entered the dance hall she removed the cover over her star, and her star lit up the entire ball. As soon as the prince saw the maiden, he danced with her and asked her for her word that she would be his sweetheart, and she gave it to him. He asked her where she lived, and she told him she lived in a place where she didn't really live. The first night when he left her for a while to go with a friend she left him and went home. The same thing happened the next night. He immediately went over to her when she appeared and took her to dance with him. And she told him that his parents should arrange for her marriage and said she had to go home. But the next night he had the door of the ball watched and declared that the doorman who let her escape would be shot. She found out and changed a lot of money into small change, into pesetas or whatever. She had a big sack and took it to the dance. The prince was more tranquil when the dance was about to end because he had told the doormen not to let her get away. When she saw that the dance was ending and tried to leave, the doormen detained her. But she threw the coins and escaped as the two doormen picked up the money. The prince had covered the stairs with tar, and one of her shoes stuck to the stairs as she ran out. She went home with one shoe on and the other shoe off.

The prince's mother asked him, "Son, what's she like?" "Mother, she's very beautiful, but she got away from me. Even though I told the doormen not to let her leave, she threw some coins. What people will do for money! They went for the money and let her escape." It turned out that each night he had given her something. One night he gave her a watch, the next night a bracelet, and the next night his gold ring.

The prince became ill from sorrow because he couldn't find his bride. And the girl dressed in a pelican suit. A woman had given it to her, and said, "Wear this suit and go where the king waters his horse. Stand there and you'll see that the king will take you home because you're a pelican; he wants to have one so much." So she went there and stood where he watered his horse. He said, "What are you doing here, little pelican?" She said, "I'm warming myself in the sun." He asked, "Do you want to go with me?" She said, "Oh, do you want me to go to the palace?" He said, "Yes, go with me to the palace and live with me in the house." The prince was ill, and she had the rings and other things he had given her at the ball. So when he asked someone to make him some soup, the maiden offered, "Oh, I'll make it for him." But his mother protested: "For God's sake!" Then the maiden pulled out something and threw it in the fire as if it were lice, but it was really salt. "Why do we want any more of this?" declared the prince's mother. But the maiden insisted, "I'm going to make him soup so he'll get better. Didn't he tell you to make him soup?" She threw the ring into the bowl, and he found the ring as he ate the soup. He called out, "Mother, the soup is delicious!" She said, "Oh, my son, I made it for you." He said, "Well, look, mother, have the person who made this soup make me another one. If you made it, make it for me again." The mother said, "Oh, my God! How horrible! Now he wants the same person who made the soup before to make him another one." The pelican said, "I'll make him another soup. You won't find anything wrong with it." The next day the maiden made him another soup and she threw in the watch. The next day the prince declared that whoever made the first two soups must make him another. So then she threw in the bracelet he had given her. His mother took the soup downstairs to him, and he ate it and said, "Send the one who made this soup downstairs." "But, my son, I made it for you. Yes, I made it." He said, "No, Mother. You didn't make the soup. She who made the soup has to come downstairs." The mother felt very bad. She said, "Now I'll kill her or . . ." It turned out that the pelican put on the clothes she wore at the ball and removed the cover over her forehead. She went downstairs, and the mother went downstairs behind her and said, "Now I'll kill her." She appeared with the star on her forehead, and the prince declared she was the maiden with whom he had danced and he loved her. He had to marry her. And his mother said, "But, my son, how can you marry her?" "Mother, I have to marry her." But they didn't get married. It turned out she went home to her father, and her stepmother put her away. And the school-teacher tried to marry off one of her two ugly daughters. She kept her step-daughter in the ash heap and that's why they called her Cinderella.

Then the prince said that everyone who had been at the ball had to go to his palace because of the shoe. The schoolteacher had another shoe made for her daughter so the prince would marry her. The prince picked her because she

covered her forehead as if not to show her star, and he thought she was the woman he loved. He took her out in his coach, and a little bird said, "The one you love is in the ash heap, and the one you take is not the one you love." The bird told him who she was, and the prince ordered the two daughters of the teacher hung. He married Cinderella, and they were happy and ate partridges and threw a bone at my nose.

Ulalia's story describes metaphorically the struggle of a maiden who competes with other women for a young man, is ambivalent about his efforts to make her fall in love, tries to get him to see her as more than an idealized woman, and struggles with his mother, who reluctantly gives up her role as the nurturer of her son. Ulalia's heroine represents a maiden more ready for courtship and marriage than Snow White: Cinderella is more assertive in attracting the attention of the man she marries. Rather than lying in a glass coffin waiting to be rescued, she takes matters into her own hands and goes to the ball, removes the cover from her forehead, and fills the hall with radiance from her star to attract the notice of the prince. She is successful: the prince spots her, dances with her, and asks her to be his sweetheart. Cinderella, like any maiden concerned about her moral reputation, tells him to announce his intentions of courtship to her parents. The prince gives her valuable gifts—a watch, a bracelet, and his gold ring—which symbolize the expressions of love that are so necessary for a woman to conquer her fear of men during courtship.

Cinderella's reaction to the efforts by the prince to create an illusion expresses how women feel ambivalent about approaching marriage and resist the compliments of a young man. Maidens in the Cáceres villages are socialized to be skeptical of the man of good appearances who attempts to win their affections. The heroine leaves as soon as the prince is distracted by his friends; she tries to throw him off track when he asks where she lives, and she escapes from the doormen by throwing coins. Although Cinderella successfully eludes the doormen and escapes, she returns to the ball and dances with the prince again. On the final night, she flees and loses one of her shoes because the prince puts tar on the stairs. The loss of her shoe and the tokens of his love that he gave her earlier are the connections between Cinderella and the prince that eventually permit each to recognize the other and turn their relationship into marriage.

One of the more curious details in the "Cinderella" stories told by Cáceres women is the heroine's deliberate efforts, sometimes with the help of another woman, to conceal her beauty and get the prince to recognize her in ugly form as the woman he loves. Ulalia and other women generally describe a prince declaring his love to Cinderella when she appears as the most beautiful woman at the ball and depict the prince as refusing to recognize Cinderella in her ugly form. Ulalia describes a woman giving

Cinderella the pelican suit and sending her to where the king waters his horse so he will take her to his palace, where she will try to get him to recognize her as the woman to whom he professed his love at the ball. The tension between Cinderella and the prince builds as the heroine, dressed as a pelican, deliberately makes herself appear ugly by throwing salt into the fire as if it were lice. Ulalia's story describes a protracted struggle to work through a woman's problems in courtship. It takes three bowls of soup, each containing a token of the prince's love, before this Cinderella reveals herself to the man who says he loves her.

The details of Ulalia's story convey the message that Cinderella is a maiden who struggles with a man who has fallen in love with her at first sight because she is beautiful and sees her as he wants to rather than how she sees herself. Men often idealize women, as will become apparent when considering a masculine Cinderella story later in this chapter, and they convey their idealized conception of women through the compliments designed to make women fall in love. The compliments in courtship ostensibly create the feeling that a maiden is the most wonderful person in the world in the eyes of the young man who courts her. Consequently, in paying those compliments the young man will convey to a woman what he wants her to be and not necessarily what she believes she is. Ulalia's story has powerful imagery—the pelican suit, representing a woman with a physical deformity familiar to many in her village, and the star on Cinderella's forehead, representing her inner beauty—to get across to her listeners the struggle over a woman's identity in courtship.

One of the reasons that Cinderella may be concerned about her identity with the man who says he loves her is because of her long and difficult struggle to establish her own feminine identity and separate from her mother. Psychoanalytic studies of gender difference stress how women as well as men develop adult relationships based on their experiences in their families of origin. Girls generally have longer pre-Oedipal attachments to their mother and remain more emotionally tied to their mother during the Oedipal period. They are consequently likely to grow into women who define themselves by their relationships with others (Chodorow 1978: 92–140). Cáceres women have extremely complex ties with their mother and are consequently likely to have struggled to establish their independent feminine identity prior to courtship. Ulalia expresses the complexity of a woman's ties to her mother (or daughter) when she places Cinderella among several women in her own and her future husband's families.[2] First, there is her stepmother and stepsisters, who represent a maiden's natural mother and sisters, from whom she must partially separate as she emerges from her parental family to form a family of her own. Second, there is the helpful woman who gives Cinderella the pelican suit and tells her how to be admitted into the king's palace; this woman probably stands for a maiden's mother as helpful intermediary agent in her daughter's marriage. If Cinderella is like many of the maidens in the Cáceres village, she will rely on her mother after marriage for help in child care and will care for her elderly mother when she is unable to care for herself. Third, there is the prince's mother, whom Cinderella will replace as the nurturer of her husband. Ulalia, like other Cáceres women, describes the ambivalent position of the mother, about to be replaced by her daughter-in-law. On the one hand, she is hostile toward the heroine, protesting when Cinderella offers to make the prince his soup, and she contemplates killing her future daughter-in-law just as her son is about to recognize Cinderella as the woman to whom he professed his love at the ball. On the other hand, the mother steps aside and allows Cinderella to take over and does nothing to block her son's marriage, much as mothers must eventually give up their role as the nurturer of their sons. The ambivalent position of a man's mother in courtship and marriage is a noted theme in family relations (Brandes 1975: 119).

Despite all of the problems a woman must overcome in courtship, Ulalia draws her tale to a conclusion by expressing faith in conjugal love. Her Cinderella eventually does lay aside her ambivalence and uncovers the star on her forhead, revealing her inner beauty to her prince; his mother steps aside and allows Cinderella to take over her role as his nurturer; and the prince eventually recognizes the woman he loves even when she does not appear beautiful and is in the ash heap in her own home.

Other women from Cáceres told the story of Cinderella and her stepsisters presenting a similar picture of women's ambivalence during courtship. Their stories (listed in the Appendix) contain details that bring out different aspects of a woman's struggle. Domitila Prieto Perez and Filomena Arivas Miguel emphasize how a woman's beauty is a superficial rather than fundamental part of her identity by describing Cinderella becoming beautiful when she puts on beautiful dresses. Ulalia, it may be recalled, stressed how Cinderella's beauty was an essential part of her being, represented by the star on her forehead, which filled the ballroom with radiance. The two conceptions of beauty—one as intrinsic and the other as superficial—probably represent the different ways women think of their identity with the men who say they love them. Some women perhaps see the aura of romantic love as revealing something intrinsic to themselves when they hear the compliments paid them by the men who say they love them. The same women at other times or different women may see romantic love as superficial to what they really think they are. If one assumes that Cinderella as beautiful is the woman in the aura of romantic love, then the alternation between beauty and ugliness stands for the waxing and waning of the feeling of being in love during a long and complicated courtship. The waxing and waning of romantic love, described as entering and leaving an illusion, is a particularly feminine conception that does not appear in stories men tell about courtship and marriage, as will become apparent later in this chapter.

Once again, Domitila and Filomena engage their heroine in relations with others as she struggles with her ambivalence, represented by her alternation between beauty and ugliness. Their stories, like that just considered by Ulalia, describe Cinderella in a relationship with her stepmother and stepsisters and a helpful parental figure who provides the dresses that make their heroine beautiful and allow her to attend the ball. For Domitila the helpful parent is the Virgin Mary, a symbolic recasting of the good mother who helps her daughter make the transition from courtship to marriage. For Filomena it is Christ, a symbolic recasting of the father who helps his daughter transfer her affections to her husband. In both stories, the endings are happy because Cinderella and the prince marry and live happily ever after.

### Cinderella in Animal Skins

Filomena Arivas Miguel told another version of Cinderella, one that adds a dimension by considering romantic love as something shared by a man and a woman. Her tale, which describes Cinderella as an orhpan dressed in animal skins, resembles a story collected by A. Espinosa (1924: 203–207) from an unknown narrator in Cuenca. The heroine represents a maiden who has broken farther away from her parental family than the heroines in the stories of Cinderella and her stepsisters. This heroine has no parents or siblings and represents a maiden who has probably developed more fully her independent feminine identity. It is significant that this Cinderella's beauty is an intrinsic part of her femininity as becomes apparent when she steps out of her animal skins. Filomena and other Cáceres women appear to say in their "Cinderella" stories that the woman who believes her beauty is an intrinsic part of her femininity is a woman who has reached a more mature stage in her development and has a stronger sense of who she is. She is a maiden who no longer needs the help of a parental figure, recast as a helpful Virgin or Christ, to make herself appear beautiful to others. Filomena's heroine reveals her beauty to a man; he appreciates her beauty and falls in love with her; and then Cinderella tries to persuade him to understand that she will love him just as she wants him to love her, even when both do not necessarily appear as physically beautiful persons.

#### "CINDERELLA," BY FILOMENA ARIVAS MIGUEL

Once there was an orphan girl and she went about the world dressed in an animal hide. She asked for water from a woman who took her in. The woman had a son, and there were dances at night. The girl went out a little at night and went to the dances. There was no one who caught the son's attention. When the girl went to the dances, she came out of her animal hide, and the son fell in love with her because of her beauty. She went to the dance, and when the boy looked at her, she left and went back into her animal hide. She came home and threw a fistful of salt into the fire and the woman said, "Oh, my, Cinderella, you have so many lice and so much misery!" And the girl said, "I sure do."

And then the boy got sick, and his mother asked him, "Son, what's wrong with you?" He said, "I don't know. Nothing is wrong with me." She insisted, "Are you sure? You're sick." "Nothing is wrong with me. Nothing is wrong with me." And Cinderella asked, "Do you want me to make him something to eat?" His mother said, "Oh, for God's sake, if he were to find out that you made him something, he'd throw me out of the house." Cinderella agreed, "Yes, it's true." And when the boy got up in the morning, the girl came and said to him, "Don't wash yourself so much. You're loved by the one who must love you. You've been seen by the one who must see you." "Hush, Cinderella. You have more lice and nits than anything else." She said, "Don't worry." And the same thing happened again the next day. "Hey! Don't wash yourself so much. You're loved by the one who must love you. You've been seen by the one who must see you." "Be quiet or I'll throw this washbasin at you." Then the next day his mother asked, "Son, what's the matter with you? You're not well." But he protested, "Leave me in peace." She insisted: "What's the matter with you, son? What's wrong with you?" He replied, "I tell you, leave me in peace." Again he got up in the morning, and again Cinderella said, "I tell you not to wash yourself so much. You're loved by the one who must love you. You've been seen by the one who must see you." "Quiet! I'll throw my comb at you Cinderella!"

On the morning of the next day, the boy was still sick. He was sad with such a sorrow that it was killing him. And Cinderella said to his mother, "Calm yourself, I'll make him some soup." "Quiet, daughter! For God's sake, if he were to find out!" But Cinderella insisted, "What would he do? I'm going to make it for him." And she took his ring off her finger and threw it in the bowl, into the soup. Then she took the soup up to him, and of course he was eating it and he looked at the spoon. He called to his mother, and she said, "What do you want, son?" "Who made this soup?" he asked. She said, "I did, son. I made it." He said, "It wasn't you." She said, "Yes, son. I made it." "I tell you that you did not make this soup. May the one who made this soup come here." "Have you found a hair?" "I tell you, send up the one who made this soup." "Son, it was Cinderella. Did you find something?" "Tell her to come up." And she went up. He said, "Come out of that hide, eh." She said no. He said, "I tell you, come out of that hide." And she came out and was missing the ring. He said, "And what is this?" A beautiful maiden appeared. He said, "I'm sick because of you." She came out of her animal hide, and they were married and lived happily and ate partridges.

This Cinderella has some of the qualities of the others because she too is ambivalent about her courtship and conceals her beauty from the man who has fallen in love with her. She covers herself in animal skins when he looks at her and she throws salt into the fire as if it were lice deliberately to make herself appear ugly. Tension develops in the story when Cinderella conceals her beauty, and her man becomes sick with sorrow because he cannot find the woman he loves. Filomena develops the tension differently than other narrators by introducing an exchange between Cinderella and her man that reveals another dimension of the meaning of love in courtship and marriage. Every morning the heroine, dressed in animal skins, comes to see her man and says, "Don't wash yourself so much. You're loved by the one who must love you. You've been seen by the one who must see you." He replies, "Hush, Cinderella. You have more lice and nits than anything else." He threatens to throw his washbasin and his comb at her. His mother asks him what is wrong, and he tells her, "Leave me in peace." When she asks him again, he replies even more sternly, "I tell you, leave me in peace."

Filomena's tale expresses how the pain and doubts of romantic love are shared by a man and a woman. Cinderella in her ugly form represents the courted maiden in a doubting phase of romantic love who wants her man to see her as the woman he loves even when she does not appear beautiful. Her doubts bring her to test his love by deliberately appearing ugly, concealing the beauty he so admired at the ball. Her man has similar concerns about his own lovableness at a crucial transition in his life, represented by his efforts to make himself appear handsome by washing and combing, presumably in order to find the woman with whom he has fallen in love. Cinderella tries to assure him that he is loved, but he cannot hear her, much as men, anxious and lost in the transition from courtship to marriage as they trade mother for wife (Brandes 1975: 119–120), may not hear the expressions of love from their courted maiden or wife.

Filomena resolves the conflict in the same way as other narrators: Cinderella takes over as the nurturer of her man, his mother reluctantly steps aside as the nurturer of her son, and the man eventually realizes that the woman he loves is in his midst. Cinderella returns his tokens of love in the soup, he orders her to step out of her animal hide, she appears to him as the woman he loves, and they marry and eat partridges at the wedding banquet and live happily ever after.

Women tell other stories expressing their concerns about men's infatuation with illusory beauty, their persistence in getting their husband to really see them, and their fidelity to their husband. Felisa Sanchez Martín, a seventy-two-year-old woman from Serradilla, told the tale of "The Three Grains of Anise" (listed in the Appendix). The heroine is a beautiful maiden who announces that if she married the king, she would smash three gains of anise on his neck without him feeling it. She marries the king and becomes disheveled, ceases to be beautiful, no longer keeps the castle in order, and loses the affection of her husband. When about to depart on a trip, he says, "If you were different, you would come with me. I'm going on a trip to Toledo, but because you are this way, I cannot appear with you in public." The disheveled queen makes herself beautiful again, goes on her own to Toledo, dances with her husband, who does not recognize her as a beautiful woman, and spends the night with him on the condition that he give her his hat, the symbol of his status. The king returns, finds the queen as disheveled and unattractive as ever, and makes a second trip, this time to Aragón, where his wife, whom he does not recognize as a beautiful woman, sleeps with him on the condition that he give her his banner. The king makes a third trip, to Seville, where he spends the night with the disguised queen who this time demands that he give her his ring. The queen secretly gives birth to three children, one for each night she spends with her husband. When the king holds a banquet in his castle at the urging of his wife, the queen brings out each child, one wearing the hat, the second carrying the banner, and the third wearing the ring. She says, "These are the three gains of anise that you wanted crushed on your neck without feeling it."

### The Father Who Wants to Marry His Daughter

Women and men describe their different perspectives on romantic love in a third variant of "Cinderella" (AT 510B), which begins when a widower wants to marry his youngest daughter because she resembles her mother. Romantic love appears in the story after the daughter flees from her father, ends up in a king's castle, and dances with a prince at a ball. The prince falls in love with Cinderella at first sight because she looks beautiful in each dress provided by her father. Maximina Castaño, a sixty-eight-year-old widow from Garganta la Olla, and Leandro Jimenez, a seventy-two-year-old married man from El Guijo de Santa Bárbara, told closely related versions of this story, which convey very different conceptions of romantic love (*la ilusión*). For Maximina, the illusion is something that waxes and wanes as a woman deals with her ambivalence in courtship. For Leandro, the illusion is brittle and can break with tragic results. Their different conceptions of romantic love have many possible sources. The waxing and waning illusion for women probably develops as maidens struggle to separate and yet remain connected to their mothers, with whom they have a continuous relationship throughout the life course.

The brittle illusion for the man is probably related to his discontinuous relationship with his parents, particularly his mother (Brandes 1975: 199–120), and has antecedents in early childhood, when a man is socialized to believe that romantic love can come to a sudden and tragic end if another man takes his honor by seducing his sweetheart or his wife.

This type of Cinderella story contains pronounced Oedipal themes: the father proposes marriage to his youngest daughter, who resembles her dead mother. It expresses important dimensions of gender relations because it circulates widely in Spanish oral tradition; A. Espinosa (1924: 204–209) collected variants from unknown narrators from Jaraíz de la Vera and Zamora that look very much like the stories by Maximina and Leandro. Bettelheim (1977: 245) believes that the existence of this kind of Cinderella tale in Europe warrants the conclusion that other kinds of Cinderellas are mistreated by their stepmothers because they are in Oedipal situations. Psychoanalytic theory stresses the connection between Oedipal entanglements in the family and conceptions of heterosexual love by explaining that adult men and women transfer their affections from their parents to others according to how they work through their Oedipal complex. Boys and girls have different Oedipal situations; they resolve them differently, and are likely to develop different conceptions of heterosexual relationships in any society in which the mother is the primary parent. Chodorow (1978: 111–130) explains that a girl develops Oedipal attachments to the father without ending her affective relationship with the mother. A boy, on the other hand, generally opts for the mother as the love object and then represses these feelings to avoid threats of castration from the father. Girls do not experience a single type of Oedipal situation and they resolve their Oedipal entanglements slowly without an "absolute 'change of object' " (1978: 127). One would expect, on the basis of psychoanalytic theory, that a woman would have a more continuous conception of heterosexual love, perhaps with undulations as she works through her evolving relationship with both parents as love objects. A man, on the other hand, would have a more finite conception because he must turn away from the mother as the love object to avoid rivalry with the father. Carol Gilligan, building on the work of Nancy Chodorow and others, discovered that North American men describe more tragic scenarios than women after looking at the same pictures of couples in situations of intimacy (1982: 41–63).

Maximina and Leandro convey in their "Cinderella" stories conceptions of romantic love that accord with the findings of psychoanalysis. Maximina, like other Cáceres women, describes Cinderella alternating between beauty and ugliness, metaphorically representing her waxing and waning illusion as she works through her relationships with her parents, the prince, and the prince's parents. Leandro describes the prince falling in love with Cinderella, who always appears beautiful, and then tells how their relationship comes to an end tragically and suddenly with the death of the heroine.

"Cinderella," by Maximina Castaño

Once there were some parents who had a daughter. And it turned out the mother died and left her daughter and told the father not to marry anyone who didn't look like her. And her daughter was the only woman who looked like the mother. So the father said to her one day at the table, "Look, daughter, I have to marry you because you know mother wished that if I marry, it has to be with a woman who looks like her. And I've traveled the entire world, and no one looks like her except you." And the girl replied, "Oh, father, you're going to marry me?" He said, "Yes, daughter."

So the girl started to cry, and a woman who lived across the street asked, "What happened to you, daughter?" The girl said, "My father told me I have to marry him. My mother told him he has to marry someone who looks like her, and no one looks like her except me." The neighbor said, "Well, daughter, that's no problem. You tell your father that if he wants to marry you, he has to bring you the dress of the stars." When her father asked her, "Daughter, have you thought it over?" she said, "Yes, father. But if you want me to marry you, you have to bring me the dress of the stars." He said, "Daughter, prepare my lunch. I'm going to get it." So he went, and three months later he came with the dress of the stars. The girl started to cry and the neighbor asked her, "What's wrong with you, daughter?" She said, "My father brought me the dress of the stars." The neighbor said, "Don't worry about it, daughter. You tell him yes, you want to marry him, but he has to bring you the dress of the sun. He won't come back if he goes to get it." And so when he asked, "Well, daughter, have you thought it over?" she said, "Yes, father, I've thought it over. But if you want to marry me, you have to bring me the dress of the sun." He said, "Daughter, make my lunch. I'm going to get it." So he went to get it, and three months later he came back again. She said, "Oh, mother of mine, what shall I do?" And the neighbor asked, "What's wrong with you, girl?" "My father brought me the dress of the sun." The woman said, "Don't worry about it. When your father comes, you tell him that yes, you've thought it over, but if he wants you to marry him, he has to bring you the dress of the moon." The father said, "Daughter, make my lunch, I'm going to get it," and spent another three months away. It turned out he got it. The girl started to cry, and the neighbor asked, "What's wrong with you, my daughter?" "My father brought the dress of the moon and so it's all over." The neighbor said, "Look, daughter, I can't do anything else. Upstairs I have a pelican suit. Put it on if you want because it's better to travel about the world than marry your father." "Give it to me," the girl said.

She put on the pelican suit and went about the world. She went to the house

of the king and knocked on the door. "Knock, knock." "Who is there?" She said, "Do you need a turkey keeper?" The person inside said, "Yes, because the turkey keeper we had left this morning. How much do you want to earn?" She said, "When you see my work, then you pay me." So they gave her some corn in the morning , and she went to take care of the turkeys. She wore the dress of the stars and said, "Yes, for my little turkey, for my turkey feeder, may the king's son give you . . . a bad seed." A dead turkey. She came back in the afternoon and said, "My lady." The lady asked, "What happened? A dead turkey! Oh, for God's sake, we're starting early." But the next morning, they gave her more food, and she went again, this time wearing the dress of the sun. She said, "Yes, for my little turkey, for my turkey feeder, may the king's son give you . . . a bad seed." A dead turkey. She went again to the house with the news. Then the master came and said, "Another dead turkey!" Again they gave her some feed, and she went to feed the turkeys. She wore the dress of the moon and said, "Yes, for my little turkey, for my turkey feeder, may the king's son give you . . . a bad seed." A dead turkey. So the king said to her, "You can't take care of any more turkeys. You stay here in the house and nowhere else."

Then the king said to his son, "It's been a long time since you held a dance to see if you can find a bride. It's time now you found one." "Whenever you want, father." They prepared for the dance, and everyone went to it. The pelican said, "Oh but I'm going too." "Whatever, filthy little pelican pig-keeper,"[3] someone in the king's palace said. The girl insisted, "Whether I'm filthy or not, I'm going to see the king. I'm going to the dance too." So she went to the dance and wore the dress of the moon. And as she appeared wearing the dress of the moon, the king's son immediately took her away to be at his side. As they danced she said, "Those windows bother me." He said, "I'll send someone to close them." She said, "No. You have to go yourself." He went to close the windows, and the girl, now dressed as a little pelican, said, "Attention, sentry, the pelican is shitting at the door." And she went home where someone said to her, "Little pelican, if you could have seen it. A maiden appeared and she was very beautiful. She told the king's son to go close the windows, and he let her get away from him." The next day the pelican said again, "I'm going to the dance." But the king said, "Stay away, so you won't shit at the door again." She said, "Whether I shit or not, I'm going again." She went again and wore the dress of the sun, lighting up the hall even more. Then the king's son took her to dance with him. And each night he gave her a ring. When they finished dancing, she said, "I could drink a little bit of water!" He said, "I'll send someone to bring it." She said, "No. You have to do it with your own hands." So he went for the glass of water, and the pelican escaped again. She said, "Attention, sentry, the pelican is shitting at the door." And again she escaped. The next morning; "Oh, my! If she was beautiful the night before, last night she was more so. But the prince let her get away from him again." And the king said, "Oh, Christ!" It was the last night of the contest, and he said, "Well, we can see how we're doing." She wore the dress of the stars, and the prince took her hand in his grasp and led her away with him. When they were dancing, he gave her the ring, and she said, "Oh, I'm so warm. I'm going to open the balcony window." He said, "Stay here. I'm going to tell someone to do it for you so you don't have to open it." "Can't you open it yourself?" So he went. She said, "Attention, sentry, the pelican is shitting at the door."

The next day the king's son became ill, and the pelican asked his mother, "Why don't you ask him if he'd like to eat a custard?" His mother replied, "Why would my son want a custard when he has so many things and he doesn't want any of them?" The pelican said, "Ask if he'd like to eat one." His mother asked him, "Son, do you want to eat a custard?" He said, "Make one, let's see if I have an appetite." With that the pelican said, "I'll make it for him if he has an appetite." But his mother replied, "Filthy little pelican pig keeper, if my son were to know it was yours, there's no way he'd eat it." "If you want me to, I'll make it. If you don't want me to, I won't make it." She made it, and his mother took it downstairs to him. He cut into it and saw the ring in the custard. And he called out, "Mother! Who made the custard for me?" She said, "I did." He said, "May the one who made me this one make me another." The mother went back upstairs, and the pelican asked her, "What did he say?" She said, "May the one who made this custard make him another one." The pelican said, "Good. I'll make it if you want." She made it for him, and the mother went downstairs again. And he said, "Mother, may she who made this custard make me another one. May she make me three." Then he said, "Mother, have the one who made this custard come down here." She said, "I made it for you." He said, "You didn't make it." His mother told the pelican to come right away. She said, "Give me a few minutes, if you don't mind." She combed her hair, she got herself ready, put on the dress of the moon, the first one she had worn at the dance. Then he said, "Mother!" She said, "Is something wrong with you, son?" He said, "Make a double portion of chocolate. There are two of us." So he married her. And this story has ended (*acabado*) and may the town's behind go about sewn with purple thread (*hilo morado*).

Maximina's closing scatological reference to sewing up the backside of her town in purple thread, thereby preventing proper defecation, is another formulaic ending designed to shock her listeners back into reality and perhaps trigger their associations between the content of her story and real village life. The heroine starts off embedded in an Oedipal situation with her father, much as many young Garganta women might find themselves as they enter the age of courtship and marriage. Maximina develops her story, however, to illustrate that the heroine's entanglement with her father and her emergence from that entanglement come about as a result of her complicated relationship with her mother. She represents two sides of the mother-daughter relationship by splitting the images of the heroine's mother. On the one hand, the narcissistic and controlling mother instructs her husband to marry only another woman who looks like her and unwittingly places her daughter in the Oedipal situation. The widowed father follows the wishes of the heroine's mother and proposes marriage to his daughter because she is the only woman who looks like his dead wife. Perhaps Maximina's story is a warning that a mother's narcissism may actually contribute to Oedipal rivalry in the family. On the other hand, the mother, symbolically recast as a female neighbor, helps Cinderella extricate herself from her Oedipal entanglement by giving her advice and the pelican suit, by which she escapes her father's incestuous proposal of marriage. Maximina makes clear that the helpful woman represents another side of the mother's relationship with her daughter by specifying how Cinderella and the helpful woman address each other using mother-and-daughter kinship terminology. The portrayal of a complex relationship between mother and daughter fits the reality of life in Garganta la Olla and other Cáceres villages, where mothers and daughters actually have a very complicated interdependence.

Maximina describes her Cinderella emerging from an Oedipal situation as a fascinating chain of events that represents metaphorically the heroine's transference of affection from her father to her husband. The heroine's father collaborates in his daughter's transference, but he plays a passive role because he merely responds to the requests of women. In Maximina's sequence the dying mother makes a request of her husband that results in an incestuous marriage proposal; Cinderella then turns to the mother symbolically recast as the helpful neighbor to escape an incestuous marriage; the helpful "mother" tells Cinderella to request three dresses from her father; and her father provides the dresses, which become the vehicles by which she eventually attracts the attention of the prince who becomes her husband. Maximina's heroine is assertive in her own courtship and transference of affection, like other Cinderellas in stories by Cáceres women, because she does not wait to be discovered by her prince charming. Rather, she takes matters into her own hands and heads off to the house of the king, where she asks for work as a keeper of turkeys.

At this point in the story, Maximina reveals her conception of waxing and waning romantic love, which looks very much like that of other Cáceres women who described their Cinderellas alternating between beauty and ugliness. Maximina adds details revealing more about what beauty and ugliness mean to a woman as she describes her Cinderella switching back and forth between wearing the beautiful dresses and the pelican suit. In this tale, Cinderella's identity as a beautiful woman is directly connected to her sexuality because when wearing the dresses she brings about the death of domesticated animals. This detail in Maximina's story is a reference to the destructive powers of women connected with their sexuality, which is part of the belief system concerning menstrual magic (Pitt-Rivers 1966: 189–201) and occurs in other stories circulating in Cáceres oral tradition. Her identity as an ugly woman is emphasized when Maximina makes a metonymical or contextual association between Cinderella dressed as a pelican and excrement. Like other Cinderellas, this one draws attention to her own ugliness, and in Maximina's story she does this by shouting as she leaves the ball, "Attention, sentry, the pelican is shitting at the door."

The alternation between beautiful and ugly in this Cinderella, like that of the others, represents the ambivalence of a maiden in courtship, and Maximina adds another dimension to women's concern about the men who fall in love with women at first sight. This Cinderella wants to make sure that the man who says he loves her is not simply infatuated with her beauty, but will also help her in the complex division of labor after marriage. So she puts her prince to the test by asking him to perform a number of tasks, and when he fails by saying he will send someone else to fulfill her requests, she escapes from the ball, takes off her beautiful dress, associates herself with excrement, and puts on the pelican suit. She turns herself from a beautiful to an ugly woman to protect herself from the man who says he loves her, much as a maiden might protect herself from the professions of love from a man she does not fully trust. Once again the heroine overcomes her ambivalence and acts in ways that express a woman's faith in conjugal love. This Cinderella, like the others, takes over as the nurturer of her husband; his mother reluctantly steps aside after voicing some criticisms of her future daughter-in-law; the heroine reveals her beauty to the man who says he loves her; and the two marry and live happily ever after.

Leandro Jimenez, speaking through the characters of his "Cinderella" story, presents a much more brittle conception of romantic love, based on an idealized conception of women. Men's idealization of women has many possible sources, including the Oedipal entanglements in the family whereby a boy develops his images of a nurturing mother who gives him her exclusive loyalty and affection (Spiro 1982: 112–140). Many Cáceres men other than Leandro idealize women in stories that describe Oedipal situations. Julio Lopez Curiel's tale of "Snow White," considered in Chapter 5, describes a maiden idealized as an icon of the Virgin Mary who rescues her brother from punishment for killing their father. According to Oedipal theory, boys and men in the midst of Oedipal entanglements sometimes project feelings toward the mother onto their sisters or even adolescent daughters (Spiro 1982: 96–98). Julio's story could be a symbolic recasting of the Oedipal wish of a boy to banish his father and possess his mother. Leandro and Julio give voice to themes that all men, to a greater or lesser degree, express in fantasy. Leandro's sudden and tragic ending of his "Cinderella" story expresses his very brittle conception of romantic love, which differs radically from the waxing and waning illusion in the stories by women. Men's brittle conception of romantic love may have a basis in the way boys must resolve their Oedipal situation by repressing their feelings for the mother to avoid threats of castration from the father (Chodorow 1978: 111–130).

"CINDERELLA," BY LEANDRO JIMENEZ

Once there was a father who had three daughters. The mother died very young, leaving her husband with their daughters and leaving her wedding ring with him. She said that she understood he would have to remarry because he was such a young widower. And she said of the woman, "This ring has to fit on her finger." The young father went here and there trying the ring on many single women to see if it fit one of them well. But it didn't fit anyone.

After so many tries, and failing to find a woman whom the ring fit, it occurrd to him to say one day when his three daughters were together, "I'm going to see if mother's ring will fit you. Let's see which one it fits well." The two older daughters tried it on, but it didn't fit them. But it fit the youngest perfectly. "I have to marry you," the father said to his daughter. She knew it was impossible for a father to marry his daughter. "Well, I have to marry you," he said to the youngest. "Oh, father, I can't. Oh, my! Impossible. No!" The father insisted so much that she said, "If you get me a silk dress for the eve of the wedding, I'll marry you." The father was in league with the devil. He bit something in a certain place and spoke of the devil, and the devil appeared before him and said, "What do you ask of me? What do you command me to do?" "Prepare me a dress of silk for the eve of the wedding." To ask for it was to obtain it, and he gave it to his daughter. "Here you have it, daughter." Again he asked her when they were going to get married. She said, "You have to prepare me a dress of gold. I won't marry you if you don't." This was for the wedding day. He bit whatever it was again, and the devil appeared before him: "What do you ask of me? What do you command me to do?" "Send me a dress of gold." He prepared it for him at once. The father brought it to his daughter. "Here, daughter, you have your dress for the wedding day." She still wasn't happy, she still didn't want to marry her father. So she said, "Look, father, if I marry you, you have to bring me a dress with all of the flowers and birds singing in the countryside." And he obtained it for her. He asked the devil, and the devil gave it to him. Now she had three dresses.

Now that the father had obtained everything his daughter asked of him, she said to her sisters—because the wedding wasn't going to take place for several days, giving her time to think about what she was going to do—"Look, I'm not going to marry father. I've thought this through. I'm going to the house of a cork maker who makes furniture and things out of cork, and he's going to make me a little bull where I can take a lot of provisions. And I'm going to throw myself into the sea inside of the bull." It turned out just as she had planned. If not today, then tomorrow or another day a fisherman would see the bull because it floated. She wouldn't drown. She would be tranquil traveling about the sea. And one day some fishermen saw this precious thing—a golden bull. Wouldn't it be worth money? They grabbed it and took it to a market in a capital city. By chance everything ended up with kings. They are the ones with the most money and they have the most whims. The fishermen took it to a square so that a queen, or the daughter of a queen, would buy it. The bull was a piece of finery that would cost a lot of money and not just anyone would buy it. Some people where in charge of buying if for the king for whatever price and they picked it up and took it to him as an adornment for one of his rooms. It was a beautiful piece of furniture, a bull varnished in gold, and they put it in the best room the king had.

The king and queen had a son who wasn't inspired to look for a bride. The maiden, whose father had wanted to marry her and who was inside the bull, was very beautiful. The king arranged to hold a ball in his home. He wanted to see if someone would appear whom his son would like and want to make his bride. He would hold the ball for three nights. On the first night of the ball, the maiden appeared wearing the dress. No one knew where she came from, nor the road she took to get there. And the king's son found her very pleasing. He danced with her for some turns, but he didn't dare court her and tell her that he loved her. He had her with him the entire time of the ball, and when he attended to some other people, she escaped and no one knew where she went. She had gone into the bull in the king's room. How would they know she was inside the house? She ate and she drank inside the bull, where she had her provisions. All of the people were in awe of the dress that she had worn. "Who is she? Who isn't she?" The next night there was another ball. She appeared at the right moment wearing the dress of gold. Oh, the prince was enchanted with her. But he didn't dare court her, though he wanted to marry her. He didn't dance with anyone but her. That night, when he attended to others, she escaped a few dances before the end of the ball. No one knew where she was. There was only one more night of the ball to see if he could court her and to see if she would stay with him. They prepared the room for the ball on the following night. This time the prince arranged to put some gatekeepers at the doors of the castle before the ball ended to see where the woman went. That night she appeared wearing the dress with the flowers and birds singing of the countryside. He liked the dress much more than those of the nights before. The dance ended, and he was left in an awkward situation, as if he were one of three in a shoe. She left and went into the room as always. The prince thought, "This woman has to be here. She has to be in the house." They extended the ball one more night to find out where the woman was hiding. Now he took a small spool of thread. She put on the dress of the roses and the birds singing, which she had worn on the previous night. And as they danced, the thread wound around the roses and other things on her dress. She did the same as she had on all the other nights: she left before the ball ended. But he found her because she left a trail of thread. He went to his room, where the enchanted golden bull was. And there she was. She had closed the door, but the thread was hanging. He saw where she was, and, of course, she saw he was with her. She opened the door, they saw each other, and during the time they were together he told the servants to bring meals for two to the room. But she didn't let anyone see her—the queen, the king, or anyone. No one except the son. And it was a secret between her and the prince. And the servants took them their meals, but they were disgusted because they had to take meals for two when only he was in the room.

They called him to war, and he left her alone in the house. She had as a signal that he pat the right horn three time before she would open the door. No one but the prince knew it. The servants went to clean the room, bring the meals, and clear the plates for two from the table. But when he was about to go away, he told the servants, "You have to bring meals to this room every day." They said, "But who will eat the food? Where will this person be?" It was a difficult situation. Day after day he was at war, and they brought her meals without knowing to whom or why. They found the empty plates without knowing who ate the food. But one day, after bringing food many times, one of them touched the right horn three times because the bull was so beautiful. The maiden opened the door, and they saw her. The poor thing, they seized her, threw her down off the balcony, and killed her. The king came and found out. Do you know what happened? Do you know what he did? He tied the servants to two horses, one pulling one of their legs and the other pulling the other, and he killed them.

Leandro, like Maximina, begins his story by describing his Cinderella in an obvious Oedipal situation. He represents the mother as setting the stage for an incestuous marriage proposal, and he makes the father the unknowing instrument of his daughter's transference by providing the three dresses that make Cinderella beautiful and attract the attention of the prince. Leandro eliminates the helpful woman present in Maximina's tale, who aids her "daughter" by giving advice and providing the vehicle for the girl's escape from her father. As mentioned in Chapter 5, in their stories men often simplify the complex, ambivalent ties between mother and daughter, and Leandro is no exception.

Leandro expresses a brittle conception of romantic love by eliminating the metaphor for a woman's waxing and waning illusion of love, represented by a heroine who alternates between the appearance of beauty and ugliness. That metaphor is an essential element in all of the feminine "Cinderella" stories I know that circulate in Cáceres oral tradition. Leandro's Cinderella is always beautiful and, if beauty represents idealized woman, then his heroine always appears in her idealized form. Instead of fleeing in an ugly pelican suit, this heroine flees in a beautiful golden bull, which the narrators describes as a valuable and beautiful object that only the wealthiest kings and queens could afford. A king buys the golden bull and places it in the best room in his castle. It becomes apparent in the rest of the tale that Leandro, more than female narrators, emphasizes the beauty of Cinderella on each night of the ball, how the prince is taken by her beauty, and how he is hesitant to declare his love for the heroine because he fears she will reject him. The prince is persistent, just as a young man must be persistent when he tries to make a maiden fall in love with him. The ball is extended a fourth night so that the prince can have another chance to court the beautiful maiden, and after several unsuccessful attempts, he discovers where Cinderella is hiding. Ironically, she hides right under his nose, much like her counterparts in the stories by women, with one essential difference. Leandro's heroine never appears ugly; she is only concealed because she hides inside the beautiful golden bull.[4]

Relative to the story by Maximina, the tale by Leandro presents a one-dimensional, idealized picture of Cinderella. The woman the prince loves in this tale is the most wonderful woman in the world. She is the woman of all illusions that a man tries to create with his compliments and shows of gallantry. But men, like women, also know that one can lose the illusion (*quitarse la ilusión*), and Leandro's conclusion illustrates in the poetic language of a story how this can be tragically sudden, unexpected, and permanent. When the prince goes off to war, servants discover Cinderella hiding inside the bull and throw her off the balcony to her death.

# CHAPTER SEVEN

## Disenchanting a Princess

STUDIES OF rural Spanish masculinity stress how men rival one another for many things, including women. Gilmore (1987a: 134–135) characterizes relations between men as "erotic aggression" in which one man competes with another for and through women. The winner in the competitive game of erotic aggression takes away the honor of another man by dishonoring his sweetheart, his wife, or any woman in his family. A young man can lose his honor in retrospect if he discovers that the maiden he courts has lost her virginity with another man (Pitt-Rivers 1966: 96). A married man whose wife does not keep her marital chastity is a *cabrón* or old goat, a term used throughout Spain to mean a cuckold who knows about his wife's affairs (Aceves 1971: 63; Brandes 1980: 88–89). The word *cabrón* is applied to a man without honor and carries such a powerful connotation that its use in casual conversation brings the glares of men and women, and its mention in a serious accusation provokes a violent response.

The young man who comes to court a maiden represents a threat to her father, who stands to lose his own honor if his daughter is seduced and abandoned by her suitor. The elaborate rules of courtship whereby a man formally requests the hand of another man's daughter in marriage, the expectation of a maiden's premarital celibacy, the suitor's frequent visits to the maiden and her family—all help to mitigate the threat. Despite these safeguards, some fathers avoid the future sons-in-law who formally court their daughters (Pitt-Rivers 1966: 100–101). Some parents go to extreme lengths to break up courtships and block the marriages of their daughters to the men of whom they disapprove. The ostensible reasons for parental interference in a maiden's budding courtship are many and include disapproval of the young man's character, dislike of his family, and the belief that a maiden can make a better marriage with a man of greater wealth and social position.

Although the father may oppose a particular man as his future son-in-law, the mother usually exerts more influence on her daughter's marital choice because of the close and interdependent relationship between the two woman in the rural Cáceres family. Florencio Ramos explained how his relationship with a maiden ended before becoming a formal courtship because the maiden's mother considered him too poor for her daughter.

The maiden loved me, but the mother didn't because they were richer than my father. And the maiden paid a lot of attention to the mother and the mother took the idea out of the head of her daughter that she loved me, to the point that she really didn't love me. We spent at least two or three months with her saying yes, yes, perhaps no, perhaps no, perhaps yes. But the maiden didn't let herself be tempted, which was her salvation. Because any woman I have allured, I tempted—not to say this to prove myself, because it is very bad to speak about another person—but any woman I have tempted has had a difficult time separating from me. But she didn't allow herself to be tempted. And we did not become sweethearts. Well, one night I went out with her and we argued. I told her to go to hell.

The conflict between a young man and a maiden's parents can become extremely intense and involve all members of her family. The case of the maiden from Barrado courted by a young man from Arroyomolinos illustrates the lengths to which parents actually go to prevent their daughters from marrying men of whom they do not approve. This anecdote comes from Teresa Nuñez, the daughter of a charcoal maker who formerly lived in Barrado but now makes her home in Piornal. Barrado is between Piornal and Navaconcejo and Arroyomolinos is near Garganta la Olla.

This is about a girl who became the sweetheart of a boy from Arroyomolinos. The girl's parents were opposed to her relationship with the boy. He was good, but her parents were opposed because the boy did not have a father and they believed he would not give their daughter a good life. The girl had seven brothers. Neither the father nor the mother wanted a relationship with the boy. They sharecropped land in Bazagona, but they brought the girl to Barrado. The boy came to see her in Barrado, and they took her back to Bazagona. If the boy went down there, they brought her back to Barrado. Then the boy and girl decided to marry because the boy was going into the army and her parents wouldn't let him write her at home. So the boy went to her parents and said, "I want to marry this girl." Her father told him absolutely no and her brothers told him no. She had a sick brother who stayed inside the house. The boy came and said, "I'm going to marry her in one week before going into the army. If you don't allow letters to come here, I'm going to take her away." Then he prepared the papers. He came to town, and her parents had left; they had gone to Plasencia on the day of their daughter's wedding. They didn't want to have anything to do with the boy or the girl. They said she couldn't return home. The boy came for her in the morning, without guests of any kind because he didn't have any close relatives. The girl's sick brother was in the house, the rest had gone away. The girl asked her brother for his blessing, but he refused. So her godmother and what there were of the invited guests, who were from among her closest relatives, arrived at the door, and the boy asked their permission to take the girl away. And there was no one to give him permission to take the girl. She was of age, so her godmother said, "If you give this woman a bad life, you'll hang for it." Then they were married. She left with the clothes on her back and nothing else. He took her to Arroyomolinos, and after a long time her parents came to accept him because they saw he was a good boy and a hard worker. They have three children and they live splendidly.

Intense rivalry between a son-in-law and his future father-in-law for the loyalty and affection of a maiden can be very costly for a woman. She may end up with a broken courtship if she sides with her parents or she may have to break with her parents if she marries a man without their approval. The maiden from Barrado paid a heavy price for the conflict between her parents and the young man from Arroyomolinos: she had to temporarily break with her mother. A woman needs the help of her mother, particularly in child care during the early years of a marriage. A man stands to lose as well because he may have to break with the woman he loves or he may temporarily lose the labor of his wife, who has no mother to free her from caring for small children and permit her to help him in the agricultural work. Male rivalry for and through women consequently requires mediation, and this chapter focuses on dialogue through storytelling that deals with conflict between a young man and the courted maiden's father.

## "THE GRIFFIN BIRD"

Men tell a number of stories about heroes who disenchant maidens, stories that express their view of courtship as intense rivalry between men for and through women.[1] Julio Lopez Curiel, a gifted storyteller from Garganta la Olla, told the tale of "The Griffin Bird" (AT 461), which describes rivalry between a king and a young man over the loyalties of the king's daughter. The story opens with a king issuing a proclamation that he who disenchants his daughter will win her hand in marriage. Although the hero succeeds, her father tries to prevent the marriage by demanding that the hero complete a series of exceedingly difficult tasks. I did not find a Cáceres woman who knew this folktale, but Luis Cortés Vázquez collected three feminine variants from the oral tradition of three communities in Salamanca (Cortés Vazquez 1979: 2: 56–69) and recalled hearing the story told to children in his native Zamora (264–265). Cortés Vázquez collected no variants from men, but the story seems to have appeal to narrators of both genders if one considers the pattern of storytelling in both Salamanca and Cáceres. Serendipity in story collection can easily affect the types of tales collected from men and women in a single region. Comparison of the stories by Julio and the Salamancan women reveals some possible contours of the dialogue through storytelling involving "The Griffin Bird." Julio probably learned his story from his grandmother, with whom he slept as a child in Garganta, and perhaps the variant originally told by his grandmother once resembled the feminine variants collected by Cortés Vazquez.

The stories of the Salamancan women also describe courtship and marriage as male competition over the loyalties of a woman. They present a father blocking the courtship or attempting to disrupt the marriage of his daughter by making impossible demands on her suitor or husband. The key element in all of the tales is that the father demands that his son-in-law bring three hairs of the devil or the feathers of a feared and ferocious griffin bird. The hero makes a long journey to complete the task and has a series of encounters with an enchanted boatman and kings who send the hero with questions for the devil or bird who is a wise man (sabio). The hero, with the help of the wife or housekeeper of the devil or bird, successfully obtains the hairs or feathers along with the answers to the questions. The kings and the boatman reward the hero handsomely, and the hero returns to his father-in-law wealthy and triumphant. The hero avenges his father-in-law, explaining that he obtained his wealth by grabbing hold of the oars from the boatman who took him across the river. The old king, filled with greed, goes with his son-in-law to the river, jumps into the boat, grabs the oars, and is enchanted, thus releasing the boatman from his enchantment. The hero's completion of the task demanded by the king takes a very long time and is very complicated, much like a long and difficult courtship.

Although the Salamancan stories vary in details, they generally describe a scenario that makes clear the costs to the the maiden's father of male competition in courtship. The narrators draw attention to the costs of male rivalry because women have little to gain and a great deal to lose when they find their father blocking their courtship and marriage to the man who loves them. If maidens acquiesce to the demands of their parents, they may lose their suitor and if they side with their suitor they may have to break from their parents. The girl from Barrado, who chose to marry the man of whom her parents did not approve, was forced to leave her home town for a while and give up the interdependent cooperation with her mother so highly valued by woman in Cáceres villages. Telling the tale communicates women's wishes that fathers and suitors come to terms.

The plots of the Salamancan stories have an ironical twist because they tell how a father who has the loyalty of his daughter may find himself totally alienated if he blocks his daughter's courtship and marriage. In no Salamancan variant does a princess initially go against her father, and in one the heroine is allied closely with her father and initially does not want to marry the hero who disenchanted her. But in all stories the father who makes impossible demands on his son-in-law finds himself enchanted in the river for an undetermined amount of time (Cortés Vázquez 1979: 2: 65–69) or until his death (56–64).

All variants of "The Griffin Bird" have some Oedipal themes in that the hero, the maiden he wishes to marry, and her jealous and demanding father are like the triangular constellation consisting of a son, his mother, and his father. Julio's tale illustrates how male Oedipal themes, which are present in all of the stories, are projected to a greater degree onto a masculine story about courtship and marriage. Julio tells many stories with particularly pronounced Oedipal themes, one of which is "Snow White" (discussed in Chapter 5). Julio's "Griffin Bird" develops the themes to a greater degree by drawing attention to the unpromising nature of the hero in the eyes of his own father at the beginning of the tale, by representing the princess as the idealized woman who is willing to side with a weaker man, and by increasing the number of demands the old king makes on his future son-in-law. His tale ends on a hopeful note, indicating that time can heal some of the differences that develop between a man and his father-in-law during a difficult courtship.

"THE GRIFFIN BIRD," BY JULIO LOPEZ CURIEL

Once there were kings for each kingdom. For example, Cáceres had a king and Avila had another. In one place there was a king who went to a witch to see about the daughter of another king, and she was enchanted. The witch put her in a wall; she couldn't speak, move, or do anything. Well, the witch knew what she had done, and after a year or two she came to see the daughter of the king. She saw that the princess was still in the same state. So the witch said, "Oh my! Your Majesty, I have a remedy to cure your daughter." The king said, "What are you saying?" She said, "Yes, sir. I know what will cure your daughter's illness." "Then you'll tell me what it is." She said, "Well, perhaps it'll be difficult for you to find it in Spain, but you'll save your daughter if you do. She'll come out of the wall to be like you are, and like I am, and like everyone is." He said, "Go on, talk." She said, "If there is a place in Spain that has an apple tree with an apple, have someone bring it here. Cut it into three pieces and give her one piece at a time. You'll see her move something after she eats one piece. When she eats another, the same thing. And when she eats the third, she'll come out of her enchantment." The king was so happy that he issued a proclamation at once that said, "He who brings an apple to cure the enchanted princess of the king will marry her."

There wasn't an apple anywhere. In a hamlet, in a small town like this one, there was a shoemaker who had three sons. He had an apple tree in his garden for his pleasure, and the tree had three very beautiful apples on its highest branches. The oldest son jumped up and said, "Father, look at the proclamation they carry over there saying, 'He who takes the apple to cure the princess of the

king will marry her.' I'm going to climb up to pick one." The father said, "Yes, go on." The father continued sewing shoes while the oldest son climbed up the apple tree, grabbed an apple, and put it in a chest. He covered it with a lid, put it under his arm, and pan, pan, pan. Ala! While he was traveling along the road, he met an old man who was sitting on a bench. The old man asked him as he approached, "Tell me, young man, what are you taking in that basket?" "I'm taking frogs haunches." The old man said, "Whatever you say, that's what it'll be." The shoemaker's son came to the palace and called out, and they came down to open the door for him. "Here is the apple." They came down right away to open the chest. At first they couldn't get it open, but then inside they found haunches of frogs. Mother! They gave him such a caning they left him half dead. "Is this what I asked for? I asked for an apple, and he doesn't bring me one." The king was like a wise man. He gave him a caning and left him half dead. The boy came dragging himself home, and his father asked him, "How did it go, son?" The boy said, "Father, they gave me a caning. Look how I come home covered with blood from the sabers they stuck into me. It turned out the apple became frogs' haunches."

The son next in age jumped up and said, "Now, I'm going to do it. Let's see if what happened to you also happens to me." He climbed up into the apple tree and picked another apple. He put it into a basket and went tan, tan, tan tan. Ala! An old woman was in the same spot. She asked, "Tell me, young man, what are you carrying in that basket?" He said, "I'm taking sausage." She said, "Well, now that you say it, that's what it will be." He came to the palace and started calling: "Come down and open up for me." The king said to the guard, "Open the door for him if you want, but if he comes with some nonsense like the other one, he'll be killed right away." They went downstairs, opened the basket, and found a sausage! For that they threw him into the street and left him for dead. He came home in the afternoon, and his father asked, "How was it, son?" The boy said, "My father, they left my brother half dead. Well, I come home much worse. They gave me such a caning." His father asked, "What happened?" "Nothing. It turned into a sausage." "Oh, my! Is that possible?" said his father.

The youngest one, who was like a fool, said, "Now I'm going to do it. Let's see if the same thing happens to me." But his father said, "My son, your brothers are so smart and you are like an imbecile. How are you going to go?" The boy said, "Well, I'm going." He went to the apple tree, climbed up, grabbed the finest apple, and put it in the basket. Pin pan, pin pan. The old woman was in the same place. She said to him, "Tell me, young man, what do you take in that chest?" He replied, "I'm taking a very beautiful apple to cure the princess of the king. I'm going to marry her." The old woman said, "If what you say is true, continue on. What you said really will be." He arrived, and the King didn't want to go downstairs. "There have been two with this foolishness. I'm not going," said the king. Then he said to the guard, "Come. Go downstairs and open for him. If it isn't what I want, put him against the wall and shoot him with three or four bullets." They went downstairs and opened the door for him. They went back upstairs and tried to open the chest. They couldn't open it, and someone had to go running for a tool and open the chest and remove the apple. The king cut it into three pieces. He gave one piece to his daughter, who was enchanted in the wall. She ate it and blinked her eyes just as the witch said she would. He gave her another. She ate it, then began to move. He gave her the other. She ate it and jumped out of the shrine her father had made for her. And she was healthy and well just as before. The fool had removed her from her enchantment.

They at once prepared a supper and the girl didn't leave the side of her groom. The truth was she had to marry him. Then the king said, "How are we going to marry our daughter to a fool? This is impossible." He told his daughter, "You can't marry this fool now. How can we arrange for you to get out of marrying him?" She said, "Yes, I'm going to marry him, whatever he is. It's enough that he took me out of where I was. I'm going to marry him." They came to eat supper, and after the supper and the dance, the king said, "I take you for an intelligent lad. I see you as truly smart. Now, I issued a proclamation all over Spain saying, 'He who cures my daughter marries her.' But before you marry my daughter, you have to complete three tasks for me. If you don't do them, you won't marry her." "Tell me what I have to do," said the shoemaker's son. The king said, "Tomorrow you have to perform the first task. We'll go to the forest where I have a house with one hundred rabbits in a room. I'm going to release them in the forest, and you have to watch them. You have to turn over the one hundred rabbits to me when you leave the forest and put them back in the room again in the afternoon." They went to the forest early the next day and released the rabbits one by one. They counted one hundred rabbits. The king said, "With the first task he won't marry her," because he had given the boy an impossible job to do. After the rabbits were out of the room, the boy sat down on a rock and became drowsy. The rabbits were everywhere. He didn't know what to do. He said, "I'm going home. How am I going to find the rabbits by myself? There's nothing more to say." Then a man came and nudged him, and the boy awoke. "Oh, my! Grandfather, what are you doing here?" The man said, "What are *you* doing, son? Tell me your story." So the boy said, "The king issued a proclamation, 'He who cures the princess of the king will marry her.' And I brought her a very beautiful apple, and she ate the apple, and now the king gave me the job of watching one hundred rabbits, and I have to deliver them in the evening at the door where he gave them to me when he imposed this condition on me." "Don't worry," said the old man. "Take this whistle. When you blow on it all of the rabbits will come dancing behind you." The old man disappeared, and the young man saw if what he said was true. There wasn't a rabbit anywhere, and he took the whistle and blew on it and all the rabbits appeared dancing in front of him. He counted one hundred rabbits, neither more nor less. But the king was a low and vicious man, a usurer. He thought, "Can he keep track of them? I don't feel confident. In the middle of the afternoon, the king sent a servant with his daughter to fetch a rabbit without telling them why. The servant and the girl went into the forest in search of the groom. The princess told him, "My father says for you to give me a rabbit for supper tonight." But he said, "No. If I have to turn all of them over to him tonight, how am I going to give one to him now?" The poor boy sadly gave a rabbit to his bride. And she gave it to the servant, who put it in her apron and covered it. They said good-bye and after they had gone far away, the boy blew on the whistle to see if more than one was missing. When he blew on the whistle, the rabbit turned the apron to dust and took off and—Ala!—went straight to where the boy was. The king came to the door and asked his daughter, "Where is the rabbit?" "I was carrying it in my apron, and this 'uncle' blew a whistle. It tore my apron to shreds and escaped." The king bit himself because he wanted to punish the boy so he wouldn't marry his daughter. When the time came to turn over the rabbits, the boy was waiting for the king. The king appeared, and the boy had all the rabbits together in a little field. The king asked, "Have you fulfilled your promise?" The boy said, "Yes, sir. They're all here." They began counting as the rabbits went inside. The king said, "Yes, sir. You are a talent, a great talent. You have won the first wager. Now tonight I'll make you another."

He gave him another condition that was even more difficult. They were having supper, and the idea was put on the table, and the daughter sat up and said, "But, cruel father, how do you have the nerve to make these demands on my groom? Don't be that way. Don't order my groom to do that. It will all turn out to be in vain for you. You study a great deal but—" "I've told you to be quiet! I'm going to order this boy to do all that he has to do. If he doesn't do it, he won't marry you. I have my sword here to crease you first," the father said. He was a very bad man. In the morning he gave the boy an adze, a saw, the tools to work wood. He said, "By tomorrow you have to make me a ship that travels on the earth the same as through water. It has to be at the door of the palace at four in the afternoon." The boy and his bride were angry. "Father, you're cruel. You love neither me nor him." The sun came up in the morning. The girl made the boy his lunch, and he grabbed the hammer and the spikes to nail together all the material for a ship. But he had never learned how to make a ship. So he said, "I'm going to rest here for a little while," and he sat down on a rock to rest and fell asleep. When he was asleep, the old man came. He said, "Son, wake up. Oh, my! What are you still doing here?" "Oh, grandfather, it's you again. Now it's worse than yesterday. He ordered me to make a ship that travels on land the same as through the water. And at four in the afternoon I have to have it ready at the door of the palace." The old man said, "Go to sleep." Another man came. He let the boy sleep until three-thirty and then called him. They built the ship, and the boy climbed into it and started the engines. When it loomed in the hallway, the king said, "Here comes the man from Seville. Look, he's bringing a palace and he's bringing a ship directly to our palace." The daughter jumped up and declared, "You deserve what you've done to many people, had them shot, had this and that happen to them. You're a cruel father. There you have it. I wonder if you have ever seen anyone as smart as yourself before." The king snapped back, "Shut up! Go cut your messy hair." The ship arrived, and the boy climbed down. The king said, "Very good. Very well done. A fine piece of work. I've never seen a piece of work like this in my life. I've been a king now forty years and I've never seen a piece of work like this. Very good." They put their hands on it, and the boy embraced the king's daughter.

They made a fine supper. They were having supper and the king said, "I see you are an intelligent boy. You do all that I ask of you. But now I'm going to send you on an errand, and if you can do it, I won't order you to do any more. This will be enough. Tomorrow you have to make a year's journey. One year! You have to go to the griffin bird and you have to bring me a feather that is the color of an eagle on top and a lion underneath. The wings underneath are the color of a lion." The sun came up in the morning, and they loaded a horse with provisions for feeding the boy on his journey. He went forth. The first place he came to was a very big river. There was a boat, and when he came to the river he called the boatman. The boatman crossed the river, and he climbed onto the the boat with his horse. The boatman asked him, "Tell me, where are you going on this road because I never see people like you, young men who come by here. You must be on a very serious journey." The boy said, "Yes, sir. It's a pledge. I've fulfilled two conditions for the king and I have to complete the last one to marry the king's daughter. First he ordered me to watch one hundred rabbits in the forest. I had to deliver them without missing any when they were put away at night. The second was that I make a boat that traveled the same on land as in water. I did that too. Now he ordered me to go to the griffin bird, and I have to bring him a feather." "Oh my! Friend, don't go to the bird. It'll devour you. It isn't a bird, it's a wild beast." The boy said, "I have to go. Be it a wild beast or whatever, I have to go." The boatman said, "You're going to a bird that knows everything. Ask him why the boatman in such and such a place is always the boatman, and there is no person to relieve him." The boy wrote it down on a piece of paper and put it in his pocket. They said good-bye. The boatman said, "Have a good trip. Don't go. Stay here with us. You won't return. The griffin bird will devour you once he sees you. But in the end, if you're lucky, you may save yourself, and ask him that question." "Very well. Good-bye."

He got on his horse. Tran, tran, tran, tran. And after nightfall he saw a light in a high place. He tightened the stirrups of his horse and came to a castle. There was a huge storm, and he arrived and knocked on the door. They came downstairs and opened up at once. A man appeared and said, "Son, for God's sake. Where are you doing in these parts? No one travels through here on these roads." The boy said, "This and that happened to me." "For God's sake, don't go to the griffin bird. Stay here with us. We'll give you a job. You'll have food here. You'll have money for whatever you want." The boy said, "No, sir. It is a promise, and I must go." They were having supper. After supper they asked him, "If you commit yourself to this, will you do us the favor of asking the bird, 'Why in the castle of such and such have they lost the key and can't find it?'" The boy wrote it down. Ala! The next morning it dawned. "Don't go." The daughters embraced the boy and they didn't let go of him. And the mother and the father and the brothers did the same. But he told them all yes, he was going. It was a vow. And if that's how he was going to die, then so he'd die. But he had to keep his promise.

He went forth—tran, tran, tran, tran. On the following night, he saw another castle. He said, "Surely there is the nest." When he arrived, it was the same thing. He knocked on the door, and a man came downstairs and said to him, "Oh, my!" He called his wife. "Fulana! A gentleman who is such a young man. We have whatever you might need in the house. We have a little girl and we could arrange things with her." When the boy arrived at the castle, he appeared as a worthless person (*caballito de Bamba*). They removed his clothes. They dressed him in new clothes. They made him a good supper, and when they were sitting by the fire, one of the women asked, "Tell me, young man, what brings you on this road?" He said, "I saved the King's daughter from enchantment. Now he orders me to complete a final task for him. I have to bring him a feather from the griffin bird, which is half lion, half eagle." "Oh, for God's sake, don't go. You're very close to the nest. As soon as he sees you, he'll devour you. One neither looks at nor escapes from him. No sooner will you arrive, than he'll devour you." The boy said, "Whether or not he devours me, I'm going on. I'm going to go to bed now. I've done the impossible. Now I'm tired." When the sun came up in the morning, they said to him, "Listen, wait a moment. Since you are committed to going, ask the griffin bird, 'Why in the castle of such and such is there an apple tree that once bore golden apples but dried up? Why has this apple tree dried up?'" The boy wrote it down on a piece of paper. They said good-bye and cried because the young man was going. Tran, tran, tran, tran.

At four in the afternoon he came to the nest of the griffin bird. The bird had a woman attending to the nest, making meals, and cleaning house. The boy came near the cave, and the witch said, "My son, what are you doing here? Run away. Get out of here. The griffin bird is going to come any moment and he'll devour you." The boy embraced her. "Mother of mine, save me from the mess I'm in. This is a condition that the king of such and such a place ordered me to fulfill. I have to bring him a feather from the griffin bird, which is half lion, half eagle. Save me if you can. I have no other recourse except to come here and throw myself at your feet." She said, "Don't worry. I'll save you." The boy caught his breath, and the woman said, "When the griffin bird comes, I'm going to turn you into an ant and I'm going to put you into the fold of my skirt so he won't see you." The boy said, "Grandmother, surely you'll speak to the griffin bird." She said, "Yes, yes, I talk with him the same as with you." He said, "Please ask him three questions that I dreamt: First, the boatman in such and such a place is always the boatman. Why does it always have to be this man? Is it his punishment or is it a vow?" The old woman wrote it down on a piece of paper. Then the boy said, "In the castle of Fulano de Tal, the king lost a key to a great room filled with gold. See if the griffin bird knows where it is." Because it knew everything. The old woman also wrote this down. "And in the castle of such and such, which is the last thing I am going to bother you with, grandmother, there is an apple tree that once bore golden apples. Why has this apple tree dried up?" The grandmother went and, pan, pan, the moment the bird came roaring like a wild beast, the woman turned the boy into an ant. The bird declared as it arrived, "I smell human flesh. If you don't give it to me, I'll devour you." The old woman said, "Yes. You're right. A schoolchild passed by here and smelled your room. He just fled, and you won't be able to put a hand on him." The bird said, "You could have shot him with my musket and prepared him for supper, because I didn't catch anything." "Don't worry." "I come exhausted. Prepare my bed for me because I'm going to lie down right away," said the bird. She prepared his bed and also made his supper from leftovers. The bird had supper and then went to bed. Now that he was asleep, she turned the boy back into a person. He grabbed a feather and pulled it, and the bird said, "I feel that I've been touched by human flesh." The old woman said, "Yes, you fool. I was cleaning the nest. How touchy you are!" "I've been shot with a very big bullet." "Yes, your feather was stuck and it pulled out when you turned yourself," said the old woman. So then she asked him, "I've been asleep and dreamt three things. Let's see if you can tell me what they mean. In the river of such and such, there is boatman who has been there as boatman for many years. How come only this man is there as a boatman?" "The only thing he can do is put the oars in the hands of someone who passes by and then push off the boat. The next one has to learn to be the boatman whether he wants to or not." Good, that was quick. She said, "In the castle of such and such, the king lost a key. Do you know where it is?" The bird said, "Yes. It's in a pile of straw in stable number twelve." The boy also wrote that down, and the witch went on: "Now for the last thing I dreamt. I'm going to ask you one last thing and I won't bother you anymore, so you can rest. In the castle of such and such there is an apple tree that once gave golden apples but dried up. Why did this apple tree dry up?" The bird said, "It's because the rats killed it and are demolishing the roots." She went away. The sun came up in the morning. The griffin bird left, saying, "If by chance a boy comes like yesterday, grab him and don't let him go or you'll pay with your health." The old woman said, "No, from now on I'll do all that one can do." The bird went away, and the boy, seeing the bird had gone, took to the road with the feather, which was higher than a house.

He took the same road by which he had come before. First he came to the palace with the apple tree. The king saw him from far away and said to his wife, "Look at that load coming toward us. What is it?" The woman said, "It's the boy we took in the other night. He brings the feather." "Hush, woman. How could he bring the feather of a bird that kills and eats all that it sees?" "Then who is it?" The boy came closer, and they saw exactly who he was. "How was the trip?" they asked him. He said, "Fine, fine. It turned out very well for me. The bird behaved very well." The king said, "What did he say about the apple tree?" The boy said, "Take a hoe and dig a hole and kill the rats. They are eating the roots." They went at once and uncovered the trunk of the apple tree. They killed all the rats, and at that moment the apple tree was loaded with golden apples. They loaded three horses with money for the boy, and he left there very happy.

He came to the other castle to find the same thing. "That looks like that boy. Could it be the griffin bird's feather? No! How could it be? It isn't him." "Yes, that's who it is." He got closer. The boy said, "What luck I've had, like I never hoped for! Everyone said it would eat me. Well, it did nothing to me. Not even one small bad thing." "And the feather, how did you arrange to take it from him?" "I caught him asleep and I pulled it out." "What did he tell you about the key?" The boy said, "You have to look in stable number twelve. It's lost in a pile of straw." They went and uncovered all the straw and found it. They went to the room that wouldn't open with anything but that key. They opened the room and it was all full of gold. They loaded another three horses with money. "Ala! For you."

He came to the boatman, and the boatman said, "I wasn't waiting for you to come." The boy said, "Well, now I'm here." He got in the boat, and the boatman asked, "What did the griffin bird tell you about my question?" The boy said, "When you reach the other side I'll tell you. I won't say it now." "Why do you wait to say it? What did the griffin bird say to you?" As they were crossing the middle of the river, the boatman implored him again, "Tell me what the bird said to you." The boy said, "I said I'll tell you when you get to the other side. But I won't tell you in the river." They reached the other side, sat down to light a cigarette in celebration, and as the boy was giving the boatman a thousand thanks, he said, "Don't trick an innocent person. I'll bring a penitent here to pay the debt he owes me. He has to pay me for all he made me suffer. Don't put anyone in the boat that I don't tell you to put in. The bird told me that when someone crosses the river, eh, you put the oars of the boat in his hands and jump to the other side. Give a push to the boat, and he has to learn to be the boatman whether he wants to or not. But don't trick anyone. I'll bring you someone. Within three days you'll have him here." Of course the boatman loaded another three horses with money for the boy, who now brought nine horses loaded with money.

And as rich as the king was, the greed he still had! The boy returned, and the daughter appeared in the hall and saw the feather and the loads on the horses. She said, "Father! Cruel father, usurer father, bandit father, you deserve the hangman's noose in place of him. You thought he was dead. There you see what the man has done. My husband. There you have him. He's bringing the feather, and he brings a multitude of horses." The king came downstairs: "But, son, what do you bring? Come, unload your horses." "I bring nine horses loaded with money. Take it up to the attic." They took it up. "From where do you bring so much money?" The boy said, "My God, the oars of the boat in the river are filled with money." "Tomorrow the boatman will give them to me so I might also have a lot of money." The boy said, "Let's get married first." They got married. Then the next day, after the king's daughter and the boy were married, they prepared for the trip to the river. They came to the river, and as they arrived the boatman came with the boat. The boy said to him, "This is the one." He gave him a sign, and the boatman recognized it. The son-in-law said to the king, "When you ask for the boat, sit between the oars and fill all of the sacks you want." Oh that king went with greed. He jumped into the boat and sat between the oars. The boatman gave a push to the boat, and the king stayed in the river, and the boatman jumped to the bank. And the son-in-law said, as he made fun of his father-in-law the king, "I suffered pain for seven years. For seven years you also have to suffer here as the boatman. At the end of seven years, I'll trap an innocent like you and I'll take you out of here. Meanwhile, I won't remove you. You have to suffer for all that you made me suffer." And this story is over [*acabado*] and may the breeches of Rosi be sewn with violet thread [*hilo morado*].

Male rivalry through and over women is a pervasive theme in Julio's story and first appears when the narrator mentions that the maiden's enchantment is the result of male competition. The princess is enchanted because one king contracts a witch to use her supernatural powers to bewitch the daughter of another king. Julio's story focuses, however, on the struggle over a woman between a younger man of low status and an older man of high status. The rivalry between two men of unequal status, a feature in many of "The Griffin Bird" stories (Cortés Vázquez 1979: 2: 56–59), is like the rivalry between a father and his son recast in terms of courtship and class relations.

Oedipal themes are particularly apparent in Julio's tale if one considers that a high-status father-in-law and a low-status son-in-law struggle for the affection and the loyalty of a woman. The king initially shows affection and concern for his daughter when she is immobilized by her enchantment and placed on a shrine as if she were an icon of the Virgin

Mary. Presumably he also enjoyed her affection and loyalty before the hero provides the apple that disenchants her, a metaphor for her sexual awakening. The king ironically issues a proclamation inviting the right suitor to court and marry his daughter and rejects the hero's two older brothers, sending them home bruised and battered when they fail to provide the apple that can remove the princess from her enchantment. The king is like a father who opposes his daughter's courtship with men of whom he disapproves but does not seem generally opposed to the idea of her marriage with the right man. The story by Julio, like those of the Salamancan women (Cortés Vázquez 1979: 2: 58–69), makes clear, however, that it is the daughter's sexual awakening that brings about a change in the father's relationship with his daughter. The very success of the hero turns the king against him, and the king imposes a series of impossible tasks to block the hero's marriage to the princess. The father's opposition to his daughter's marriage turns the princess against the king, and his affection for her changes to anger. In the context of the storytelling dialogue, a listener to Julio's tale could easily conclude that the king has brought about the change by jealously wanting his daughter for himself. After all, it was the father who proposed marriage to his own daughter in the Cinderella tales considered in Chapter 6. From the point of view of those who identify with the unpromising hero, the change in the relationship between the king and his daughter gives expression to an Oedipal wish; the daughter turns against her high-status father and gives her exclusive loyalties to the unpromising hero, much as a young boy might wish that his mother would support him in a conflict with his own father. The Oedipal wish is very conspicuous in Julio's tale because the king's daughter, who declares her loyalty to her suitor and openly opposes her father's efforts to block her marriage, is a detail absent in "The Griffin Bird" told by the women from Salamanca. Julio tells a number of tales about older and younger men competing for the loyalty of a maiden who sides with the younger man. As mentioned in Chapter 5, his "Snow White" told of a heroine who rescues the man who kills her father. The heroines in his "Snow White" and "The Griffin Bird" are idealized when represented as icons, and in terms of Oedipal theory, they stand for the good mother that all men in an Oedipal struggle hope will come to their rescue.

The unpromising nature of the hero as the stupid and youngest son of a shoemaker and his struggle with an extremely powerful king who has sent many to their death is a further embellishment of the Oedipal theme in Julio's story. The third or youngest sibling as hero is extremely common in European folktales (Lüthi 1984: 127), including many tales told by storytellers in Cáceres. In terms of Oedipal theory, the youngest and least competent sibling in a group of three represents the child in relation to his more powerful and competent parents. The third dumb child, who improves over the course of time, is a common metaphor for psychological development as a child works through the Oedipal struggle toward maturity (Bettelheim 1977: 106). Improvement often comes with the help of an older person (106), and Julio's story follows this general pattern because the hero, with the help of several older parental figures, manages to overcome many obstacles and win the hand in marriage of the king's daughter. Julio's tale includes helpful old men as well as old women. The helpful father figures are old men who enable the hero to round up the one hundred rabbits and build the ship that travels on land as well as through water. The helpful mother figures are an old woman (who Julio later identifies as the Virgin Mary) encountered on the way to take the apple to the king and the witch who cleans and attends to the griffin's nest. Even the griffin turns out to be an extremely important and helpful agent, despite its ferocious appearance: it provides the hero with the information used to obtain his wealth from the two kings and the boatman. The helpful characters are, according to Oedipal theory, projections of positive sentiments toward parents. The negative sentiments that a son might feel toward a demanding father are censored by the value of filial piety and projected onto the maiden's father, who demands the completion of many impossible tasks. The recasting of Oedipal competition in terms of rivalry between a young man and a maiden's father is a result of the actual tension between fathers and future sons-in-law during courtship of the maiden. Moreover, women generally have close ties with parents, which probably threatens many young men who desire that the women they court and marry make a complete transfer of their loyalties upon marriage.

Julio's tale comes to a satisfying conclusion from the point of view of the hero. After years of fulfilling impossible conditions, the hero finally completes all of the tasks, becomes just as rich as his father-in-law, and marries the maiden. The hero's acquisition of wealth expresses Cáceres men's belief that they must acquire wealth in order to win the approval of a maiden's parents. Although the hero manages to overcome many ordeals and win the hand of the maiden, there is an incomplete resolution of the family conflicts created in this courtship. The hero never really makes peace with his father-in-law, although Julio indicates that peace might be possible sometime in the future. The old king replaces the boatman for seven years, and the hero promises to replace him with someone else at the end of that time. This represents the possible resolution of Oedipal conflict when a young man finally attains maturity, marries, and no longer sees his father, the father figure, or the father-in-law as a threat.

In the context of the dialogue through storytelling, Julio's "Griffin Bird" acknowledges that men will compete through and over women in ways that parallel the Oedipal struggle in a family. Male competition is very threatening to women and interferes in courtship, marriage, and family relations in many ways. Maidens who run into the sexual predator stand to lose their moral reputation even when they guard their premarital chastity. Married women as well as maidens are sometimes the victims of male slander particularly if they appear at the wrong place at the wrong time. Julio provides a message of some comfort to women concerned about rivalry between their father and their suitor because he suggests that, although male competition is a fact of life, a maiden has cause for hope, because sons and fathers-in-law can learn to forgive each other in time, much as the hero of his story promised to disenchant his father-in-law. The concluding message of Julio's story appears to reflect the actual relaxation in the relationship between a man and his son-in-law after a courtship has turned into a marriage: the older man no longer perceives the younger one as a threat to his masculine honor (Pitt-Rivers 1966: 100–101, 117) and the younger no longer perceives the older as blocking his marriage. In the following section we consider a story that circulates more widely in Cáceres oral traditon and also depicts courtship as male competition through women. The versions by women suggest other ways for men to view courtship, ways that mitigate the conflict in family loyalties when a son-in-law clashes with his father-in-law.

## "The Grateful Animals"

One of the most popular stories about heroes disenchanting maidens is "The Grateful Animals," a tale about an unpromising man who acquires the power to change into four different animals, slays the animal counterparts of an ogre, kills the ogre in human form by cracking an egg on his forehead, and marries the maiden held prisoner in the ogre's castle. The stories, which have a variety of titles depending on the region and the storyteller, contain several story elements that folklorists call "The Grateful Animals" (AT 554), "The Dragon Slayer" (AT 300), and "The Ogre's Heart in the Egg" (AT 302).[1] I shall use the title "The Grateful Animals" because all variants circulating in Cáceres oral tradition feature a protagonist who helps four different animals and receives in gratitude the power to change into each.

"The Grateful Animals" is a dragon-slayer tale, a common type of story in European folktale tradition. Bettelheim (1977: 111–113) suggests that dragon-slayer stories generally represent male Oedipal conflicts and their resolution. The ogre and the maiden are symbolic recastings of the father and mother, and the unpromising hero who kills the ogre and takes the maiden for himself is acting out a boy's wish to banish his father and possess his mother. In a culture in which men compete through women, dragon-slayer tales are likely to have a broad appeal, and "The Grateful Animals" is a very popular folktale in the oral tradition of Extremadura and other provinces in Spain. I collected four closely related variants from narrators in Serradilla and Tornavacas in northern and central Cáceres, and Curiel Merchán collected additional tales in southern Cáceres (1944: 108–112) and northern Badajóz (305–307). Outside Extremadura, A. Espinosa published two closely related stories from narrators in Seville (1924: 297–300) and Valladolid (1924: 295–297), and Llano Roza de Ampudia obtained another from a storyteller in Asturias (1975: 34–37).

"The Grateful Animals" addresses the theme of men's competition for women, and men and women develop the plot differently as they mediate the disharmony that male competition can create in courtship and marriage. The stories by José Díaz Sanchez and Felisa Sanchez Martín of Serradilla illustrate best the contours of the dialogue between women and men because the narrators live in the same community, are about the same age, and know many of the same tales circulating in oral tradition. José's tale appears, first, to present the masculine view of male competition in courtship. José was in his early sixties when he told the story and appears to have learned it from his grandparents, particularly his grandmother. His tale has many elements in common with other versions of this story circulating in the oral tradition of different parts of Cáceres. I collected another masculine version from Pedro Cuesta Martín in Tornavacas (listed in the Appendix), and Curiel Merchán collected a third masculine tale from a storyteller in southern Cáceres (1944: 108–112).

José has many things in common with the hero in his story. Like the hero, he was unpromising because he came from a very poor family among the agrarian working class of a stratified agrotown. In a society where wealth means power, José was comparatively powerless to win the hand in marriage of the first maiden he courted. Land is the single most important symbol of wealth in Serradilla, and José's father owned none. José's first courtship came to an end because the maiden's parents considered him too poor to marry their daughter. He courted and married another woman and described to me how he supported his young wife and infant son by working as a charcoal maker (*carbonero*), an occupation many narrators use to represent men of humble social position in stories:

> As for my life, I married and then of course I had a very bad time of it. The first thing that happened was we had a son and there wasn't any work. Nothing. I went about setting up enclosures for making charcoal, those broken pieces of coal they call them. I sold them at five or six pesetas [a sack]. And I went carrying the charcoal over my shoulder. I didn't have any horses whatsoever until later, after I had been married for some time. At first, neither horses nor any-

thing. I went carrying charcoal over my shoulders and I carried a big sack, which made one big one and one little one. One day I sold one sack and the next day I sold two, until later, when I bought some horses and things improved and I went on pulling and pulling and pulling.

Eventually José was able to use his horses to plough land owned by the aristocracy in Serradilla, and his economic position improved, much as the destiny of his hero became brighter when he acquires the supernatural power to change into four different animals.

### "THE GRATEFUL ANIMALS," BY JOSÉ DÍAZ SANCHEZ

One time there was a man who was going down a road. He came upon an eagle, a lion, a greyhound, and an ant quarreling over a beast of burden that had died. So he said, "What are you doing?" "Look here. We're eating this beast and we can't agree." So the man divided the meat and went on, and they called him again: "Please come back here." The man thought, "They're calling me back to kill me now that they've eaten the beast." But one of the animals said, "You're probably wondering why we called you." The man replied, "It'll be for whatever you want." The animal said, "Since you have divided the meat for us, we want to thank you." First the lion came forth because the man had given the rump to the lion. He had given the shoulderblades to the greyhound. He threw the intestines to the eagle. He tossed the head to the ant. Then the lion pulled out a hair and gave it to him and said, "Take this little hair and when you say, 'Man to lion,' you'll turn into a lion that no one in the world will vanquish." "Oh, good," the man said and put the hair away. The grey-hound came and removed another hair and said, "Take this other hair and when you say, 'Man to greyhound,' you'll become the fastest-running grey-hound in the world. There'll be no one who'll leave you behind." The eagle appeared and plucked out a feather and said, "Take this feather and when you say, 'Man to eagle,' you'll become an eagle no one will vanquish flying." Then the ant appeared and said, "Look, I don't have any hair. I'll pull out one of the little horns that I have here and give it to you. And when you say, 'Man to ant,' you'll turn into an ant and you'll go through wherever you want. You'll enter through a small hole or whatever."

The man went on walking farther and farther and farther. After walking for a long time, he said, "Is it true what they told me?" So he said, "From man to lion." With the hair of the lion, he became a lion. He was a lion no one could vanquish. "From man to greyhound." And [one by one] he became all of the animals. He came to a place where three maidens were enchanted in a castle. He went looking for work, and a swineherd was looking for someone to care for some pigs. The man said, "Man to eagle," and turned into an eagle. He circled up in a spiral. He climbed up in a spiral into the castle. And there in the hall was a little hole. He said, "From man to ant." He became an ant and went inside. He came to where the enchanted maidens were, and one of them saw him after he had turned back into a man. She said, "How did you get in here? If the giant comes, he'll kill you. Get out of here right away. To disenchant us from the castle, you have to go to a field where no livestock goes, no one goes. There is a serpent and it kills all the animals or people who enter. And you have to kill that serpent to disenchant us. And a hare will appear after you kill the serpent. And after you kill the hare, a dove will appear, and you have to catch the dove and kill it. Then open the dove. It has an egg inside. And you have to come here with that egg. And the giant will be very ill when you come with the egg. And the egg has to be broken on a white spot on his foreheard."

So that is what he did. The owner was looking for someone to care for his pigs and he said, "You be careful. Don't go into that pasture over there. There is a serpent that kills all who enter—livestock, people, everything." "Ah, now I know where the pasture is." He came to the pasture and went inside with the pigs. There was a lot of grass to eat since other livestock hadn't been grazing because of the bad thing that was there. The serpent appeared when the man went in with the livestock. The serpent came making a sound like brrr, and the man said, "From man to lion." He turned into a lion and he began to fight the serpent. He threw himself into the struggle and he fought and he fought. And the two of them grew very tired. And the serpent said, "If I were to grab a glass of water from the lake of the Gredos,[2] I would smash you between my fingers." And the lion said, "If I were to grab a hot loaf of bread and a cup of brandy and the kiss of a maiden, I'd take a slice out of you that would be bigger than an ounce." They left each other. He came back to the swineherd on the evening of the next day, and his boss said, "Look, he brings the pigs well fed. Oh, Christ! Where has he been? They must have been somewhere inside." And he said to his daughter, "Tomorrow you follow him from afar so he won't see you. Make sure he doesn't see you." He left the next day with the pigs, and—Pum!— the pigs went straight there. Then the serpent came again. The maiden was hiding so the man wouldn't see her. They fought again. And when the serpent grew weary, it said, "If I were to grab a glass of water from the lake of the Gredos, I would smash you between my fingers." And the man who turned into a lion said, "If I were to grab a hot loaf of bread, a cup of brandy, and the kiss of a maiden, I'd take a slice out of you that would be sweeter than an ounce." Once the girl saw what happened, she came back to town and told her father, "He put the pigs inside, and the serpent came. They were fighting, and he turned into a lion and fought the serpent. And then after they had fought long enough, the serpent said, 'If I were to grab a glass of water from the lake of the Gredos, I would smash you between my fingers.' And he said, 'If I were to grab a hot loaf of bread and a cup of brandy and the kiss of a maiden, I'd take a slice out of you that would be bigger than an ounce.'" The girl's father said, "To-morrow you're going to take him those things." So he went off again. Then the serpent appeared and went brrr. The man said, "Man to lion." He became a lion. He started fighting with the serpent. He fought until they were tired of fighting, and the serpent said, "If I were to grab a glass of water from the lake of the Gredos, I would smash you between my fingers." And the maiden was very close to the lion. She was very close to him when he tired and said, "If I were to grab a hot loaf of bread . . ." Then she said, "Here it is." He ate a bite. "A cup of brandy." "Here it is." He drank it. "And the kiss of a maiden." So then she gave him a kiss, and he threw the serpent down. He turned it into dust, he killed it. A hare came running out after he killed the serpent. He caught the hare, and a dove flew out when he killed the hare. He turned into an eagle and went after the dove. He caught it. And the egg appeared after killing the dove. He had the egg of the dove. When he killed the dove, the giant in the castle became ill, and one of the enchanted maidens said, "He killed the serpent."

So the man arrived. The boss and his wive loved the man who took care of their pigs. They said, "Stay here with us." "No, sir. I am not taking care of livestock anymore. I am not taking care of any more pigs." And he went off to the castle and turned into an eagle. He flew in a spiral and flew and flew and flew until he climbed up high. And the giant was very ill. So the man turned into the ant. He went in through a small hole and went down to where the giant was. He was in bed now. He could no longer move. The man grabbed the egg thus. He gave it to him on the white spot he had on his forehead. And smash! The giant died, and the man disenchanted the maidens. And he married one of them, the one he loved, and they made a good stew and ate it. They ate rabbit and partridges and lived happily, and I came home.

The order of events in José's story expresses what men believe they must do in order to court successfully the maiden of their choice. First they must acquire the resources to appear attractive to the maiden and her family, much as the hero acquires the supernatural power to change into four animals. The power of animals probably represents many sources of power, including inner resources harnessed through socialization. Friendly animals, according to psychoanalytical critics, represent the constructive natural energies of the id (Bettelheim 1977: 76), and acquiring the power to change into four friendly animals could stand for the socialization of natural energies according to the ideals of gallantry of a young man ready for courtship and marriage. It is interesting that the hero in "The Grateful Animals" acquires supernatural power by doing a good deed that brings peace to quarreling animals. The performance of the dead and the peaceful result could represent the social responsibility and capacity for leadership in conflict resolution that Spanish men should learn in preparation for their status as head of the family. Socialization as the harnessing of animal energies and the development of social responsibility is a theme in other popular folktales from Spanish oral tradition. The plot of "Juanito el Oso" (AT 302) is a complex metaphor for male socialization according to which a masculine protagonist begins as half bear and half human and learns to harness his initially destructive animal strength and fearlessness and develops into an entirely human adult. Juanito's social responsibility is apparent when he disenchants the maiden who eventually becomes his wife. Storytellers in Garganta la Olla,[3] Navaconcejo, and Serradilla told this story, which is widely circulated elsewhere in Spain (A. Espinosa 1924: 275–283; Larrea Palacín 1959: 141–148; Cortés Vázquez 1979: 2: 130–154).

The acquisition of power, regardless of its source, is a vital element enabling the hero of José's tale to take a woman from another man. The narrator emphasizes how important power is in the competitive life of his village by describing the power acquired from animals in superlative terms. The hero can turn into a lion "no one in the world will vanquish." He becomes the "fastest running greyhound in the world." He becomes the "eagle no one will vanquish flying." The order of the animals is a significant feature of this tale because a different sequence is mentioned in stories by women. José begins with the most powerful and ends with the least powerful animal because relative power is so important to a man in his competition with other men over women. Pedro Cuesta Martín from Tornavacas, whose tale is listed in the Appendix, also emphasized the acquisition of power from animals that enables a man to excel in competition with other men. He describes the hero trying out his new power to catch game, much as men need to test themselves as they enter the fray of male competition through women. He also placed greater emphasis on the lion as the source of the hero's strength by mentioning the lion first and the ant last in the series of animals, and by giving the lion a more prominent place in the plot of his story. Pedro's lion makes two requests of the hero; he asks him to remove a splinter from his paw and to divide the dead animal's carcass among the other animal companions.

The power acquired through animals enables the hero to slay the animal counterparts of the ogre and kill the ogre in human form to release three princesses from enchantment. The Oedipal themes in the story are very clear: the ogre could be a symbolic recasting of the father, and the princesses held prisoner in his castle could be the mother. The acquisition of power by the hero is therefore necessary to fulfill a boy's wish to surpass the strength and power of his own father and possess his mother. The Oedipal themes, however, are mixed with class consciousness: the hero appears as a man of humble social position who takes women from men of much higher social position. Relative wealth is a very important consideration in courtship, and Serradilla is a rigidly stratified community. As mentioned, the narrator's first courtship came to an end because he was considered too poor by the maiden's parents.

Symbols of socialization are mixed with class relations in the description of the hero's defeat of the animal counterparts of the ogre. The ogre as serpent, in the context of socialization according to Judeo-Christian values, could stand for phallic aggressiveness, which all gallant men should tame in their relations with innocent maidens and which Gilmore (1987a: 134–135) argues is the basis of male competition through women. Defeating the ogre as serpent by obtaining three things from a maiden—bread, brandy, and a kiss—stand for what men aspire to in their relations with women. A maiden who serves bread and brandy to a man represents a woman as nurturer, and her kiss is one way of representing a woman's love, which all gallant men hope to obtain during the age of courtship. The kiss is what actually gives the hero the power to throw the serpent to the ground and turn it to dust despite the hero's other sources of supernatural power acquired from animals earlier in the story. The power of a woman's love enabling a man to perform incredible tasks is a common theme in stories circulating in Cáceres oral tradition and will be discussed again in Chapter 9.

The symbolic recasting of Oedipal themes in terms of class relations in courtship becomes particularly apparent when one considers the occupation of the hero before he takes the maiden from the ogre. José says the hero is a swineherd, a lowly occupation in many tales circulating in Cáceres oral tradition. The lowly occupation of the hero is a characteristic of all grateful-animal stories in Cáceres because relative wealth is an important consideration in courtship even in communities where land is more evenly distributed than in Serradilla. The hero is a swineherd in the stories from northern Badajóz and southern Cáceres (Curiel Merchán 1944: 108–112, 305–307) or a goatherd in the story by Pedro Cuesta Martín. Pedro also spent most of his eighty-nine years herding goats in the mountains surrounding his community. Jose's and Pedro's heroes act out the wish of many humble men to acquire the means to take women from other men wealthier than they. The social aspirations of the hero emerge as an important theme in José's story when the hero rejects an offer to settle permanently with the swineherd and his family. The hero announces his intention to herd swine no more, and he heads off to kill the ogre in human form and rescue the maidens held prisoner in the castle.

The ogre in human form can be any powerful man who blocks women from more humble men. According to Oedipal theory, he is the father, and one would expect that a Cáceres man would symbolically recast his father as a rich man blocking the marriage of his daughter to a man of more humble social position in stories about courtship. Filial piety prevents a man from openly acknowledging his negative sentiments toward his father, and when a man enters the age of courtship and is ready to transfer his affection from his mother to his wife, he may run into a potential father-in-law who is paying particular attention to the wealth and social position of the men who court his daughter. For these reasons I suspect that Pedro Cuesta Martín has described his ogre with imagery that could easily remind his male listeners of courtship rituals. Pedro's orgre guards the enchanted princess at the door of his castle just as a father stands at the door of his house and greets a suitor asking for access (*entrada*) to his daughter to commence a formal courtship.

The wealth and social position of the ogre holding the maidens prisoner are made apparent by describing the ogre living in a castle high atop a mountain. José describes how the hero as an eagle "flew in a spiral and flew and flew and flew until he climbed up high" in order to reach the ogre's castle. Height is also a symbol of social status in the dance of the Giants and the Big Heads mentioned in Chapter 5 (Brandes 1980: 17–36). José, whose community is more stratified than those of other Cáceres narrators, accentuates the class symbolism by increasing the number of enchanted maidens held prisoner in the ogre's castle from one to three. The increase in the number to three is a small but important change that makes the ogre appear more like a wealthy father controlling access to all of his daughters or all of the women in his social class. José tends to emphasize class themes in other stories by splitting the images of men to make a sharp distinction between a father and men who represent the power of the landed aristocracy in his village. In his story "The Father and Son Who Went Out Looking for Work" (listed in the Appendix), he separates the images of masculine characters into the hero's good father and a bad, wealthy land owner who becomes the hero's employer. The tale, which is a variant of type 325 known as "The Magician and His Pupil" (Robe 1973: 58–59), describes a humble hero who sets out with his father to find work, and the two men come upon a wealthy employer who hires the son but not the father. The hero collaborates with his father against the employer when the son studies the powerful man's book of magic and acquires some of his supernatural power for himself. The splitting of paternal images, like that of the good mother–bad stepmother in "Snow White," shows the ambivalence of children toward their parents as they attempt to mature and establish independence through marriage.

## Feminine Variant

Women have a great deal to lose in male competition through women, and Felisa's tale illustrates how women modify the details of the plot to protect their relations with parents. Felisa and other women recast the rivalry between a suitor and a maiden's parents into sexual rivalry between two men who desire to court or marry the same woman. They also present the maiden's parents as allies of the hero or intermediaries who promote rather than block the marriage of their daughters. Felisa said she learned her story when she was a young girl and sat around the fire with other girls and women who told stories. She mentioned that men often joined their storytelling groups, and it is very likely that some boys and young men heard feminized versions of "The Grateful Animals" in which women presented their views of male competition. Felisa and José know many of the same stories circulating in Serradilla oral tradition and borrow story elements from each other and weave them into various tales in their repertoires. Felisa's version of "The Grateful Animals" begins with an episode resembling the first part of José's story "The Father and Son Who Went Looking for Work." She describes her hero finding an employer who reads from a book of magic. Her tale adds some unusual elements that protect a daughter's relationship with her mother. The hero enters into an alliance with the mother of the enchanted maiden and offers to remove her daughter from the castle and the ogre. Felisa turns male rivalry in courtship from competition between a suitor and a maiden's parents into sexual rivalry between two men, one of whom takes the wife of the other.

"The Grateful Animals," by Felisa Sanchez Martín

There was a soldier coming from the war, and he came walking along a road. He had to find work to feed himself before reaching home. He spotted a sign on a door that said, "servants are welcome." He went in, and they said yes when he asked for work. But his boss said, "You have to heed everything I say." The soldier said, "Yes, of course. I'll heed you." Everything was well prepared and well taken care of in the house. His boss told him, "Saddle two horses. We're going into the forest for a ride." They went off and came to a very high mountain, and his boss said, "You have to climb that mountain." The soldier asked, "Where?" His boss said, "I said you had to obey me." "Fine, fine." So his boss pronounced some magic words, and the mountain came down. And lo and behold, the soldier went onto the mountain—that is, he rode his horse onto a plain. The boss pronounced magic words, and the plain turned back into a very high mountain. And the soldier asked, "Now what do you want? What shall I do up here?" The boss said, "Kill the horse and clean the bones thoroughly and throw all the meat inside the hide down to me here." The soldier threw down the meat and asked, "All of the bones well cleaned?" His boss said, "Yes, all of them. Just as yours will be as well." His boss picked up his things and went off, leaving the soldier there.

And the poor thing, there he was asking himself, "What's going to happen to me here?" He had to urinate very badly. He peed, and a hole opened up as he peed with a great deal of force. He said, "Oh, my! It's hollow." He dug and dug until he spotted a light below. He continued to dig and was very hungry. He had been there for several days when he saw a ham hanging. He was good and hungry. So he continued to dig and dig and dig. And he saw before him a bed. He ate the ham until he was full and then slept in the bed. A woman came in while he slept. She was an old woman like us [the storyteller and her friends]. She said, "Oh, my! What are you doing here?" He told her what had happened to him. The woman said, "I have a daughter. They have enchanted her in a place very far away from here." He asked, "Where?" and she said, "In such and such a place." He said, "I'm going to see if I can rescue her."

He went off, and while he was walking along the road, walking and walking and walking, he saw a lion, an ant, a greyhound, and I don't remember what. And they had a goat. They had caught it and were eating it and had made a division. The soldier scattered them as he passed. But they said to him anyway, "You come here." He said, "What do you want of me?" One of the animals said, "Divide this goat for us so we all agree with the part you give us." So he cut off the head and gave it to the ant. He gave the body to the lion and the intestines and all of that to the eagle. That's how he made the divisions for them. "Are you in agreement?" "Yes." They called him again just as he was leaving. He thought to himself, What? They aren't satisfied with the goat, and now they want to put their hands on me. But one of the animals said, "We forgot to ask you where you're going." The soldier said, "I'm going to this place." The ant said, "Then take this horn and when you say, 'God and the ant,' you'll become an ant." The eagle said, "Take this feather. When you say, 'God and the eagle,' you'll become an eagle." The greyhound gave him another hair. He said, "Say, 'God and the greyhound,' and you'll become a greyhound." And the lion did the same thing, he gave him a hair. That's how they thanked him for dividing the goat and they were very happy, and he went on.

After walking and walking and walking he came to a town very far away. That's where the maiden was enchanted in a castle And he said, "God and eagle." He appeared as an eagle and flew by the castle and the maiden said, "Oh, my! What a beautiful eagle! It probably brings news from my mother." It landed, and the maiden was alone on the roof of the house. The eagle turned back into a man and said, "I come to rescue you." She said, "Oh, my! But you have to kill a serpent that is in a nearby town." She told him the serpent gives strength to a black man who holds her prisoner. She said, "It gives him strength. If you don't kill the serpent, the black man won't die." So he said, "Good, I'm going to that town."

He went forth, looking for work so he could eat. He found a man who had a lot of pigs, and he started taking care of them. The boss said to him on the first day, "Don't go to the pasture in such and such a place. There is a serpent and it eats everything that passes by." The soldier wasn't afraid of it. He went to the serpent's pasture. There was a gate. Plum! He put the pigs inside, and the serpent appeared. He said, "God and lion." As a lion he fought the serpent all that he could, but neither vanquished the other. He went back with the pigs in the afternoon to the house of his boss. "Oh, my! How he has fattened up the pigs! Where have you been?" asked the boss. He said, "I have been where there is a lot of grass." But the next day, without the soldier knowing, the boss sent one of his daughters with the instructions, "Go see where he puts the pigs. I hope he doesn't put them in the serpent's pasture." The daughter followed the young man without letting him see her. And the young man removed the gate, he put the pigs inside and came to see the serpent. They fought again, and the serpent said, "If I had a bottle of tar, I'd make you bleed." The protagonist said, "If I had a loaf of soft bread and a piece of soft cheese and the kiss of a maiden, I'd also make you bleed." The maiden, who had heard it all, told her father and he said, "Tomorrow go with him and give him a kiss." And her father threw in a chunk of soft cheese and tossed in a piece of soft bread. The serpent appeared again, and the soldier fought and vanquished it. He cut off its head because the king had issued a proclamation saying he would give the pasture to the one who kills the serpent. One had to present the head of the serpent. So the soldier took out a knife, cut off the serpent's head, and took it with him. His boss said, "Present it to the king because you killed the serpent." The soldier said, "No, I won't because I'm going somewhere else." Oh, I forgot. After killing the serpent, he opened its stomach, and a hare came running out. Then the soldier said, "God and greyhound." He tore out running after the hare. He caught it, killed it, opened it, and a dove came out. He said, "God and eagle." He caught the dove because he had to take the egg out of the dove and break it on the forehead of the black man. He killed the dove, removed the egg, put the egg in his pocket, and said, "The rest I leave for the boss."

After he presented the head and the pasture and everything to his boss, he came back to the top of the roof, and there the maiden was sitting. She saw him when he landed. She said, "The black man is going to come up very soon. He's taking his siesta. Get out of here at once. The black man is going to come up and he'll kill you if if he catches you here." But the soldier said, "Don't be afraid." Then: "God and ant." He became an ant. He went under the caldron, gave her the egg, and then the black man came up. She said, "Sit down so I can remove your fleas," because every time he rose from his nap, she combed him and removed his fleas. He said, "You really seem to want to comb me today." He was already very ill because the serpent was dead. But she had to break the egg on his forehead to finish him off. She replied, "No, today is just like every other day." So he sat down. When he was just about asleep, she broke the egg on his forehead and killed him. Then the ant turned back into a young man and said, "Come. Let's get out of here right now." She said, "I'm going." He told her, "Take this hair. Say, 'God and ant,' and you'll become an ant." He said, "God and eagle" and turned into an eagle. The ant grabbed the eagle's claw, and they went flying off to the castle, where her mother was. She was sitting at the door and said, "Oh, my! What an eagle! It appears to bring news of my daughter." They landed, and the soldier said, "God and young man and God and maiden." They married, and everyone was very happy, and they tossed the bones of their wedding feast at our noses.

Felisa presents a very different picture of male competition than did José in his version of the same tale. Felisa focuses less attention on the acquisition of power, which men believe they must have to excel in male competition. She changes the order of the animals that give the hero his supernatural power and places physical power lower on her scale of values. She makes the ant, the smallest and weakest animal, the first and the lion, the largest and most powerful, the last. The change in the order of the animals is a significant detail; it expresses a different hierarchy of values in a woman's view of human relations. The power to excel in male competition assumes less importance because, as mentioned earlier, feminine narrators stress the heavy costs to women of male sexual rivalry. Abilities unrelated to power, represented by the capacity to change into an ant, assume greater importance.

José depicted his hero as an unpromising man of low social position who takes a maiden from a wealthy and powerful man, who probably represents a maiden's father. Felisa turns the plot around by making her hero an ally of the enchanted maiden's mother and a person willing to take the maiden from a suitor of whom the mother does not approve. Felisa represents the disapproved suitor as a wealthy man in a disapproved relationship with a maiden. This aspect of the story accords with actual experience in Serradilla, where several men of the landed aristocracy have dishonored the daughters of working-class families. Felisa remains loyal to her agrarian working-class background by representing the hero as a man of humble social position, and presents a scenario that contradicts the often-mentioned male view that a maiden's mother disapproves of young men only because of their poverty. The suitor is a lowly man—he is a soldier who becomes a swineherd—who has the approval of a maiden's mother, who lives in a castle high atop a mountain. The location of the mother's castle and the mention of hams hanging from the ceiling have a number of possible connotations. They could represent her high-class status in a stratified society and her exalted social position as the nurturing mother in a family. Felisa places the maiden's mother, rather than her father, in an alliance with the approved suitor for several reasons. The maiden's mother is important to Felisa because mothers and daughters have a close relationship throughout the life course. The father is absent as an ally because fathers regard the young men who court their daughters as potential threats to their masculine honor.

It is preferable from the point of view of women that men avoid competition over women during courtship. Felisa consequently directs the male competition away from the father and son-in-law relationship by making the rivalry between the two men that of equals by describing spouselike intimacy between the ogre and the enchanted maiden. She tells how the maiden instructs the black man to kneel so she might remove his fleas and comb his hair, enabling her to smash the egg on his forehead. Furthermore, Felisa reduces male competition by making the daughter, not the suitor, the one who kills the ogre. This perhaps symbolizes a woman's belief that it is she who must chose her husband and not her husband who must choose her.

Other Cáceres women also tell "The Grateful Animals," recasting the competition between men as sexual rivalry between suitors for the same women and presenting the maiden's parents as helpful intermediaries in their daughters' marriages. Julia Lobato Gil, also from Serradilla, told a slightly different variant in which male competition through women is directed away from the son and father-in-law relationship. The identities of the ogre and the maiden's father are kept distinct, and the father promotes rather than blocks his daughter's marriage to the young man who comes to court her. The maiden's father is a king who offers his daughter in marriage to the man who slays the ogre. Male competition is presented as male sexual rivalry when another suitor steals the heads of the ogre, a seven-headed serpent, and presents them to the king. The hero, however, has cleverly taken the tongues out of the heads and uses them as proof to take the false suitor's place at the side of the princess. Julia's tale (listed in the Appendix) resembles another story that Curiel Merchán collected from a woman in northern Badajóz (1944: 305–307). Specific elements in the stories by Felisa and Julia appear in some of the masculine versions of "The Grateful Animals" and other stories circulating in Cáceres oral tradition. Male sexual rivalry, for example, appears in a version of "The Grateful Animals" that Curiel Merchán collected from a man in the southern Cáceres community of Madroñera (1944: 108–112). In this story, the enchanted princess is married to the ogre, and the hero sleeps with her before killing the ogre and taking the woman for himself. Moreover, the same masculine tale features an assertive woman who takes the egg from the hero and kills her ogre husband, much like her counterpart in the tale by Felisa. One can also find parallels between the tale by Julia and another story called "The Fisherman" by Julio Lopez Curiel (listed in the Appendix). In Julio's story, a usurper takes the heads of an ogre and presents them to the king to win his daughter's hand in marriage. In spite of some overlapping plot elements in male and female stories, the sum total of all changes to the plot shifts the direction of male competition in stories told by women compared to those told by men.

In the dialogue through storytelling, men cast their picture of male competition in accord with their actual experiences. Many of the storytellers I met, who are comparatively poor, can easily identify with a humble suitor who runs up against the stiff opposition of a father protective of his daughter's moral reputation and his own masculine honor. Men with little property can easily see the need to acquire supernatural power to win the approval of a courted maiden's parents. On the other hand, women need their mother throughout the life course, and they are loyal and caring with both parents, especially when they are unable to care for themselves in their old age. A woman faces a serious conflict in her loyalties when her parents and suitor are in opposition. For example, life during courtship was very difficult for the woman from Barrado and the young man from Arroyomolinos (described earlier in this chapter). Women can mitigate against some of the conflict in loyalties by presenting a picture of a humble man, a swineherd in the stories by Felisa and Julia, who is the approved suitor in the eyes of a rich maiden's parents. Such a picture is likely to appeal to humble men hearing feminine versions of "The Grateful Animals" and perhaps calm their fears about approaching a maiden's father with a wine bag and asking for the daughter's hand in marriage. The feminine stories might facilitate accommodation in marriage by encouraging older men to view their parents-in-law as potential allies rather than enemies in a culture where women have strong ties to parents.

# CHAPTER EIGHT

# The Animal Groom

MEN AND women tell one another how they can bond in heterosexual love when they tell and retell animal-groom stories. In the tales told by women, a maiden with strong loyalties to her father transfers her affections to a prince enchanted in animal form. The heroine disenchants the prince by showing him compassion and devotion and thus transforms him from an animal into a man. Animal-groom stories are very popular in the European folktale tradition, and Bettelheim (1977: 310) believes they teach women and men to change radically previously held attitudes toward sex in order to love. The story has meaning for men as well as women because both genders have sexual anxieties learned in early childhood. The heroine, who transforms the beast into a man by showing him compassion and devotion, is the woman who conquers her feelings, learned through socialization, that sex is a beastly experience. The animal, who turns into a handsome prince, is the man who learns to replace phallic aggression with heterosexual love and thus no longer sees himself as repulsive to women.

Animal-groom stories (AT 425) are very popular in Cáceres and Spanish oral tradition probably because men and women have so much to transcend during courtship and marriage. A man must establish his position among other men by competing through and for women, temper sexual assertiveness with gallantry, come to terms with his fear of women, and transfer devotion from his mother to a wife. A woman must conquer her fear of safe-appearing but dangerous men, be willing to endure defloration, develop an independent identity, shift the balance in her loyalties from parents to a spouse, and contend with the waxing and waning of her illusion of love as she deals with a jealous and critical mother-in-law. I collected six versions from narrators in northern and central Cáceres villages; Curiel Merchán (1944: 82-86, 142–144) reports two more from southern Cáceres; and folklorists have collected at least eleven others from regions in Spain outside of Extremadura (Cabal 1924: 66–71; Cortés Vázquez 1979: 2: 110–114; A. Espinosa 1924: 256–274; Llano Roza de Ampudia 1975: 29–32; Larrea Palacín 1959: 55–63).

The contours of the dialogue through storytelling between men and women are particularly apparent in animal-groom stories told by narrators from Garganta la Olla and the neighboring village of Piornal. I found storytellers who knew animal-groom tales in several villages, but narrators from Garganta and Piornal voluntarily told more animal-groom tales than their counterparts in other villages. This chapter focuses on four stories by men and women who describe in metaphorical language how conjugal love can work. I shall refer to other stories collected from different narrators to provide a fuller picture of the dialogue through the animal-groom stories, and the reader can find the remaining northern and central Cáceres stories that I collected listed in the Appendix.

### "Beauty and the Beast"

Teresa Herrero of Garganta la Olla, a twenty-four-year-old unmarried woman, told "Beauty and the Beast," which expresses a maiden's anticipation of marriage. "Beauty and the Beast" has a wide geographical distribution; other women of northern and central Cáceres know this tale, as do women in southern Cáceres (Curiel Merchán 1944: 142–144) and northern Salamanca (Cortés Vázquez 1979: 2: 110–111). A. Espinosa (1924: 271–273) collected a "Beauty and the Beast" story in Soria in the early 1920s, illustrating the stability of this tale over time in Spanish oral tradition. Teresa said she learned "Beauty and the Beast" from her now deceased maternal grandmother, who was in the same generation as the younger women Espinosa met during his folklore expedition earlier this century.

An examination of all the stories told by older women to younger women reveals that maidens hear two contradictory messages from their mothers and grandmothers. On the one hand, they hear stories of maidens and thieves depicting in graphic language the horrors of defloration to reinforce the premarital chastity of women. On the other hand, they hear "Beauty and the Beast," which prepares maidens to conquer their fear of sex, consummate their marriage on their wedding night, and enter into a permanent bond of heterosexual love with their husband. Both types of tales are necessary in a culture in which women must guard their premarital chastity, maintain their moral reputations, preserve their father's masculine honor, and enter a permanent monogamous marital relationship. Teresa's story describes a heroine who learns to conquer her fear of sex by transferring her love from her father to a prince enchanted as a lion. Her tears of compassion and love remove the prince from his bewitchment and transform him from an animal into a man.

#### "Beauty and the Beast," by Teresa Herrero

Once there was a father who had three daughters. He was going to a fair in a nearby city, and he asked his daughters what they wanted him to bring them. The oldest asked for the most beautiful dress, and the middle one asked for the most beautiful necklace he could find in the city. The youngest asked him to bring her a white rose. The father went to the fair and bought the dress and the necklace, but he couldn't find the white rose. He started for home disgusted and came to a castle along the road. He went into the castle and found a table set with every kind of thing to eat. He ate and lay down. He got up in the morning, looked through a window, and saw a rosebush with white roses in the garden. So he went downstairs and cut one of the roses. But when he cut the rose, he heard a voice say, "Ingrate! Weren't the dinner and the bed enough for you? Now you cut the roses in my garden." A lion appeared. The man explained that his daughter had asked him for the rose and he couldn't find one in the city. The lion told him he had to bring his daughter, and if he didn't, he would kill him. So the man came home very worried. He gave the gifts to his daughters and explained that a lion appeared when he cut the rose. The lion told him that because he had cut the rose for his daughter, she had to go to the lion. His daughter told her father not to worry because she would go, even though she was afraid. She went to the lion's castle. The lion gave her a kind of mirror in which she could see everything that happened, everything that she wanted to see.

One time, when she was looking into it, she saw that her father was very ill. She told the lion that she had to go see her father because her sisters were not taking good care of him. He told her, yes, she could go see him, but she had to return after a given period of time. If she didn't, he would die of sorrow. She went, and her father recovered. But her sisters were envious of her because they saw her fine clothes. She was very well off. One of them persuaded her to stay: "Why do you want to go? You're living with a beast. No, you are not going back to him." One day when she was looking in the mirror she saw that the lion was very ill, he was dying of sorrow. So she left her father's house, left her sisters, and went to the lion's castle. She saw him lying on a table nearly dead. She loved the lion a great deal, and she began to cry. Her tears fell on him as she cried, and he was transformed into a prince. He told her he would not have been transformed into a prince if someone had not shed tears of love for him. They were married, and they threw their bones at our noses.

Teresa's story has many of the elements found in other "Beauty and the Beast" stories, including the written fairy-tale versions of this tale.[1] Teresa's heroine is the youngest of three daughters in a family with a father and no mother. The absence of the mother possibly is a poetic device focusing attention on Beauty's special relationship with her father which, according to Bettelheim (1977: 307), shows that a "child's oedipal attachment to a parent is natural, desirable, and has the most positive consequences for all, if during the process of maturation, it is transferred and transformed as it becomes detached from the parent and concentrated on the lover." The father in Teresa's story is an instrumental agent for his youngest daughter's transference of love by inadvertently delivering

Beauty into the hands of her husband. The father's search for the rose requested by Beauty leads him to the garden of the enchanted prince. The representation of the father as intermediary in his daughter's marriage is likely to have appeal to a maiden in a Cáceres village because women need the support of their father in courtship not only to transfer their affections to their spouse, but also to avoid a terrible conflict in loyalties that would require a woman to choose between her parents and her suitor.

In the context of messages delivered in the storytelling dialogue, the prince in the form of a lion, a wild and ferocious animal, probably represents a maiden's fear of defloration. The heroine tells her father she'll go to the lion even though she is afraid, much as many maidens might tell their parents that, despite sexual anxieties, they are willing to go ahead with their wedding and consummate their marriage. It is a cultural norm for women to express a fear of defloration even in retrospect; many older married women openly admitted crying uncontrollably on their wedding night when left alone for the first time with their husband.

The heroine in Teresa's story feels a conflict in her loyalties as she makes the transition from daughter to wife. Beauty shows her strong ties to her father when she tells the Beast that she must return home because her father is ill and is not receiving good care from her sisters. The pull of the heroine's filial loyalties almost results in the death of the prince, much as a young married woman would actually have marital problems if she could not shift her loyalties from parents to spouse. Teresa depicts the heroine taking the initiative in returning to her husband when she sees him sick and dying of sorrow. Her return symbolically represents a maiden's transference of affection from father to husband. As she makes the transference, she shows compassion for her husband by shedding a tear of love, and her tear removes him from his enchantment. Her love transforms him from a beast into a handsome prince and symbolizes that she no longer sees sex as bestiality.

A maiden hearing this story can make many associations with other stories of courtship and marriage. The lion is an animal that lives in the forest and is metonymically associated with thieves who personify women's fear of men. His transformation represents how appearances differ from reality, but in this case appearances are dangerous and reality is safe. In the dialogue through storytelling, men tried to present themselves as dangerous appearing but actually safe in other stories told to persuade women to love men. "Beauty and the Beast," in the context of Cáceres storytelling, illustrates that women who are ready to separate from parents and make the transition to marriage can accept the messages of men. It also shows that for a girl taught to fear men, love is an essential element in enabling this transition and acceptance.

Women describe metaphorically their sexual anxieties at the time of marriage in various ways. Some older women depict life with the beast during his enchantment as a blissful period, much like Pitt-Rivers (1966: 109) reported older couples in Alcalá recalling with nostalgia the time of their courtship when "everyone was happiest." Florencia Real Cobos of Serradilla, a mature married woman in her mid-fifties with two grown children of her own, told a version of the story in which the enchanted prince never takes animal form. The prince is a handsome young man and his bewitchment means only that he cannot leave his territory. He and Beauty fall in love and live happily in the prince's realm, where they and everyone else are very well off. Florencia's tale (listed in the Appendix) is like another variant collected from a woman in southern Cáceres by Curiel Merchán (1944: 142–44) in which the enchanted prince is never an animal and appears only as a very well-dressed, elegant (*gallardo*) young man who treats Beauty with every consideration and kindness. On the other hand, Cortés Vázquez (1979: 2: 110–111) collected a story from a woman in northern Salamanca emphasizing the fearful nature of the Beast. He is a wild animal (*fiera*), and a fearful Beauty must be mute and communicate with her Beast by lettered signs lest she startle him with the sound of her voice. A fearsome Beast also appears in a story A. Espinosa collected in Soria from a narrator whose gender he did not report (1924: 271–273). The range in images of the Beast undoubtedly captures the range of feelings of women anticipating or recalling their defloration and their first years of married life. All stories nevertheless include happy endings, indicating that despite their fear of men, women can learn to change their attitudes toward sex through love of the men they marry.

## "THE SOLDIER"

Animal-groom stories appeal to men as well as women in Cáceres because men also have sexual anxieties likely to surface as courtship turns into marriage. Bettelheim (1977: 295–299) suggests that animal-groom stories appeal to men because they fear their coarseness will repel women. Morever, some rural Spanish men fear sexual intimacy as a part of their general fear of the power of women (Brandes 1980: 77). Men express a different perspective in their telling of animal-groom tales, illustrated by the version of "The Soldier" that Julio Lopez Curiel performed in Garganta la Olla on a warm evening in front of neighbors resting after a hard day of work. His story reworks many of the themes in "Beauty and the Beast" from a masculine point of view. To be sure, sufficient differences between Julio's "The Soldier" and Teresa's "Beauty and the Beast" warrant their classification by folklorists as different stories. Ralph Boggs (1930: 52) reports no Spanish stories like "The Soldier" in his *Index of*

*Spanish Folktales*, but Stanley Robe (1973: 67–68) identified a tale like "The Soldier" in Mexican oral tradition. He categorized the story with a different Aarne-Thompson tale-type number (AT 361) than is normally applied to animal-groom stories. Julio's story, however, appears to be a retelling of "Beauty and the Beast" from the perspective of the Beast. The hero is like the Beast because he appears as a fearsome lion and marries the youngest of three daughters. Julio's story presents an explanation for why a man is like a lion and expresses what a man needs from the woman who loves him.

The stories by Julio and Teresa taken together form a dialogue through storytelling in Garganta in which men and women tell one another how conjugal love can work in a culture in which men are different from women and each gender fear the other. It is possible, even likely, that Julio, age seventy-four, and Teresa's now deceased grandmother knew many of the same stories circulating in Garganta oral tradition and participated in the dialogue through the telling and retelling of the same stories. I could not verify this because Teresa's grandmother died several years ago, and Julio had moved to Barcelona before I returned to Garganta for a second period of fieldwork and collected the "Beauty and the Beast" story from Teresa in the spring of 1984. The two families are friends, Teresa has learned other stories from Julio's sister, and Julio and Teresa's grandmother were about the same age.

### "THE SOLDIER," BY JULIO LOPEZ CURIEL

Once there was a young lad of fourteen, and when he turned twenty, he went into the army. Because he didn't have a father or mother or brothers or anyone at home, he said, "Where shall I go after my tour of duty? They feed me well here and they take good care of me, they dress me well." And each time he ended a three-year tour of duty, he signed on for another three and stayed in the army.

His tour of duty ended, and the soldier could no longer could stay in the army because he was fifty years old. He had no other recourse but to take to the road and go home. In those days there were no cars, no airplanes. He had to walk home. After walking and walking, he entered a forest of oaks and cork trees. Night had fallen, and a huge storm broke. The man climbed up into the shelter of a cork tree. So much hail fell that he was confused. The hail wounded his face and hands and turned them black. He jumped up and went out into the storm, saying, "I'd give my soul to the devil if he'd take me out of the straits I'm in." Plum! The devil presented himself. He said, "What do you want, what do you desire? I'm your slave for all you command of me." The soldier said, "Who'll take me out of these straits?" The devil replied, "I'll to take you out, but I'm going to give you no more than seven years to live, and at the end of seven years you have to come back to this same spot. Then we're going to say good-bye. I'll fix you a suit of clothes, and you'll have to wear it during the seven years for which you'll sign an agreement." The devil spotted a lion. He drew his sword, killed the lion, and skinned it. He pierced the hide and made a greatcoat with sleeves and pockets and said to the soldier, "Look at this. Each time you put your hands in the pockets, they'll be full of money. But there is one more condition. You can't shave for seven years (just as I [the storyteller] am starting not to shave). You may not shave, or cut your hair, or your nails." After four or five years, of course, the man had nails like this. And he went from inn to inn in all the towns telling everyone to pray to God for him to live for more than seven years. He asked everyone to make the sign of the cross. Before he had left the oak forest and after he said good-bye to the devil, he dug a huge hole. His pockets were always full of money, and he buried money there.

Now, one day he came to a little town and asked for lodging. The authorities were pursuing an innkeeper who didn't have any money to pay the rent on the inn; the owner of the inn wanted to throw him out. That's the way things were when the soldier came to the inn and spoke to the innkeeper: "I say, can you rent me a room so I can come here to live?" He said, "Yes, sir. Why not?" But the soldier frightened him. He had a beard this long, nails this long, and his hair fell way down. It had been five or six years since he had shaved. The soldier was sitting in a chair when the owner of the inn came to ask for a year's rent. The innkeeper didn't have the money to pay the rent, and his three daughters started crying because the Civil Guard took their father away to jail. The soldier asked, "What's happening?" No one answered. He asked again, "But what's happening here?" One of the daughters said, "The inn belongs to this man, and my father doesn't have the money to pay the rent. They took my father to jail so he'd get the money to pay." Then the soldier asked, "Let's see. How much does this man owe?" "This much," said one of the daughters. He thrust his hands into his pockets, which were always full of money. He started counting and counting and counting out the money for the owner, and he saved the innkeeper.

The innkeeper came home and didn't know how to repay the soldier for the favor. The soldier said he had done only what he wanted to do by removing him from the straits he was in. The innkeeper and his daughters invited him to have supper one night. He came downstairs to the supper, and the innkeeper said to him, "I don't know how to repay you because I don't have money. All I know is that I have to repay you for this favor, which no one else in the world would do for me. I don't have money but I do have three daughters. Take the one you want and marry her." Then the innkeeper asked the oldest, "Come, daughter. Do you want him?" "Why would I want him when he looks like a lion? I don't want him! Don't even mention it." He asked the one who followed in age, "And you? Do you want him?" She said, "Me? He looks like a demon. I don't want him either." And he went to the youngest: "And you, daughter? Do you want this man?" "Yes, sir. I want him, father. Let him be whatever he is, but I want him. It's enough he removed us from the straits we were in. I want him." The soldier had a gold ring on his finger. He removed it and cut it in half and put her name on one half and his name on the other half. He gave the half with his name to her so she would recognize him one day by the sign of the ring.

One of her sisters declared, "You're crazy! Marrying a demon!" And the other one said, "You with a lion. Don't you see that if he looks like a lion, he's going to tear your skin with his nails? And one can't even see his face!" It was covered with hair. Then the soldier said good-bye. He left plenty of money with the father, and the girl prayed to God for him to live more than seven years. The soldier told her he would marry her. And her older sister said to her, "Oh, you're silly! You're not really going to marry him." But she insisted, "I've said I would." She went into the darkest corner of the house and always prayed for the soldier. She got the worse for not eating. She didn't eat anything but her spirit. She sustained herself with that.

The seven years were up, and the soldier had to keep his date with the devil. So he left and went to the oak tree where he had battled the storm. The soldier had come early to fill the place with crosses and waited for the devil to appear. The devil couldn't get in to where he was. When the devil got close, one of the crosses seized him and grabbed him as if he were beef jerky. The devil tried to remove himself, and the soldier declared, "Listen, you're going to undress me, but before you remove this greatcoat, you have to buy me a good suit of clothes. You have to shave me. You have to cut my hair and nails. Then we'll say good-bye to each other like good friends. But nothing more, you devil pig." The soldier sat down, and the devil cut his hair and shaved him. He bought him the suit of clothes. The soldier was dressed like a doctor now.

Then he said good-bye to the devil, and they went their separate ways. The soldier went to a small town nearby and rented a yoke of oxen and a cart and took the money directly to the inn of his bride. But now they didn't recognize him. No one—not the father, not his daughter—recognized him because he came shaved like a young lord. He asked, "Who is the innkeeper of this house? My servant, can you rent me two rooms?" "Which ever ones you want." But the innkeeper didn't recognize him. They went upstairs. He showed him the room. The soldier said, "It's fine." The same beds were there. They took all the sacks of money upstairs—there was a pile of sacks of money—and they locked the door. The soldier went about the town to amuse himself and wasn't recognized. Then the older daughters fell in love with him, and one day when they were of a mind one of them asked their father, "Why don't you invite this gentleman to dinner? We've fallen in love with him. He must be very rich because he seems well placed in town as a gentleman. Let's see if one of the two of us can catch him." And the poor youngest one was in a corner crying. The soldier said to her tenderly, "Don't you worry, daughter." Her father said, "I've had the pleasure of your being here for several days now. Come eat with us."

B. Taggart '89

"Yes, sir. Delighted." "Come eat with us tomorrow when we'll all be together." "Very well." The innkeeper laid out a banquet. Everything was ready—the dinner, the table settings. And the oldest one sat there, the other who followed her in age was here, and the groom was in the middle. They wanted to see which of the two the groom would choose. But the groom wouldn't go for them because he knew there was another one. When he came, he asked the father, "Sir, don't you have another daughter?" The father said, "Oh, yes, sir. I have a daughter, and she is always hidden away." He was ashamed to ask the soldier to make way at the table for his daughter. Her oldest sister declared, "That fool! One time a soldier came here dressed in rags who looked like the devil because his nails were this long and he had long hair. That girl is a fool. She believes the soldier is going to come back here." Then the soldier said to the father, "If that girl doesn't come out to eat with us, I'm leaving. I won't eat here." Then one of the daughters declared, "Oh, don't let that fool come out because she's so weak. She's always crying." "She has to come," said the soldier. The father went to her saying, "Look, my daughter, we have a gentlemen eating here at the table with us who will probably marry one of your sisters one day. He'd be pleased to have you come and eat too." She didn't want to but she finally yielded. The soldier got up, went to the room where she was, took her hand, and said, "Come and eat and don't be ashamed. And don't cry anymore." She sat down and the groom changed his seat. The bride sat between her two sisters, and he sat facing her. While she was eating with tears in her eyes, her fate was decided. He lifted his glass of wine and said to her, "Take this, my love, and drink it." And he placed the ring down on the table between them. When she saw it, she said, "Father, our savior!" She jumped up as she saw it and embraced him. Mother of mine, the oldest hung herself, and other one drowned herself. The soldier and his bride arranged for their wedding and were married at once. After they were married, the devil appeared at the door in the night. He tapped on the window. Tan, tan. "Who is it?" He said, "It's me. I'm the devil. I've come to give you a thousand thanks. Instead of taking your soul, there are more in your place." And the story has ended [*acabado*] and may the britches of Rosi be sewn with purple thread [*morado*].

Julio's story provides a masculine perspective on how and why a man is like a lion. The devil, who forces the hero to appear frightening to women, represents a force bringing out a man's animality. Such a force could be a man's anxiety about appearing coarse to a woman, the expectations of manliness that require a man to be sexually assertive like an animal and enter into the game of "erotic aggression" (Gilmore 1987a: 134–135), or an Oedipal conflict with the father symbolically recast as the devil. Julio draws particular attention to the dehumanizing effects of the expectation that a man must become wealthy to succeed in winning the approval of a maiden and her father in courtship. He makes this point by representing the devil as the source of the money that the soldier used to save the innkeeper, win his gratitude, and earn the hand in marriage of his daughter. Whatever the source of the soldier's fearsome appearance, the story is another masculine attempt to persuade women to love men by drawing their attention to how the appearance of a man is different from the underlying reality. The soldier is one of many men in masculine stories who appears dangerous but actually is safe. Other examples include the apparently cruel father in José Díaz Sanchez's "The Innocent Slandered Maiden," the thieves in José's "The Maiden and the Thieves" and in Vito Flores's and Julio's "Snow White." The tendency of men to represent male characters as dangerous appearing but actually safe is an apparent response to women, who personify their fear of men in the safe-appearing but actually dangerous male characters in their stories.

Julio's story expresses how a man needs to believe that a woman will love him for what he is, despite his appearance of ugliness. Julio makes this point in metaphorical language by describing how the two older daughters of the innkeeper refuse to marry the soldier in return for saving their father. The oldest daughter rejects him because "he looks like a lion," and the next oldest refuses him because he "looks like a demon." The youngest, however, agrees to marry him and says, "Let him be whatever he is, but I want him." The idealized conduct of the youngest daughter, who remains loyal to the soldier despite his appearance and the criticism of her sisters, expresses how men need the loyal devotion of women and want to be loved in spite of their physical and material shortcomings. Julio's language is particularly dramatic when describing the loyal and virtuous bride of the soldier rejecting food as if she were a deeply religious woman showing her devotion to Christ by fasting. Such women became the stuff of legend in Spain (Christian 1981: 57–59), and Julio follows legendary tradition by depicting the bride as constantly praying, weeping, and starving. She lived only on her spirit while her husband was away confronting the devil. Julio dramatically splits the images of the sisters, depicting the older, greedy ones delivering themselves to the devil by taking their own lives. They represent the greedy women whom men fear only want them for their wealth and their appearance, whereas the good sister represents the ideal bride who loves a man loyally for his true self.

## "Cupid and Psyche" by a Woman

Juana Moreno also of Garganta la Olla, a married woman of sixty-five with grown children, told a composite animal-groom story combining "Beauty and the Beast" and "Cupid and Psyche" themes. Her story acts as a feminine response to the tale by Julio; in it Juana describes a heroine who shows her man the untiring devotion that men like Julio say they need from women. Her heroine not only conquers her fear of sex but also demonstrates a willingness to look for her lost husband, wearing out seven pairs of iron shoes in the process. Juana's tale also speaks to a maiden anticipating her marriage with anxiety over her defloration. Juana's story is reassuring because she presents a blissful image of her heroine's life with the enchanted prince. Although he appears first as a snake, he quickly turns into a king during his enchantment. He and the heroine fall in love and live happily as long as Beauty is faithful to her oath of secrecy about his human form.

"Cupid and Psyche," by Juana Moreno

Once there was a father who had three daughters. He was going to go to the fair. He asked, "Daughters, what do you want me to bring you from the fair?" The first one said, "Father, bring me a very beautiful dress." The second said, "And some shoes for me." The youngest said, "And three singing roses for me, father." And the father went to the fair and bought the dress and the shoes. But he couldn't find the singing roses anywhere at the fair. When he was on his way home, he saw a garden in which all of the roses were singing and he asked himself, "Shall I go in or not?" He asked himself this question because the garden wasn't his. He went in and cut a rose and then, after he cut the rose, a huge snake appeared who was an enchanted king. The snake asked, "Who told you to come in here?" He said, "I have three daughters, and one asked me for a dress, the other asked me for some shoes, and the youngest asked me for three singing roses. I couldn't find the roses at the fair, but I saw these singing roses and came in here." The snake said, "Tell your daughter to wait for me at my door at eight o'clock tonight."

The daughter went and on the first night the snake turned into a king while speaking with her. He told her, "Don't tell your father or your sisters or anyone until the last night that I've become a person, that I'm a king. You have to keep this a secret." She went the next night, and he talked with her again. The two of them fell in love, and she didn't tell anyone.

But one night her father and sisters insisted, "You have to tell us. What does the snake say to you?" She didn't say at the time that the snake was a king. She said, "It doesn't say anything to me. It just lays at my feet and doesn't say anything to me." But they made her tell, and she she told them that the snake turned into a king, and the two of them had fallen in love. Then he was enchanted for another period of time. The third night she went again, and he said, "Well, now, it's bad for me and worse for you. If you want to find me, you'll have to wear out a pair of iron shoes. When you have worn out the pair of iron shoes, I'll be there."

After he told her this, she went upstairs to her father and said, "Father, you have to make me a pair of iron shoes. I have to go look for the snake. He is a king, and I'm going to look for him." But her father said, "No daughter! How are you going to go?" She said, "You make my lunch and the shoes." So he made the shoes, and they made her lunch, and she went about the world looking for the king who was a snake. One night she came to the house of the wind and asked, "Can you take me in for the night?" The woman inside the house replied, "No. I'm the mother of the wind, and if my son comes, he'll devour me." The girl said, "Even if I'm in a little corner thereabouts? He won't smell me." The woman took her in, when the wind came home, he said, "Mother, I smell human flesh! If you don't get it for me, I'll devour you." His mother said, "It's a young woman who is going in search of the king-snake, and I took the poor thing in, these nights being as cold as they are." He said, "Good. Have her come out." She came out. They gave her supper and a walnut for desert and went to bed. Instead of breaking the walnut open, she put it away and didn't eat it. They told her, "You'll reach the house of the moon, and there they'll give you a little more information about where he is." She went to the house of the moon, but he also didn't know where the king-snake slept. He also gave her an apple when they ate supper, and she got up in the morning and went off again. She walked and walked and walked and she came to the house of the sun. The sun came home saying, "Mother, I smell human flesh! If you don't get it for me, I'll set whomever it is on fire." The mother said, "Oh, my son, it's a young woman. She comes looking for the king-snake, and I took her in." "Tell her to come out." He didn't do anything to her. They had supper and after supper they gave her a pomegranate. She put it away, and the sun said, "He's in that town over there, that's where the king-snake lives." He found another woman and touched her and married her. She had disenchanted him and now he was a real king.

The girl arrived and split open the walnut and went down the street where the king lived, saying, "Who'll buy this twist of gold from me?" And the king's servant appeared at the window and said to the king's wife, "Oh, my lady! Holy mother of mine! What a beautiful thing that woman is selling! Buy it from her!" The queen said, "Oh, come now! How am I going to buy it?" But the queen said, "Call her." And she asked, "How much to you want for it?" The girl said, "I don't want anything. Just let me spend one night with your husband." She went upstairs that night, but the queen and her servant had given the king a sleeping potion, and he didn't wake up all night. The girl said, "Rey Culebrón [king-snake], here you have Rosita Rosaura to ask you pardon." So it went all night, and he didn't wake up. She got up in the morning and—ala!— she went away. She split open the apple, and it turned into a spool of golden thread. And she went about selling it as well, and the queen's servant said, "My lady. Oh, my! If you thought what she was selling last night was beautiful, you'll think this is even more so. Buy it." The queen said, "Call her." And girl said again that she wanted to spend the night with the king. The servant said, "Oh, buy it. We'll give him the potion again. Don't you see? He didn't hear what went on." It was the same thing all night as before. "Rey Culebrón, here you have Rosita Rosaura to ask your pardon. Rey Culebrón, here you have Rosita Rosaura to ask your pardon." And because the apartment walls were as thin as tambourines, one of the neighbors was listening. And in the morning he said to the king, who had slept through the night again and hadn't heard anything, "What do you have at the head of your bed? Every night, for two nights now, it says, 'Rey Culebrón, here you have Rosita Rosaura to ask your pardon.'

It's that way every night." And the king remembered his first love. The next day she split open the pomegranate, and it turned into a golden hen with golden chicks. She walked down the street with the hen and the chicks. The servant said, "Oh, Holy Mother of mine! Lady, if you thought the other things were beautiful, you'll think this surpasses them. You have to buy this." The lady said, "And by chance what if my husband hears her and wakes up?" The servant said, "He won't wake up because we'll give him a stronger dose." They gave him a stronger dose, but now he knew and he threw the potion behind the bed and didn't drink it. And the woman came at nine o'clock and sat in the chair and started, "Rey Culebrón, here you have Rosita Rosaura to ask your pardon. Oh, my God. It's been two nights now that I'm telling you this, and you don't hear me. What will happen to me if you don't hear me?" And she continued, "Rey Culebrón, here you have Rosita Rosaura to ask your pardon." And then he grabbed her and put her in bed and placed a two-edged sword in the middle of the bed so they wouldn't touch each other. And when it was nine in the morning, the servant called, "Madam, leave now. It's time. Get up. It's time now." The king answered, "This morning it's a double ration of chocolate in bed." They took him the chocolate, and they got up and held a party. He invited a lot of people, all of the rich ones. It was a big celebration. Then after they had eaten, he said, "Now we're going to tell some stories. Each one will tell one." They told many stories, and he went last. He said, "Well now, I'm going to tell you mine." "I had two keys and I lost one. Which one do I keep? The one I lost or the one I got later?" And then everyone answered, "The one you lost." No. He said, "I had a trunk, and it had two keys. Let's see which one I keep. The first one or the second?" And then everyone said, "The first one." So he stayed with Rosita, and they lived happily and threw their bones at our noses.

Juana's heroine is like Beauty because she is the youngest of three daughters and asks her father to bring her three singing roses. Her father is an intermediary who sets the stage for his daughter's marriage by cutting the roses from the garden of a prince enchanted as a serpent. The heroine is like any maiden who feels the pull of conflicting loyalties between her family and the man who courts and marries her. The enchanted prince who demands that the heroine conceal his identity and the secret of their love is like the young man who demands proof of the loyalty of the woman he courts and marries. In this respect, he is like the hero in Julio's tale, considered earlier. Juana's heroine loses the prince because she yields to her family by revealing the secret to her sisters and father. Once again, however, her father is an intermediary who helps transfer her loyalties and affections to her husband. In this case, he makes his daughter the pair of iron shoes and helps prepare her lunch (*merienda*) so she will have something to eat on her long and difficult journey. The father as instrumental agent in a story by a woman illustrates how women at-

tempt to persuade their fathers to support rather than oppose their courtship and marriage.

The heroine's journey to find her lost husband is a common feature of
"Cupid and Psyche" stories in European folktale tradition. Bettelheim
(1977: 295–299), intepreting a similar tale from Romania, suggests that
the search for the lost husband represents the struggle of personal growth
required to overcome sexual anxieties. For a woman to overcome her sexual anxieties in the context of Cáceres gender relations, she must transcend her fear of men personified in stories by women as safe-appearing
but dangerous predators from the periphery of the world. Juana illustrates, in the dramatic language of her story, how this takes place for her
heroine as she learns to see men more as men see themselves. Her heroine
ventures into the periphery and encounters dangerous-appearing but actually safe and helpful masculine characters. They are the wind, the
moon, and the sun and all come home roaring, smelling human flesh, and
threatening to eat the heroine. They are like the cannibals who came roaring home and smelling human flesh in Vito Flores's "Snow White," and
they even look like the griffin bird in Julio's story, considered in Chapter
7. The message of Juana's tale is that if a maiden can see a man as men
see themselves, then she can conquer her sexual anxieties and learn to
love her husband. She makes this message clear by describing how the
wind, the moon, and the sun all become kind and provide the heroine
with the golden objects necessary to regain her lost husband. To a
younger maiden, her messages might be an important way to illustrate
how a woman anxiously anticipating her defloration can transcend her
fears to facilitate her adjustment in marriage.

Juana's tale concludes with an episode common to many "Cupid and
Psyche" stories, one that metaphorically describes how a woman must
not only conquer her sexual anxieties to love her husband but also contend with rivals for her husband's affections, to whom her husband will
be particularly susceptible if she falters in her loyalty, as the heroine did.
Juana's story, in the context of the dialogue through storytelling, is an
effort to persuade men to transfer their loyalties to the woman who loves
them. Juana delivers her message by illustrating that the second wife really does not love her husband because she is willing to place her marriage
in jeopardy in return for precious golden objects. The competition between the heroine and her lost husband's second wife is described according to the ideals of femininity. The heroine is justified in taking her lost
husband from another woman because she, not the other woman, is his
original wife. The second wife has an untenable position because she has
taken a man from his original spouse in a society that did not permit legal
divorce until recently. Juana makes the untenable position of the second
wife clear with her allegory of the man who asks those assembled at a
banquet whether he should open his trunk with the first or the second

key. The guests tell him to use the first key, representing how he must leave his second wife and return to the heroine. The allegory is a detail appearing in a number of "Cupid and Psyche" stories collected in other parts of Spain (A. Espinosa 1924: 258–264, 267–271; Cortés Vázquez 1979: 2: 111–114). If Juana were to tell a story about a triumphant heroine who takes a man from his original wife, then she would express in public the image of a shameless woman and would fail to uphold the monogamous moral order.

Other versions of "Cupid and Psyche" from adjacent areas give a fuller picture of the nature of a prince's enchantment, and the stories suggest that men's parents interfere with sons' marriages as well as those of daughters. In a masculine "Cupid and Psyche" from southern Cáceres, the prince is enchanted by his father the king, who opposes his son's marriage to the heroine because she is the daughter of a humble shepherd (Curiel Merchán 1944: 122–125). In a feminine variant from Cádiz, the heroine finds her lost husband living with his mother, who then becomes the intermediary in restoring her son's relationship with his wife (Larrea Palacín 1959: 55–63).

## "Cupid and Psyche" by a Man

Zacaria Iglesia from Piornal told a "Cupid and Psyche" story that resembles the second half of Juana Moreno's tale. The two stories are remarkably similar probably because the narrators learned them at similar times and places. The two storytellers are close in age—Juana is sixty-five and Zacaria is seventy-four—and they learned their tales while working in the paprika-processing teams of Jaraíz de la Vera. Zacaria said that he learned most of the stories in his repertoire from women, and so his "Cupid and Psyche" is probably a masculinized version of a feminine tale. Zacaria also describes a heroine in a conflict of loyalties who loses and then finds her husband after wearing out seven pairs of iron shoes. In the storytelling dialogue, Zacaria affirms that women will show their untiring devotion to the man they love and he concurs that men are sometimes slow to transfer their loyalties to the woman who loves them. The heroine in his story, like her counterpart in the tale by Juana, must compete with another woman to regain the loyalty and affection of the man she loves. Zacaria's tale also differs in subtle but interesting ways from the story by Juana, illustrating how men view courtship differently despite the many areas of agreement with women. The discussion following his tale focuses on how Zacaria's story differs from the second half of Juana's tale.

### "Cupid and Psyche," by Zacaria Iglesia

Once there was a maiden who married a donkey, and he said, "If someday you allow someone to say I'm a donkey, you'll have to look for me where the waters are borne by themselves." Well, her friends grew weary of her. One of them asked, "How come you married a donkey? What do you suppose he is? A fine young man?"

He disappeared, and she had to wear out seven pairs of iron shoes to find him. She came to a house where there was an old woman who said, "Oh, my! What do you come here for? I'm taking care of a very ferocious bull." But the donkey's wife said, "If it wants to get hold of me, let it get hold of me. If it doesn't, then it won't." The woman put her under the stairs, and the bull came leaping violently and saying, "I smell human flesh." The old woman said, "It's a poor thing who is looking for her husband who is in a place where the waters are borne." They took her out from under the stairs and had supper. The next morning the young woman continued walking. Now she came to a house where there were seven crows. A woman who was taking care of them said, "For God's sake, don't come here. The crows will come and they'll eat you tonight." The old woman had to take her in. She put her in a room. The crows started arriving one by one, and each one said, "I smell human flesh. If you don't give it to me, I'll kill you." The old woman said, "A poor thing came looking for her husband, who is where the waters are borne by themselves, and I had to take her in." The crow said, "Bring her out here." She removed her as all of the crows were arriving. Now came the last one, who was lame. It said, "I smell human flesh." The old woman explained, "It's a poor little woman who came here looking for her husband, who is where the waters are borne by them-selves." "I ate the tripe of a rabbit today that her husband threw away. Tomor-row we'll go to see him. You have to buy a goat and throw it on top of me flayed and butchered. When I say, 'Meat!' give me a quarter of it. And when I say, 'Meat!' another quarter." He started talking about where her husband was. So they went there.

They told her where he lived, and the woman bought a golden hen. She went down the man's street saying, "Who will buy this hen, this golden chicken?" And a woman, who was the donkey's new wife, appeared and asked, "How much do you want for it?" "To sleep with your husband for one night." The second wife exclaimed, "Oh, my! Get out of here, woman!" But the second wife was told, "Let her sleep with him. We'll give him a glass of sleeping potion. He'll fall asleep, and nothing will happen." The first wife went to bed with her husband and said, "Donkey-prince, here you have me. Donkey-prince, here you have me." But he was asleep and didn't get up. In the morning a neighbor asked him, "What happened in your house last night? I heard, 'Donkey-prince and so on and so forth.'" The donkey-prince suspected something. He went to work and came back again before his first wife could talk to him. She went with the golden hen again asking, "Who will buy this little golden hen from me?" The other woman said, "Look at that devil of a woman! What do you want for it?" "To sleep with your husband." "You didn't have enough last night and you want to sleep with him again tonight? You will be well satisfied. No, no." But the second wife was told, "We'll give him another glass of sleeping potion and he'll fall asleep." But the man didn't drink it. They didn't see him hide the glass. His first wife went to bed with him and started in again, "Prince, here you have me." They got up, and he told the other one, "Everything is over because you bought the hen. I'm going with my wife, and you stay here."

In many respects, Zacaria's story is like the second half of Juana's tale because both narrators describe a heroine who conquers her sexual anxieties as she transfers her affections and loyalties from her parents to her spouse. The heroine in Zacaria's tale, as in the one by Juana, learns to see men as they see themselves when she ventures into the periphery where she comes upon dangerous-appearing but in reality kind animals—a bull and seven crows—who help her find her husband. The bull and crows also appear as cannibals recalling the images of cannibalistic thieves in stories of safe-appearing but actually dangerous men told by women to reinforce the norm of premarital chastity. And like the heroine in Juana's story, the wife finds her husband after proving to him that her love for him is truer than the love of his second wife.

Zacaria changes some details in his story, however, according to a masculine view of courtship and marriage. He draws particular attention to how men can become excessively possessive when competing for and through women. He places emphasis on the excessive possessiveness of the husband who makes demands on his wife that do not fit the reality of life in a village where a woman has close and interdependent ties with other women. Zacaria describes the donkey-husband telling the heroine, "If someday you allow it said that I'm a donkey, you'll have to go looking for me where the waters are borne by themselves." The wife cannot meet his demand as long as she continues to have any other relationships because someone will inevitably ask her, "Why did you marry a donkey?" Men's possessiveness of women is part of a context of male competition for women, and that competition makes it difficult for men to see male cooperation in a courtship. Zacaria's story makes this point clear by eliminating the father's help in his daughter's marriage and the restoration of the relationship with her lost husband. Masculine versions of "Cupid and Psyche" from southern Cáceres and other provinces in Spain (Curiel Merchán 1944: 82–86; Llano Roza de Ampudia 1975: 29–33) also lack the presence of the helpful father, probably because male possessiveness and competition are widespread patterns.

## THE GENDER DIVISION OF LABOR IN COURTSHIP AND MARRIAGE

Despite their differences, Juana and Zacaria both affirm the power of a woman's love to humanize a man and restore the rifts in a marital relationship. Their animal-groom tales are part of a series of stories that metaphorically describe a gender division of labor in courtship and marriage. Men initiate courtships and entice women to enter an illusion of love necessary to conquer their fears of men. Women initially take a more passive role in courtship but are expected to assume the responsibility of maintaining the marital relationship once courtship turns into marriage. The metaphorical description of the woman's role in maintaining the marital bond appears in the "Cupid and Psyche" stories told by women as well as men, in which heroines endure long and difficult ordeals to restore their relationships with lost husbands. The role of men in maintaining the marital tie is substantially less, judging from the stories circulating in oral tradition. No Cáceres storyteller told a "Lost Wife" (AT 400) tale, which metaphorically describes a husband enduring difficult ordeals to restore his marriage. "Lost Wife" tales are comparatively rare in all of Spanish oral tradition, although they do exist in other parts of the Hispanic world.[2] Llano Roza de Ampudia (1975: 53–58) collected the only Spanish version I know of from a woman in Asturias. Judging from the popularity of "Lost Husband" (AT 425) tales and the rarity of the "Lost Wife" (AT 400) stories in Cáceres and Spanish oral tradition, the gender division of labor in maintaining the marital bond is a widespread pattern in Cáceres and other parts of Spain. Women are particularly well suited to maintain the emotional bond in a marriage because their waxing-and-waning illusion of love allows them to deal with the flux of marital and family relations. Men are less suited to this struggle because their illusion of love is brittle and can shatter with threats to a man's personal honor. The gender division of labor has many possible sources, including the continuous relationship between a woman and her parents. A woman is prepared to deal with the long-term vicissitudes of married life because she learns to balance over the long run her conflicting family loyalties as she transfers some of her affections to a spouse while remaining close to her father and particularly to her mother. Balancing loyalties and learning to accept heterosexual love are undulating processes for women more than men.

# CHAPTER NINE

# "Blancaflor"

MEN AND women tell one another the story of "Blancaflor," which presents a model for how courtship and marriage can work in a culture in which men are different from women. "Blancaflor" is a grand narrative with male and female protagonists that encapsulates many themes presented individually in other stories considered earlier. The hero makes a long journey to find the heroine, much as a young man must travel a long road to maturity before he is ready for courtship and marriage. The hero runs up against the heroine's father, who demands that his future son-in-law perform many impossible tasks, just as a father has high expectations of the man who courts and wishes to marry his daughter. The tasks metaphorically stand for the accumulation of property necessary to set up a new household and the proof of competence a man must demonstrate to a maiden's family to win their approval. The hero performs the tasks with the essential help of Blancaflor, illustrating how a man depends on a woman. The heroine's father acts with ambivalence because he is an intermediary as well as an obstacle to his daughter's marriage. On the one hand, he sends the hero to perform a task that symbolically represents the defloration of his daughter, setting the stage for their marriage. On the other, he attempts to kill his daughter and her husband the day after their wedding. Blancaflor consequently flees with the hero, just as a young married woman must separate from her parents and live with her husband, transferring her loyalties and affections from her parents to her spouse. A husband has his own conflict in family loyalties and the hero temporarily forgets about Blancaflor when embraced by a member of his family. The heroine must unlock his memory to restore the marriage, just as in the gender division of labor a woman is given the task of maintaining the marital tie. The story ends happily, testifying to faith in the conjugal bond and the power of a woman's love in Cáceres Spanish culture.

The story of "Blancaflor" (AT 313) circulates widely in Cáceres and Spanish oral tradition because it describes in metaphorical language a model of courtship and marriage that fits many themes of gender relations. Cortés Vásquez (1979: 2: 265) considers the story one of the most popular folktales in Spanish oral tradition, and folklorists have collected versions from many provinces in Spain (Cortés Vásquez 1979: 2: 70–99; A. Espinosa 1924: 240–255; Llano Roza de Ampudia 1975: 97–103). Four men and two women in the Cáceres villages told versions of "Blancaflor," and their stories illustrate how men and women talk to each other through storytelling about the details of courtship and marriage. More Cáceres women undoubtedly know this story, but I did not happen to find them among the narrators I knew. A more even balance between masculine and feminine versions exists for the stories collected in other provinces (Cortés Vázquez 1976: 62–66; 1979: 2: 70–99; Llano Roza de Ampudia 1975: 97–103), and I know of no reason why the balance in the Cáceres villages should differ from that of other regions in Spain.

The versions of "Blancaflor" that illustrate best how men and women talk to each other through stories are the tales by Florencio Ramos of Navaconcejo and Gregoria Ramos Merchán of Piornal. Although Florencio and Gregoria do not know each other and live in different villages, their communities are close to each other and have numerous social connections that would enable their storytellers know many of the same stories in oral tradition. Many Piornalegos have settled in Navaconcejo to take advantage of the fertile land for growing cherries in the Plasencia valley. Florencio and Gregoria told very closely related masculine and feminine variants of "Blancaflor," perhaps because of the social connections between their two villages.

## THE MASCULINE MODEL

Florencio Ramos, speaking through the characters of his "Blancaflor," presented an extremely competitive view of male relations in courtship and marriage. Blancaflor's father is particularly aggressive toward his future son-in-law: he gives him many impossible tasks and repeatedly threatens the hero with death if he does not complete them. Men generally project a competitive view of human relations onto their stories of courtship and marriage as part of their agonistic worldview. The origins of that view are complex, but one likely source is the Oedipal struggle in the family whereby the father and his son are in competition for the loyalty and affection of the mother. Florencio's "Blancaflor" illustrates how a man projects censored Oedipal themes onto a story by splitting the images of paternal figures to personify the negative and positive sentiments a son has toward his father. Splitting parental images is necessary because it is threatening to acknowledge anger toward a parent and a man cannot publicly express negative sentiments toward his father in a culture that values filial piety.

Florencio splits his parental images into a good natural father and a demonic father-in-law. Florencio's own father is similar to that of the hero: both are independent men who worked for themselves rather than earned a wage by working for others. The hero's father is an autonomous fisherman, and Florencio described his own father as a man who worked for himself raising livestock and farming his small plot of land.

> My father was a very hard worker, but he always liked working for himself. He didn't like working for anyone else because I heard him say many times, "It is very bad to clean oneself in front of another." And he was that way even though he was poor. The rich ones of this town wanted to dominate him, but they couldn't. He didn't think of anyone, not even the Virgin Mary, and he always went forward. And he knocked down a few in the sense that they did not make a fool out of him. And he made some money. He always lived off of his own property. He never worked for a wage. Sometimes he hired a worker, but not very often. And he was very honest. My father did not like to eat anything off of anyone else, but they did not eat off of him either. He told me several times, "Son, you're better off taking care of just one pig because it's yours than going to work for someone else."

Florencio's version of "Blancaflor" describes the hero's father-in-law as extremely demanding because he requires that the hero perform a large number of tasks. He tells of Blancaflor's father asking the hero to perform eight impossible tasks, nearly twice the number in other versions of this story by narrators in northern and central Cáceres. In this repect, the hero's father-in-law is like the narrator's own father, who demanded a great deal of Florencio as a young boy.

> I went to school, it seems to me, at about six or seven years of age. And I was some three or four months in school and I had just learned to recognize block letters. When there were more than two letters, I didn't know what they said. And my father got hold of calves, which he raised by halves (he split the profit from their sale with the owner of the animals), those black calves around here, and he took me out of school. The teacher said to my mother, "Why are you taking the boy out? Right now is when he is going to learn something and he learns well." My mother said, "His father got hold of two calves by halves and, of course, he needs his son to care for them." And the teacher said, "What a shame to take the boy out of school." I worked a great deal, as a boy, with my father. And my father also worked a great deal, more than I, of course.

The picture of a maiden demanding that the hero prove himself by performing several difficult tasks is a common theme in Cáceres stories of courtship and marriage told by men.[1] The tension between a father and his son-in-law in masculine stories is a projection of men's competitive view of male relations. What makes "Blancaflor" special is its message that the competition between men in courtship and marriage, when the men are a father and son-in-law, is more apparent than real. Florencio presents Blancaflor's father as simultaneously appearing to promote and oppose his daughter's marriage to the hero. One of the most dramatic examples is the first task the heroine's father requires of the hero, which symbolizes Blancaflor's defloration and creates a lifelong bond between the hero and the heroine. This task appears in all known versions from Cáceres and other provinces in Spain, probably because of the widespread symbolic significance of defloration in a culture that places so much emphasis on the premarital chastity of women.

In the context of the storytelling dialogue, Florencio's message is the key to understanding how courtship and marriage can work in a culture in which men compete for and through women. A boy hearing Florencio's message might conclude that he will eventually enter a courtship in which a maiden's father will appear more opposed to his daughter's marriage than is actually the case and he should not necessarily view the maiden's father in the same terms as he might view other men. A woman hearing Florencio's message might take hope that the apparent competition between her father and her suitor in courtship does not necessarily mean she will have to choose between the two men and sacrifice her relationship with her mother. Women frequently describe a maiden's father as a helpful intermediary in his daughter's marriage to persuade men to mitigate their competition through women in courtship, and Florencio's story illustrates how some men may have heard this message from women.

In a culture placing emphasis on the difference between the genders, one would expect that men would tell the story of "Blancaflor" differently from women. Storytelling styles differ for women and men in many cultures, including our own, where gender differences are not such an ostensible part of the culture (see Baldwin 1985: 149–162; C. Mitchell 1985: 163–186). Florencio told his story with a very masculine flavor apparent in his use of language and his reworking of details of the plot. He delivered his "Blancaflor" story in a style of narration markedly different from the style of any woman who told a story of courtship and marriage in the Cáceres villages. He peppered his tale with words and expressions that are part of masculine speech and are common linguistic markers of the agrarian working-class identity of many men in rural Cáceres. He is not the only masculine narrator whose words and expressions differ markedly from those of women, but he relies more heavily on male expressions than other narrators considered up to this point. I recorded Florencio's version of "Blancaflor" in front of his sons, and a man who tells stories only in the company of other men will generally use more masculine expressions than when telling a tale to a mixed audience.

Peppered throughout his tale is the obscenity coño, which Cáceres informants define as "female genitals." The word appears in the speech of many men in place of the exclamation ¡Hombre! (Man!) used by women as well as men. Florencio also uses the term cojonudo, derived from the word for testicle (cojon) and that literally means "big balled." The term, which has widespread use in Spain (see Brandes 1980: 93), is a substitute for "beautiful" (*bello* or *hermoso*). I never heard a woman use this term in a story or in ordinary speech, although every woman knows what it means. The word *cojonudo* sometimes has a blasphemous connotation when used in the comparative expression *más cojonudo que el copón*, which means "more beautiful than the sacramental chalice." Florencio liberally sprinkles his story with the obscenity *Me cago en diez* (I shit on ten), which is a euphemism for the phrase *Me cago en Dios* (I shit on God), a common scatological and blasphemous masculine expression that Malinowski (1929: 105) believes has an Oedipal meaning because it expresses a man's wish to defile his father, symbolically recast as God. Florencio masculinizes feminine speech when he projects the expression "I shit on ten" as words spoken by the feminine protagonist of "Blancaflor." He describes the feminine protagonist using the masculine expression when she sees her father in hot pursuit as she tries to escape with the masculine protagonist: "The maiden says to him, 'I shit on ten! That horse coming down there now, I think it's my father.' " Although some feminine narrators make scatologial references in folktales (see "Cinderella" by Maximina Castaño in Chapter 6), few women use the obvious blasphemous expression *Me cago en Dios* or its euphemistic form *Me cago en diez* as an exclamation in discourse or when telling a story. Some women utter *Me cago en la mar* (I shit on the sea), which is a euphemism for *Me cago en la madre que le parió* (I shit on the mother who gave birth to him/her), an expression used by men. I never heard a man utter, "I shit on the sea," just as no woman said, "I shit on ten." "Mother" sometimes has a blasphemous reference when she is the Virgin Mary; she may also be the mother of an ordinary human, or a factory (*fábrica*) that manufactures a defective piece of machinery. When uttered by a woman, the expression "I shit on the sea" could have an Oedipal meaning, given the accounts of rivalry among women for men in the "Cinderella" stories considered in Chapter 6.

Many men in the Cáceres villages use identical masculine blasphemous and scatological expressions in ordinary speech to voice astonishment, fear, pain, surprise, frustration, and other strong emotions. Humble women as well as men defend men's use of obscenities when they tell "The Two Ploughmen," a story that is a regional variant of AT 759, known as "God's Justice Vindicated" (Robe 1973: 124). The masculine and feminine variants (which are listed in the Appendix) illustrate that humble men use scatological and blasphemous expressions because they face difficulties and frustrations not faced by richer men, who do not use the same expressions because they face fewer hardships. In the opinion of the narrators, however, humble men who utter obscenities are often more virtuous than richer men who do not.

The story by Alvino Bravo Sanchez of Serradilla features two men, one of whom has a good pair of mules and the other a very bad pair because he is poor. The one with the bad pair repeatedly uses the expressions *Me cago en Dios* and the related obscenity *Me cago en la hostia* (I shit on the host) in frustration as he tries to make his weak animals pull a plough through the ground. Along come Christ and Saint Peter, who are very hungry, and they decide to ask for a bite to eat. They avoid the humble ploughman because of his rough speech and walk over to the rich one and ask for a piece of bread. "No, the lunch I bring from home is for me," says the man with the good pair of mules. So Christ and Saint Peter go over to the humble ploughman, who is uttering every form of blasphemy and who says, "Look in that Corsican pine tree over there where I have my lunch. Eat the whole thing." Christ and Saint Peter reward the humble but blasphemous man with a prosperous wheat crop and they punish the rich and greedy one with a crop of horns. The stories by Casiano Miranda and Esperanza Cozas of Garganta la Olla develop along similar lines except that Casiano explains how the scatological expressions of the humble ploughman are really not blasphemous because no man can actually shit on God, who is in heaven high above mortal humans. He explains that God can defecate on a man, but a man cannot defecate on God. "I shit on God," says the narrator, does not literally mean that one intends to shit on the Almighty but is a way of thinking about God. Esperanza further illustrates the moral superiority of the humble, blasphemous man when she describes how he refuses to harm a crucifix that his clean-speaking counterpart is only too willing to destroy.

Florencio also introduced a number of changes in the plot of his story, which he invented or borrowed from other tales and which seem to reflect his own family background, his marital history, his position in his community, and widely held beliefs about women and men. The large number of unusual elements in Florencio's version of "Blancaflor" facilitates the task of linking details to the experiences of this particular masculine storyteller. Relative to women who tell the same story, Florencio projects a much more combative image of the relationship between father and son-in-law during courtship and marriage.

### "Blancaflor," by Florencio Ramos

Once there was a fisherman whose name was Pedro. He went fishing and, after he finished his catch, a fish appeared. The fish pleaded, "Pedro, don't kill me." So he let it go. He went home and told his wife what happened, "I shit on ten! What happened to me today!" "What happened?" his wife asked. He said, "After I finished my load, I shit on ten, a fish appeared, and it was a huge fish. It spoke to me as I was going to lay my hands on it; 'Pedro, don't kill me.' I felt sorry for it and let it go." His wife said, "You did well if you had finished your catch. But if you don't have any luck some other day, and don't have enough of a catch, grab it and that'll be that." It turned out that the fish appeared again the following week as Pedro was on his way home. It was a big fish, a beauty. He reached out with his arm, and it pleaded, "Pedro, don't kill me." The fisherman replied, "Look, my wife told me the other day I should kill you if you appear again. And I've had bad luck today, I'm not bringing home a worthwhile catch. So today I have to kill you." The fish said, "I'm going to ask you a favor. The first thing that greets you at home will have to go with me in a year." The fisherman said, "Man, it's a deal." His boy's dog nearly always jumped up to meet him. "I'll give him the dog at the end of the year and that'll be that." The man caught the fish. He put it in his boat and headed for home. But as he came home his little boy appeared. The boy's name was Joaquín. I shit on ten! He was a lad eight or nine years old, maybe ten. I shit on ten! His father was very sad. He didn't say anything to his son. He came home and emptied out the fish. The father got sick, no one knew what ailed him, and they asked, "What's wrong with you, Pedro?" He replied, "Nothing." "I shit on ten! It's like he's upset." The father told the boy, "Joaquín, this is what happened to me. A fish told me you have to go with him at the end of the year. I don't know why, but it's not bound to be for something good." Joaquín replied, "Father, don't worry about it. I'll go with whomever." No one was a better lad than he. Now that the father had told his son and the boy had taken it well, the father quickly began to recover. The next year—tan!—a man came. "Pedro." "What?" "I come so you'll make good on what I told you last year." "Fine. Joaquín." "What?" "Come downstairs. Go with this man." The boy said good-bye.

The boy went away with the man, who was really the devil. They arrived where the devil had his abode, and the devil said to the boy, "If you're a good servant, if you take orders well, you'll do fine with me." "Whatever you say," the boy said. The boy was bigger now, fourteen or so. The devil said, "Now you'll see what I'm going to tell you to do. I'll kill you If you don't do it well. These three maidens are my three daughters. You have to kill one of the three." "I shit on ten!" said the boy, who then added, "Whatever you say." "You have to kill one and you have to chop her up." "I shit on ten! I shit on ten!" So they drew lots, and it turned out to be the youngest. Her name was Ursula, and the boy said, "I shit on ten, I'm not going to kill you." The maiden said, "Tell him you'll kill me." "I shit on ten! But I don't have the heart to kill you." She said, "It's nothing for me. You tell him yes. If you don't, my father will kill you. You say yes. You have to ask him for a guitar and a demijohn. Kill me, chop me up, put me in the demijohn and throw me into the sea, and start playing the guitar, but don't go to sleep. If you fall asleep, I won't come out." The boy did it because the devil said he would kill him if he didn't. I shit on ten! The boy did it. He grabbed the maiden. I shit on ten! He killed her. He chopped her up. He put her into a demijohn. Splash! Into the sea. He began playing the guitar, triki triki triki triki triki triki. When the maiden, inside the demijohn, was about to come out of the water, Joaquín was almost asleep and was just playing like this, tin tin tin. She said, "Play." I shit on ten! He began to play. The maiden appeared just as beautiful as before, if not more so. Then she said, "You lost a drop of my blood when you put me into the demijohn. Look how I have this finger a little shorter than the others." The maiden told him about her right hand. That's why women have their little finger smaller than men. They say they have a little finger that's thinner and more beaten up than men's.

"Very well. You're a great servant," the devil said. The devil seemed delighted but he really wanted to murder the boy. "Tomorrow I'm going to give you another task." He went to the window and said, "Come. See that hill? You have to dig it up, you have to plant grapevines, and I want to see a bottle of wine on the table when I go eat tomorrow. If not, I'll kill you." The boy said, "I shit on ten! And how am I going to clean up the ground, plant the vines, cut the grapes, and make the wine for tomorrow so he'll have wine by midday?" The boy went outside half crying. He said, "Oh my! For God's sake." "What did he tell you?" asked the devil's daughter. Joaquín said, "I have to clean that hill and plant it with vines and cut the grapes and make the wine so that tomorrow, when your father goes to eat, he'll have a bottle of wine to drink. He said he'd kill me if he doesn't." She said, "Tell him yes. Don't worry. You tell him yes." So the devil asked him that night, "Well? Have you thought it over?" Joaquín said yes. "You're going to do it?" Joaquín replied, "Yes, I'll do it." "Now, I've told you. I want to see the bottle here by midday." The girl's name was Saint or Ursula. She went to a little patch of abandoned grapevines and said to Joaquín, "Lie down." But how could he just lie down? She had a needle case with a number of little devils inside. I shit on ten! Some were digging, others were planting the vines, others were cutting the grapes, and others were making the wine. Before midday—pum!—the bottle of wine was on the table for the devil. "Good, good. You're a superior servant. Good servant. We've done very well."

The next day, the devil said, "Downstairs in the stable are a she-mule and a he-mule. I want you to go bring two loads of wood that don't have a span of straight pieces, eh. I'll kill you if they have a straight span." "I shit on ten! Who brings two loads of wood without some straight pieces?" The girl appeared and asked, "What did he tell you?" "Boy! What did he tell me! About the same as yesterday. He said I have to bring two loads of wood with the she-mule and he-mule he has in the stable, and he says there can't be one span of straight pieces. It all has to be crooked. Let's see how!" "It's nothing. It's done. This is easy. See where you planted the vines yesterday? You still have them. Go there. The little devils will cut two loads of vines for you." In fact, she sent three little devils. They cut the wood with fury. One took it upon himself to load up and—tras!—more crooked than the host. Plop! There were the two loads of wood. Joaquín said, "Here's the wood." "Oh. I've seen it," said the devil. "I shit on ten!" The man seemed happier than anything.

The devil said to Joaquín, "Tomorrow I'm going to give you another task, eh." "Good." "Tomorrow you're going to go for two loads of straight pieces that don't have a palm length of crooked pieces, eh. Straight as a candle." "I shit on ten!" The girl asked again, "What did he tell you?" "What did he tell me! The same as yesterday. Except just the opposite. I have to bring two loads of wood that are straight, that don't have even a span of crooked pieces. As straight as a candle." She said, "Tell him yes. Go to a field of reeds and cut them." So in fact—plop!—the two loads of wood. "I shit on ten!" said the devil. "Well, you know, you're terrific. I've never seen a servant like you. You're a man of accomplishment." The man seemed so happy, but he couldn't kill him now.

Then he said, "Tomorrow you're going set the mules free because it's a holiday. You're going to set the mules free in a certain place. When you go there tomorrow, you're going to take these iron shoes. When you come back here at midday, they have to be all broken." Joaquín said, "I shit on ten! I'm to set free the mules, the she-mule and the he-mule. And how am I going to break the shoes?" The maiden asked him, "What did he tell you today?" "What did he tell me today! Worse than yesterday or the same. I have to take some iron shoes and set free the he-mule and the she-mule in a certain place, and when I come home the shoes have to be broken. And they're iron shoes!" She said, "It's very simple. When you go there, the he-mule is going to pee first. Be careful the he-mule doesn't splatter a drop on the shoes. They'll get stronger if he splatters the shoes. The she-mule is going to pee a little farther on. You be where the she-mule pees and then scrub the shoes in the she-mule's pee. You'll see how fast the shoes will break apart." Said and done. He left with the she-mule and the he-mule for the place, and, in fact, the he-mule peed some distance from there. I shit on ten! He made sure it didn't splatter even a little. A little farther on— plum!—the she-mule. I shit on ten! He dismounted because he rode on the she-mule. I shit on ten! And pin pan, pin pan, the shoes had some broken places underneath. He said, "It's done." He came back and the devil asked, "How did it go?" "Fine." "And the shoes, how are they?" Joaquín said, "Look for yourself. See how they're broken." "Fine. It's done."

The devil said, "This afternoon I'm going to send you on another job. You have to go get those mules, the she-mule and the he-mule, which are loose. You have to go get them in the afternoon." Joaquín said, "Fine." The devil continued, "See this helmet." It was like one of those bronze military helmets. "See this helmet. You take it. When you come back here, you have to have the helmet broken." I shit on ten! He knew how to scrub the shoes. They were scrubbed this way. But how would he scrub the helmet? "Well," the maiden asked him, "what did he tell you?" He replied, "He has an iron helmet, one of those bronze ones, and he told me he's going to give it to me. He told me to get the mules in the afternoon, and I have to bring the helmet all broken when I come back." She said, "Tell him yes." He said, "Fine. I'll look for a way to break it." "It's nothing. He has the broken shoes, eh." He took the helmet. He went to her, and she said, "When you're on your way back here, you put the he-mule in front and the she-mule in back of the halter. There is a little hill in a certain place. The she-mule will fart when climbing up the hill. Put the helmet like this, and each time she farts, a hole will appear in the helmet. But don't change the she-mule around and put the she-mule in front because then the helmet will get stronger." He said, "Good. I shit on ten!" He was careful to put the he-mule in front and the halter on the she-mule. In fact there was a little bit of a hill. As the she-mule got there—bam! again bam!—the helmet was broken. Bam! Bam! She had three more farts. Bam! Bam! Bam! Another three holes in the helmet. He came back. I shit on ten! The damn thing had holes like the sacramental chalice. "Here is the helmet." "Very good, very good. Beautiful servant."

Then the devil said, "Tomorrow I'm going to give you another task." Joaquín said, "Whatever you want." "You're a superior servant, a dream. I've had various servants, but no one like you." Joaquín was growing into a young man. The devil said, "You must really want a woman, just like all men." "Me, no." The devil insisted: "How can you not like women? You have to want one just like everyone else in the world. Seeing I have three maiden daughters, you're going to marry one of them. The one you want, eh. I won't tell you the crooked one, or the white one, or any other one. The one you want, eh. You have to marry one, but I don't care which one. They're going into a room. Each one will put her hand through a cat hole. You'll marry the one you like the best. You see, I don't care which one you marry." "Oh, well, fine." Ursula asked, "What did he tell you?" "Oh, my! Better than anything so far. He told me I have to marry one of you." She said, "Good. You're going to tell him to give you a few days to let you think about it." The devil asked, "What?" "I'll marry one," Joaquín said, "but I have to think about it a little." "Very well. It seems very good to me. Yes, yes, that's how I like men." The devil was happier, more content than I don't know what.

"Tomorrow you'll have another job only because you're a useful man. You're going to take a little stroll tomorrow to where there is a batch of fish. You have to fry them tomorrow. Tomorrow we're eating some fried fish." "Fine." The devil continued, "But I'm going to tell you something, eh. There are a lot of cats in my house. Don't lose a single fish. I'll kill you if you're missing a single fish. The cats will want some of the fish." Joaquín said, "Fine." The maiden asked, "What did he tell you?" "He said I had to fry some fish. It isn't anything." She said, "This is the most dangerous thing." Joaquín said to the maiden, "I don't know why." She said, "All of us will become the cats. There are five of us in the house. The first one you'll see will be a big black cat. It'll have a very fat head. That'll be my father. Then you're going to see a black cat with a little white tie and that one will be my mother. Then there will be a yellow one and that will be my older sister. The other sister will be the red one." It was like the one we have here daubed with pineapple [an aside by Florencio]. She said, "I'm going to be the white one. I'll be the smallest one. You get a pan ready to fry the batch of fish and a bowl with water to wash the fish. Don't throw out the water because it'll smell of fish. When the big cat gets near—it'll be the first one that goes there and it will go creeping toward you— you have to be very careful because he'll snatch the fish from you very quickly. Get a good-sized cup of oil ready, and when the oil is very hot and as soon as you see the cat appear—zas!—you throw it on him. Then a little while later it'll be my mother, and you do the same thing. Keep on going. But not as hot for my sisters because the worst ones are the other two. I'll also go to see if I can take a fish away from you because I have to go. But you throw the water on me so I'll smell like fish. Throw it on me instead of oil. Throw spoonfuls of water from washing the fish and, of course, I'll run out of there. They'll think I was just like them because the water smells of fish." Joaquín did exactly as the maiden told him. He put the fish on to fry. In a little while, meow, meow. A big black cat came. I shit on ten! Joaquín grabbed a spoonful of oil. Zas! It fled because he threw oil on it. A little while later the black one with the white necktie appeared. Meow, meow. Joaquín grabbed the oil. Zas! It flew out of there. Then the other smaller ones came. Also—zas!—he threw a little oil on them too. Those cats also ran away. The last one, the white one also came. Meow, meow. He grabbed the water. Zas! I shit on ten! The other one also fled with a little bit of water. So, pum! When the devil went to eat—plop!—there were the fried fish. "Well? Are you missing any?" Joaquín said, "No. I don't think so. There were more cats than anything else and—I shit on ten!—I threw a little oil on them. They all ran out of there lickety-split."

"Very well. Tomorrow I'm going to give you another task. This is going to be good for you because I see you're a real man, a brave and useful man. Down- stairs in the stable is a colt, a black one. It's wild of course. At seven in the morning you have to begin goading it. I'll go downstairs at twelve to mount the colt. It has to let itself be mounted." The boy said, "Well, good." The maiden asked, "What did he tell you?" He said, "Nothing today. He has a colt, and I have to tame it." She said, "Today is a very bad day." He insisted, "No, it isn't anything." She said, "Look, the horse will be composed of all of us. The head will be my father. The neck and the shoulderblades will be my mother. My two sisters will be the ribs. Each rib will be a sister. And I'll be the haunches. If you are a little careless, they'll all eat you in one bite." "I shit on the mother! The horse." She went on, "Strike all the blows on its head, its neck, and on the shoulderblades. But hard, eh. You hit that part of the horse hard. The horse has to pee three times. Don't mount it until it pees three times. It'll kill you If you mount it before. Now hit the ribs in back but not as hard and hit the haunches too. I'll get a club ready for you so it'll have one thin end and the other end blunt. Beat the head with the thick end. And also the neck and the shoulder- blades. Then turn the club around. Take the thick end and hit my sisters with the thin one. And the haunches in back, hit me too but less because it's me." He went downstairs. I shit on ten! There was a colt in the stable, a colt more beautiful than the sacramental chalice. He grabbed the club. Brum! The animal at first—I shit on ten!—was a wild beast. He grabbed the club—I shit on ten!— which was like the handle of a hoe. Bam, bam! A blow to the head. I shit on ten! And on the neck. He struck it with more blows, he hit it on the head more times than the sacramental chalice. And now the horse peed. Brum! Blows to the head and the neck and the shoulderblades just as the maiden had told him. He hit the ribs some but less. But he struck blows to the head. They were strong blows, and a little while later it peed again. More blows, more blows. I shit on ten. He struck it with more blows than the sacramental chalice. In a little while—tan!—it peed again, and he mounted it. The horse went with its head down like this and didn't move. It was beaten. He put it in the stable and went upstairs. There was the devil. "The horse is tamed now." "And have you mounted it? Yes, yes. I know it." The man was all covered with wounds. His entire head was bandaged because of the blows.

He said, "Very good. Now I see you've done a great piece of work. Now we have to celebrate the wedding. Have you thought all about it?" Joaquín said yes. "It's done, eh. Now I'll tell you today what I told you the other day. I don't care which one you marry. It must be one of them, but any one. They're going to put their hands through a cat hole, and you say which one you want." Ursula said, "I'll show you my hand, which has the missing finger. You say, 'That one.'" One showed her hand, and the devil asked, "Do you like this one?" Joaquín said no. Another hand appeared, and the devil asked him, "Do you like that one?" He said no. The other one appeared, and the devil asked, "And that one?" He said, "Yes, this one." "Huh. She's the most arrogant, the young-est, the most this, the most that." I shit on ten! Joaquín did the worst thing to the devil he could by picking her. Well, they held the wedding. They were married. The maiden and the young man went to bed, of course, and the young man asked, "And what is that on the ceiling?" It looked like a bomb, like one of those darts with a banderole for baiting the bulls, one of those very colorful round things. The young man asked, "What is that?" She said, "Oh! If you only knew what it is!" He asked, "But what is it?" She said, "It's a bomb my father put here to kill us." "Let's get out of here." She said, "Go downstairs to the wine cellar, and there are two hides. One has wine, and the other has vine-gar. Bring them upstairs." He went downstairs, and he put the two hides in the bed. The maiden told him, "Go downstairs to the stable. There are two horses. One is thin but the other one is even thinner. You take the thinnest one. We're getting out of here. If we don't, the bomb will explode and will kill us." He went downstairs. "I shit on God! The thin one will fall down by itself. It's better to take the other one, which is a little healthier." There were two horses. One was called Wind and the other was Thought, and he took Wind. The young man took Wind, the one that was a litter fatter, because the other one looked like it wouldn't be good for anything, it was so thin. Then the maiden, who was a woman now, spit some of her spittle in the room. Her parents were in bed, and her father called, "Ursula." She replied, "What, father?" "Ursula." "What, father?" Each time the maiden answered in a softer voice. It was her spittle that answered. Then it began drying up. He called her, "Ursula." "What, father?" He called her a little while later, "Ursula." Now she didn't answer because her spittle had dried up. He said to his wife, "It sounds like they're asleep." I shit on ten! So the devil went for the bomb. The bomb exploded. Boom! Knives and a hell of a lot of grapeshot fell—boom!—onto the bed. I shit on God! He came right away to see. He tasted what he thought was their blood: "How sweet is the blood of my daughter! It's delicious." He tried the other. He said, "Oh, my! How sour! How sour is the blood of my son-in-law!" I shit on ten! The man was happier than the sacramental chalice because he believed he had killed them. Then he uncovered the vermin. I shit on ten! There were two wine bags. "Come on! What is this? Those two have gotten away from me. I shit on ten!" He went downstairs, and his wife said to him, "Go open up the stable. They've taken one of the horses." Then he came back upstairs and said, "It's not so bad. She left me Thought. They took Wind. I shit on ten! I'll catch them with this one."

He mounted Thought. I shit on ten! The others had gone some distance because they'd left earlier. But now he went on the other horse saying, "Yes, I'll catch them; no, I won't catch them." And the maiden said to Joaquín, "I shit on ten! I think that horse coming down there now is my father." So she grabbed a square comb she brought with her and threw it. She said, "May one of those very thick fogs appear in which you can't see your hand in front of your face." In fact—bum!—it turned into a thick fog. I shit on ten! Neither the devil nor his horse could turn around. And the other horse couldn't be seen. He said, "I shit on ten!" He went back. He arrived, and his wife asked, "What? Did you get to them?" He said, "Huh! You, what do you know? A fog surrounded me in a certain place, and I couldn't see my hand in front of my face. Neither I nor the horse could see. We had to come back." "Those were they. They were nearby," said the devil woman. "You have to go out again and get them." He went forth on his horse again. I shit on ten! Yes, he'd catch them; no, he wouldn't catch them. The maiden said, "That horse that's coming is my father." "I shit on ten! He's going to catch us." She said, "No, I'll turn into a chapel, and you become the monk." A hermitage was built, and Joaquín was there like a friar or a priest. And the devil came and asked, "Have you seen a woman and a man mounted on a horse passing by here?" Joaquín said, "What did you say? They're going to ring the bell for mass. If you want to come in to mass . . ." "That isn't what I asked you. Have you seen a woman and a man mounted on a horse pass by?" Joaquín said, "This is the last time they're ringing the bell for mass. If you want to come to mass . . ." "Damn the devil. You'll become a serpent for seven years." He cursed his daughter.

So the devil returned home the next day, and his daughter turned into a serpent. And she said to Joaquín, "My father put a curse on me. I have to complete

it. He said I must be a serpent for seven years. You go home to your town. You're going to be here for seven years. But don't forget about me." He said, "Oh, my! I won't. I won't." The young man was very happy with the maiden. She said, "Look, I'm going to tell you one thing. Don't let anyone kiss you. You'll forget about me if they kiss you." He said, "Don't worry, no one is going to kiss me."

So the lad came home to his town. Everyone was very happy because the boy had come home. "Pedro's son is coming. It's Joaquín." Another said, "Well that's who he is." The other said, "He's come." His family was all there, and they went to kiss him, but he said, "No one can kiss me." The lad didn't let anyone kiss him. He had gotten married with good intentions. Then his grandmother came. I shit on ten! She was a woman more than eighty years old. The lad was asleep, lying down, and she came saying, "Oh, my! Son, where have you been? How long it's been since I've seen you!" She gave her grandson two or three kisses. I shit on ten! Her grandson didn't remember anything about the serpent. I shit on ten! So he was a big lad. A bride appeared for him, or he went looking for a bride, because he no longer thought about the serpent. He became the intended of another one. With the passing of one, two, three, or four years, he became the intended of a maiden in the town, and they arranged to get married within a few years. The lad's father was rich, and so was the maiden to whom he was the intended. And so the people in that town, who had money, had the custom of giving some of those little pigs and some goats to whomever they wanted to raise for butchering in the next year or two for the wedding. And the family also gave some calves, little ones of course. By now the serpent had completed her sentence and she knew which was the lad's town and she went there. The maiden walked about as if she were begging and said, "I think they're giving away calves. A lad is going to get married." She said, "Yes, they're giving cattle away. I'll see if they give me something." Someone said, "What! Give you one? You have no way to take care of it!" But the maiden announced, "I've come here to see if you'll give me some cattle." Those fat cats said, "I shit on ten! To her! How are you going to take care of it? How is she going to care for it?" They said the same about the worthless ones. She said, "Eh, that worthless calf over there?" "The one that no one wants. That's the only one we can give the poor thing. This calf is going to die, so if it dies, the poor thing won't cost anyone anything." She said, "This is the one I want." And they gave her the little calf that no one had wanted. It was the worst one of them all. The poor thing walked up and down with the calf. It was always at the poor thing's feet, and the calf started to prosper. One or two years later Joaquín and the maiden were going to get married and they went to collect the cattle from the people and were talking about those worthless ones. "Don't you know that *one* is missing? You have to go get it." Someone else said, "Which one is missing?" "*Which* one is missing! The one we gave that poor thing last year. Don't you remember? We gave her a calf that no one wanted because it was going to die anyway. But at least one has to ask her if you should go get it." The other one said, "Yes, that's right." "One has to go get it." They went there. "Eh, we've come for the calf, the one we gave you last year. If it hasn't died on you, of course." She said, "No. The calf didn't die. The calf is fine. This is it." Someone said, "This! This is the calf!" One of them put his hand on it to take it away, and the calf wouldn't get up. He said, "Grab it by the tail, let's see if it'll get up that way." She said, "No. Don't bother the animal because it won't get up if I don't tell it to." She spoke to it: "Little calf, little calf, don't forget to walk (*andar*), like your master forgot the serpent in the olive grove (*olivar*)." The lad Joaquín was there, and again she said, "Get up, little calf, get up; don't forget how to walk (*andar*), like your master forgot the serpent in the olive grove (*olivar*)." I shit on ten! She said it again, and he answered her, "Serpent of the olive grove, I'm your Joaquín, your husband." The two of them embraced each other. I shit on ten! He said, "This is my wife." Those other worthless ones said, "But I shit on ten! What is this?" There they embraced and divided up the animals for the wedding with the other one in town he was going to marry. He went for Ursula, for the saint. Of course they prepared a huge wedding, since they had divided up all of the animals. They ate in the style of a marquis. They were very well off. Well, red dot [*punto colorado*], the story is over [*cuento terminado*].

The first episode of Florencio's tale sets the stage for the departure of the hero, Joaquín, from his home and his journey to hell where he will meet Ursula and her family. In his departure from home Joaquín is like other heroes who separate from parents and travel long distances to disenchant maidens. Florencio makes the hero's mother the instrumental agent in her son's departure, perhaps because marriage for a man means the trading of a mother for a wife. Joaquín must go to hell because his mother insists that his father catch a giant talking fish, which turns out to be an animal manifestation of the devil. The mother unknowingly promotes her son's courtship and marriage by inadvertently acting to send her son off with his future father-in-law, just as women seem to promote the *Donjaunismo* of their sons and encourage them to marry.

Florencio offers a complex image of the mother because her actions appear selfish, while actually resulting in her son's marriage. The mother appears to act selfishly by demanding that her husband kill the giant fish if he fails to bring in a good catch. Several men present a picture of a wife who brings on negative consequences by demanding that her husband kill a talking fish in their opening episodes of "The Fisherman," from which Florencio apparently borrowed the initial episode of his version of "Blancaflor." The "Fisherman" (AT 303) circulates widely in the oral tradition of Cáceres and other provinces in Spain (Curiel Merchán 1944: 279-281, 352–357; Cortés Vázquez 1979: 2: 21–40; A. Espinosa 1924: 289–292,

319–320; Llano Roza de Ampudia 1975: 74–77). The motif of the wife who demands that her fisherman husband kill a giant talking fish appears in "The Fisherman" by Bernardo Ramos, Miguel Chorro Hernandez, and José Díaz Sanchez (listed in the Appendix).

Florencio's account of the hero's mother is a comparatively unusual addition to "Blancaflor." No other narrator living in Cáceres or other parts of Spain started the "Blancaflor" story with an episode borrowed from "The Fisherman" and reworked to make the hero's mother appear selfish and demanding. Perhaps this narrator's description of the hero's mother mirrors his first failed courtship when the mother of the maiden dissuaded her daughter from marriage with Florencio because he was from a poorer family. Despite his difficulties in his first courtship, Florencio offers an optimistic scenario: he presents the mother as setting in action a chain of events that results in the happy marriage of her son to the woman who loves him. After all, if the hero's mother had not demanded that her husband kill the giant talking fish, Joaquín never would have gone away with his father-in-law and met Ursula. Florencio is one of many Cáceres narrators who play with the appearance and the reality of the actions of parents in their children's marriage. Hearing his description of the hero's mother in Florencio's story of "Blancaflor" reminds one of José Díaz Sánchez's account of the apparently cruel father in "The Innocent Slandered Maiden," whose actions resulted in the marriage of his daughter to a marquis.

Florencio continues to play with the theme of appearances versus reality when describing the actions of the demonic father-in-law toward his future son-in-law. Ursula's father seems extremely cruel and demanding, telling Joaquín that he must perform eight impossible tasks or suffer the penalty of death. The first task demanded of the hero, however—cutting the daughter into pieces—represents taking the heroine's virginity and creates an enduring bond between Joaquín and Ursula resulting in their marriage, because the drop of blood he spills becomes the means by which he later recognizes her. Florencio offers an image of the heroine's father that also makes him the intermediary in his daughter's transference of affection from her father to her spouse. Very dramatic language describes the heroine's defloration and picks up on the theme of a woman's first sexual experience as a violent act first presented in the stories older women tell younger women about maidens and thieves. The older women describe defloration as a brutal act to reinforce premarital chastity for women not yet ready for sex and marriage. Ursula, however, represents a maiden at a more mature stage of development and she encourages the hero to go ahead and take her virginity despite his reluctance and fear. The audience to this story is bound to be affected by imagery that suggests that a maiden may be willing to endure defloration, providing it takes place at the right time and with the right person.

Ursula's ordeal, which appears in all variants of "Blancaflor," is described in powerful metaphorical language that captures the meaning of a woman's defloration in Cáceres Spanish culture. Ursula sheds her blood when Joaquín chops her up and attempts to put all of the pieces of her body into a demijohn, much as a woman loses blood with her defloration. Ursula is physically marked by her ordeal because Joaquín accidentally spilled a drop of her blood. She is like any woman who is physically changed after losing her virginity. Ursula undergoes death and rebirth, much as in Cáceres women are believed to undergo a major transition when they have sex for the first time with a man. Ursula's physically changed form allows Joaquín to pick her for marriage from among her sisters, just as a woman is believed to have a special bond with the man who takes her virginity. Ursula requests that Joaquín play the guitar without falling asleep, just as a women needs the untiring devotion of the man with whom she has a sexual relationship.

Florencio, like all narrators, has the hero perform a series of impossible tasks with the indispensable aid of the heroine. These metaphorically represent the provisioning of a new household and the proof of competence a young man must show his father-in-law; they also symbolize men's dependence on women. Florencio, relative to other men who told "Blancaflor" stories, expands the number of tasks to draw attention to the degree to which the hero must prove himself to his father-in-law. He describes Ursula's father demanding that Joaquín (1) plow a hill, plant grape vines, and produce a bottle of wine the next day; (2) bring a load of wood without a span of straight pieces; (3) bring another load of wood with only straight pieces; (4) break a pair of iron shoes; (5) put holes in a bronze helmet; (6) fry a batch of fish keeping it from the cats; and (7) tame a wild colt.

Florencio presents a model of family relations based on gender differences in his account of the hero's performance of several impossible tasks. He draws attention to the gender differences when describing how the hero breaks the iron shoes and puts holes in the bronze helmet. He tells how the hero can break the shoes and put holes in the helmet by utilizing the destructive powers of the she-mule's urine and flatulence. Florencio's metaphor is complex because it expresses a common belief that women have intrinsic sources of destructive power not possessed by men. This part of his story is an allegory delivering the message that a man must learn in marriage to turn to women and utilize their special powers. Florencio makes this point clear to the listeners of his tale by saying that if the hero were to rely on the masculine principle and scrub the shoes in the he-mule's urine or place the helmet in the path of he-mule's flatulence, he would not successfully perform the tasks required of him by his father-in-law. The whole point of the "Blancaflor" story is that the hero must learn to rely on women, despite the gender differences in Spanish Cáceres culture.

The roles of the feminine and masculine protagonists in the performance of the tasks are complementary, as are the roles of wife and husband in the organization of work in the family. Before her illness, Florencio's wife helped him sell cow's milk and harvest cherries in addition to preparing meals, washing clothes, and caring for the couple's four small children. Other married women from Navaconcejo whose family depends more on farming than on domesticated animals perform a number of other roles complementary to those of their husband when raising potatoes, peas, cherries, and olives. If the couple plants potatoes or peas, the husband prepares the land for planting, makes holes in the soft ground, and his wife walks behind him inserting the crop. If the husband works on the estate of another, the wife may cultivate and irrigate the couple's vegetable gardens. Most families in Navaconcejo grow cherries as their main cash crop, and women work in complementary roles with men in the cherry harvest. Normally women collect the cherries from the ground and the lower limbs of trees while men shake the fruit from higher limbs and transport the crop to the cooperative for sale. Men and women harvest olives in similar fashion—men beat the branches with sticks, women collect the fruit from the ground—and men transport the crop to the press and remove the oil.

The "Blancaflor" story, however, involves more than a model for the organization of work by a man and a woman because the heroine has supernatural power, which represents the power of a woman's love for a man. Different narrators represent the power of a woman's love in various ways; women have the power to heal through their nurturance in "The Maiden and the Thieves" by José Díaz Sanchez and in "Cinderella" by Filomena Arivas Miguel, Umbelina García Castaño, and Maximina Castaño; a woman can humanize a man in "Beauty and the Beast" by Teresa Herrero, Florencia Real Cobos, and Juana Moreno. For Florencio, Ursula's love gives Joaquín the ability to surmount difficult obstacles and saves him from death.

Ursula has supernatural power not shared by Joaquín, just as women in many parts of rural Spain have extraordinary powers specific to their gender. Pitt-Rivers (1966: 189–199) describes how wise women (sabias) of Alcalá (Andalusia) have the power of grace (gracia) by which they cure with a touch, locate lost objects, discover the names of thieves, discern the sexual fidelity and well-being of one who is absent, cause one to fall in love or restore an old, waning love relationship, and protect another from acts of nature. Women also have involuntary destructive powers caused by contamination of their menstrual blood. The source of Blancaflor's power is complex because it derives from her demonic parents, and yet in a number of variants, including the one by Florencio, she is described as a saint. The ambiguous source of Blancaflor's supernatural power accords with the ambivalent attitude of men toward women; men need and fear women, and so women appear both saintly and demonic to men.

Florencio develops his model of marriage and family relations further when he describes how the hero, acting on Ursula's instructions, tames the colt and fries the batch of fish. The parts of the colt are the metaphors for the family, and their parts and their required treatment symbolize the organization of authority in the Cáceres Spanish family. The father is the head of the colt, just as he is the jural head of the family; but he shares power with his wife, represented by the shoulderblades. Florencio describes how Ursula tells the hero to beat the head and the shoulderblades vigorously with the blunt end of the club she provides for him because the father and the mother are the ones who may appear opposed to a maiden's marriage as they try to protect their daughter's premarital chastity. Florencio presents similar imagery by representing the cats who come to steal the fish as the components of the patriarchal family. The black cat with the big head is the father, the black cat with the white necktie is the mother, the yellow and the calico cats are the heroine's sisters, and the white cat is Ursula. Their color, shape, and required treatment are in accord with the lines of authority in the family, with the father as the jural head.

The conversion of Ursula's family into animals appears in many "Blancaflor" stories and is based on beliefs about witchcraft widespread in Cáceres and other parts of Spain (Pitt-Rivers 1966: 189–201; Caro Baroja 1973). According to these beliefs, a witch can become an animal to harm another or convert others into animals with diabolical intervention. Florencio did not know exactly how the conversion works, but he offered what he knew.

I have always heard it said that the devil does what he wants. Because I heard once that a couple got married and when they were going to bed, and they say that a cat went there, and when the cat appeared it went meow, meow, meow. The cat was meowing, and the woman said, "Sometimes the devil sounds like a cat." The husband said, "Look how fast I'll get this cat out of here." He got up and grabbed a stick, but he didn't return. And they say the devil went there in the form of a cat and took him away. . . . The devil makes himself into a dog, he makes himself into a cat, he makes himself into an ox, he makes himself into a goat, he makes himself into whatever he wants. That's what they say. I haven't seen it. It's something, I think, that's like a dream. I dream something, and it seems real to me, but of course when I awake there is nothing.

Florencio presents Ursula in a conflict of loyalties as she gives the power of her love to Joaquín. The apparently hostile attitude of her father makes it appear that she must renounce her loyalty to her parents as she develops loyalty to the man who will become her husband. She takes the first step in breaking from her family when she uses her supernatural power and her advice to help Joaquín perform the impossible tasks, and she takes the second step when fleeing from her father after her wedding. Ursula escapes from her father by casting away items that represent her former identity as a daughter as she develops her new identity as a wife. She leaves her spittle and casts away her comb, which becomes a thick fog blocking her father's pursuit. She changes form, becoming a hermitage, and she makes Joaquín the priest. The flight of Ursula and Joaquín is a particular expression of the widspread motif of "The Magic Flight," which appears in many stories around the world. The Jungian critic Marie Louise von Franz (1982: 131), when discussing a Siberian tale that has a flight episode like that of "Blancaflor," suggests that flight motif represents "a situation where it is better to flee from the unconscious than to seek to overcome it, and by so doing avoid being devoured." In the context of a woman making the transition from courtship to marriage, Ursula fleeing from her father could represent a woman's efforts to escape from the powerful feelings stirred up when making a major life change.

Florencio warns of the difficulties in overcoming the feelings raised in separating from parents by describing the devil uttering his curse to Ursula: "You will become a snake for seven years." Florencio makes the point that the lingering loyalties of a woman to her parents and parental influence in her marriage can create a breach in a woman's bond with her husband. This storyteller also warns, in the language of his story, that a man as well as a woman may have lingering filial loyalties of his own that may interfere with his marriage. Florencio presents Joaquín as a man who has an equally difficult time making the transition from a son to a husband because he fails to hold true to his promise not to let anyone kiss him lest he forget about Ursula during the seven years of her bewitchment. His grandmother's kiss erases Joaquín's memory of Ursula, who must make her lost husband remember their common bond created with the shedding of her blood, her physical change, and their cooperation through an arduous process of separation.

Despite all of the problems confronted by the hero and heroine, Florencio concludes his tale by expressing faith in conjugal love. He describes Ursula using her supernatural power one final time to restore her relationship with Joaquín, who is about to marry another woman, by nurturing

a frail calf into a sturdy animal, which will not budge unless she tells it
to. When she twice says to the animal, "Don't forget how to walk (*andar*)
like your owner has forgotten about the serpent in the olive grove (*olivar*)," Joaquín and Ursula are reunited.[2]

Telling a story is a personal as well as a collective expression of experience in narrative form, and other Cáceres men tell the story of "Blancaflor" in different ways to draw attention to their particular concerns in
the model of conjugal relations. I collected three other versions of this tale
from Leandro Jimenez of El Guijo de Santa Bárbara, and from José Díaz
Sanchez and Eugenio Real Vázquez of Serradilla (their stories are listed
in the Appendix). The men from Serradilla incorporate more class-related
themes into their telling of this story because class consciousness is much
greater in the stratified agrotown of Serradilla than in the more egalitarian villages of Navaconcejo and El Guijo de Santa Bárbara. José, a member of the agrarian working class in a very class-structured community,
describes the hero as a worker and the heroine's father as his master
(*amo*). Eugenio, who is a member of the same social class in the same
community, conveys class consciousness in a different and more subtle
way when he describes the hero leaving his parental home because he
cannot find anyone to marry, much as many a humble man of Serradilla
believe that a maiden's parents may find him an unworthy candidate for
marriage.

Leandro and Eugenio describe in detail their heroe's journey to hell and
his encounters with ferocious-appearing but helpful characters on his way
to meet Blancaflor. The journey and the encounters with menacing but
helpful characters represent courtship as a difficult struggle. The helpful
characters are animals or personified forces of nature and, in the view of
psychoanalytic critics, represent the natural and constructive energies of
the id (Bettelheim 1977: 76). For Leandro the helpful character is a royal
eagle with an unspecified gender, and for Eugenio he is the wind.

Leandro and Eugenio describe the hero's first encounter with the heroine in ways that express how men view initiating a courtship. In Eugenio's story Blancaflor greets the hero with a threat when she tells him, "If
you hadn't come today, my father would have killed you tomorrow." Perhaps the heroine's threat represents how a maiden and her father expect
a man to turn a relationship into a formal courtship within a relatively
short period of time. Leandro describes the hero and heroine falling in
love at first sight, perhaps representing the male romantic wish that a
woman accept his compliments, fall in love, and make an immediate
transfer of her affections and loyalties. Leandro is particularly prone to
describing heroes and heroines falling in love immediately, as the reader
might recall from his version of "Cinderella," but this represents a general
wish of Cáceres men.

Leandro, José, and Eugenio describe their heroes performing many of the same tasks except that they change the order and reduce the number. Their heroes must plant wheat and make bread, plant vines and make wine, in an impossibly short time to prove themselves good providers to the heroine's father. The men change the order of the tasks by placing last the symbol of the heroine's defloration, which they also represent by the loss and retrieval of a ring requiring the chopping up and reconstitution of the maiden. Most narrators, male as well as female, make the retrieval of the ring the last or the penultimate but never the first in the series (Cortés Vázquez 1976: 62–66; 1979: 2: 70–99; A. Espinosa 1924: 240–255; Llano Roza de Ampudia (1975: 97–103), warranting the conclusion that its place in the order of tasks has widespread significance. The ultimate or penultimate position of the retrieval of the ring probably represents the idea that a maiden should guard her premarital virginity during most if not all of a long courtship. Blancaflor's defloration takes place prior to her marriage in all of the variants from Cáceres and in other parts of Spain perhaps because many courted maidens actually have premarital sex toward the end of their courtship and just prior to marriage. Florencio made clear in Chapter 3 that a courting maiden who loses her virginity and becomes pregnant does not necessarily lose her moral reputation, providing she marries the father of her child. The heroine's defloration, however, is also a poetic device to illustrate dramatically the special connection created between a woman and the man who takes her virginity. That connection becomes apparent when Blancaflor's physical change allows the hero to recognize her from among her sisters.

José and Eugenio have Blancaflor's mother rather than her father pursue the fleeing couple, an unusual feature of "Blancaflor" stories. Llano Roza de Ampudia (1975: 97–103) collected a masculine variant in Asturias in which the mother pursues the fleeing couple after the father fails to catch them in several attempts, but most other stories have the couple pursued by the father. The mother as the pursuer in the masculine Serradilla stories is a detail that enhances the split images of women. On the one hand, there is the good Blancaflor described as a saint, and, on the other, there is the bad mother who is the devil. The mother of Blancaflor as a devil appears in many variants, but she rarely takes any action against the couple. Splitting images of women can occur in stories for a variety of reasons, including unresolved male Oedipal feelings from childhood (Spiro 1982: 113–124). Although many men may have Oedipal feelings that they project onto stories, not every masculine narrator presents those feelings in the same way. Eugenio and José may recast common Oedipal sentiments in their "Blancaflor" stories by enhancing their split images of women relative to other masculine narrators from different communities because of the class-conscious context of courtship and marriage in Serradilla. The active bad mother in their tales probably represents the women in wealthy families who restrict the access of their daughters to agrarian working-class men such as Eugenio and José. It is understandable in the context of Cáceres family life that men would place emphasis on the mother blocking the daughter's marriage because mothers have the primary responsibility in socializing their daughters and influencing their marital choice. The two narrators make the wealthy status of Blancaflor's mother clear when they introduce class consciousness into the opening episodes of their stories.

Most of the masculine narrators in Cáceres describe the pursuing parent of Blancaflor uttering a curse when giving up the chase. The curse bewitches Blancaflor by turning her into an animal for seven years or makes the hero lose his affection for the heroine when embraced by a member of his family. The curse is a poetic device used by many men who tell the "Blancaflor" tale in Cáceres apparently because men are concerned about the lingering filial loyalties of women. The curse does not appear in all masculine versions of "Blancaflor," including a variant by Eugenio Real Vázquez listed in the Appendix. Moreover, Cortés Vázquez collected masculine stories without the curse from men in Salamanca (1979: 2: 83–89) and Zamora (1976: 62–66). This device drawing attention to the lingering filial loyalties of women, however, appears more often in masculine tales than in feminine ones, particularly in the villages of northern and central Cáceres that I worked in. None of the women from this part of Spain included the curse in their versions of the story, and Cortés Vázquez found the curse in only one (1979: 2: 70–83) of the four feminine (90–99) variants from Salamanca. Men, understandably, are more concerned about the lingering filial loyalties of women because women have such close and lifelong ties with parents. The masculine narrators also acknowledge that men have their own conflicts in loyalties because most heroes in the masculine tales forget about the heroine when embraced by a member of their own family.

Nearly all Cáceres stories told by men as well as women describe Blancaflor regaining her lost husband by restoring his memory just as he is about to marry another woman. Leandro is the exception among narrators from the Cáceres villages because he depicts the hero acting on his own to remember the woman who did so much for him. In Leandro's tale, the hero heads for church to marry another woman and kicks and kills the dog that embraced him, causing his loss of affection for the heroine. His tale notwithstanding, the masculine narrators express a great deal of faith in the power of women to restore broken love relationships, a power expressed in widely held beliefs about women (see Pitt-Rivers 1966: 189–199).

## THE FEMININE MODEL

The version of "Blancaflor" that Gregoria Ramos Merchán told presents a model of conjugal love that shares many features with the masculine stories. Gregoria's tale is one of two "Blancaflor" stories I collected from women in the Cáceres villages and is the more complete of the two feminine versions. The second feminine "Blancaflor" story is by Evarista Moreno (listed in the Appendix). One can take the common elements in the stories by Florencio and Gregoria as affirmations of their areas of agreement about how conjugal love can work in a culture of sharp gender differences. Both affirm that a man must break with parents in preparation for marriage by describing heroes leaving home and making a long journey to find their brides. They agree that the competition between a father-in-law and his future son-in-law over the loyalties of a maiden is more apparent than real. The two narrators dramatically illustrate how a father, who is apparently opposed to his future son-in-law, is really only asking him to prove himself, and they dramatically describe how a maiden's father may actually act to promote his daughter's marriage. Gregoria, like all men and women who tell this tale, describes the heroine's father demanding that his future son-in-law retrieve a ring lost in the ocean. The father's demand results in the heroine's defloration and the creation of a special and enduring bond with the hero, setting the stage for their marriage. Gregoria, like the other narrators, represents the power of a woman's love as a heroine using her supernatural powers to enable the hero to perform impossible tasks required by her father. Her heroine, like the others, must separate from her parents; she flees with her husband, casting away the items representing her former identity as daughter as she assumes a new identity as a wife. She, like her counterparts in all of the other stories except the truncated tale told by Evarista Moreno, temporarily loses her husband when he faces a conflict in his own loyalties, and she takes on the responsibility of maintaining the marital tie by unlocking her lost husband's memory. The areas of agreement affirmed through the retelling of "Blancaflor" by men and women are powerful testimony to the faith in the conjugal bond in Cáceres Spanish culture. That faith is based on a complementary division of labor between women and men and culturally based assumptions of gender difference and interconnection.

The long and complicated ritual of courtship, the creation of an illusion of love, and the dialogue through storytelling do not eliminate all of the interlocked contradictory and discordant themes in gender relations in Cáceres Spanish culture. Gender differences run deep because men and women have such contrasting antecedent family experiences. Gregoria consequently retells the story of "Blancaflor" differently from Florencio to present a scenario of gender relations that accords with the experiences of women. She told her tale to persuade her listeners to understand the position of the woman in courtship in a culture in which women highly value and protect their relationship with their mother and in which male competition for and through women makes courted maidens vulnerable to male slander.

### "Blancaflor," by Gregoria Ramos Merchán

Once there was a married couple. They had three sons but the husband was very addicted to cards. He threw away all the capital he had playing cards. And one day he played until he lost the clothes off his back and said, "If the devil would give me a deck of cards to win money, I'd give him my oldest son." One day the devil gave him the cards and, of course, he won a lot of money. And the devil said, "Your son has to go to the castle 'Where One Goes and Never Returns.'" At first the father was very content because he'd won a lot of money. But as the time was approaching when his son had to go, he began to think and think. He was getting thinner, and his sons didn't know what had happened. They asked, "What happened to you, father? You're going to get very sick." He said, "Oh, sons, if you only knew. One day when I was playing I found myself in a bind and had to ask the devil for a deck of cards to win money. And now the oldest has to go to the castle 'Where You'll Go and Won't Return.'" The oldest said, "Oh, my! Yes, father. I'll go. No problem."

Well, the day came for the oldest son to go. No one knew where the castle was, and he had to ask along the way. But no one knew. He came to a place where a man or a woman said, "Oh, my! No one ever heard of that. But we've heard that a lame she-wolf goes to the castle 'Where One Goes and Never Returns.'" He left and walked a little way. He found the lame she-wolf and asked, "Little wolf, do you know of the castle 'Where You'll Go and Won't Return'?" "I come from there," said the little wolf. The boy asked, "Would you please take me there?" The wolf said, "Oh, my! It's a little far." "How can we go there?" asked the boy. "You have to kill a bull for me and you have to climb on top of me and give me meat the entire way." The wolf went the entire way saying, "Give me meat! Give me meat! Give me meat!" They came to a certain place, and the meat ran out. "Give me meat!" And the boy said, "For God's sake! There's no more for me to give you. What shall I do? If you want, I'll cut off a piece of my buttocks and give it to you." The wolf said, "No. Let's see if we can make it."

They came to where there were three maidens bathing. They had laid down their clothes, and the youngest had hers separate from the others. The two older ones had theirs separate too. The wolf told the boy, "You have to take the clothes of the youngest and keep them. She'll look for them when she comes out of her bath and she'll have to say, 'Oh, my clothes. Oh, my clothes. Who has my clothes? I'll get whoever has my clothes out of all the straits he's in.'"

Well, that's what he did. They arrived. The wolf let him off, he took the youngest girl's clothes and kept them from her. The two older ones came out and got dressed, but the youngest was nude. "Oh, my clothes. Oh, my clothes. Where are my clothes? I'll remove whoever has my clothes from all of the straits he's in."

The boy gave her the clothes he had taken, and she got dressed. Then she asked him, "What's going on with you?" He said, "Well, this and this and this. Is your father going to scold me because I'm late?" She said, "Yes. Tonight when you arrive, he's going to scold you. But tell him it's because you didn't know the way and had to come asking." They arrived, and the devil said, "It seems you've taken a long time." "Sure! Because I came asking the way. I didn't know the way, and all of that took time." The devil said, "Fine." They ate supper, and before they went to bed the devil said to him, "Go to that window. What do you see?" The boy said, "I see a plot of land that's very big, very, very big." The devil said, "Tomorrow you have to plant wheat, and I have to have a loaf of bread to eat on my table tomorrow at midday." The boy said, "Oh, my God! How am I going to do that? It's impossible!" The youngest daughter asked, "What did my father tell you?" He said, "This. I can't! I can't do it. I'm not able to. I'll kill myself. I'll do myself in." She said, "No. Take this needle case. Sprinkle the needles." And he sprinkled them. Some were for ploughing, others for planting, others for threshing. The devil had a loaf of bread to eat on his table by midday.

He came back at night and they ate supper. The devil said to him, "Go to the window again." He went. "What do you see?" "Oh my! A plain that's very big. There's a lot more land than yesterday!" "You have to plant vines on this, and I have to have wine to drink on my table tomorrow." The devil had given him an impossible task. Well, he had wine to drink on his table. The devil began to get suspicious. He said, "Maybe you're a devil or maybe you're a saint, but you're with one of my daughters."

They ate supper that night, and the devil said, "Tomorrow you have to go take care of the dogs." The youngest daughter asked, "What did my father tell you?" He said, "Tomorrow I have to go take care of the dogs." She said, "Well my father is the big dog. My mother is the black-and-white one. My sisters are the other dogs. And I am the little white dog." Her name was Blancaflor. "Don't be afraid to hit them with sticks. But threaten me without hitting me." And that's what he did. He went out and started with the sticks. He slapped some, he wasn't afraid to hit the others, pin pon, pin pon. But he threatened her without hitting her. Then he came back at night, and the devil asked, "How did it go with the dogs? How did you take care of the dogs?" The boy said, "Oh, fine, fine."

"Good. Let's have supper." The devil said, "One hundred years ago my great-great-grandfather's ring was lost in the sea. I have to have it on the table at dinnertime." "Oh, my! Holy Virgin Mother! For God's sake! What road have I taken? I'll kill myself. I'll do myself in. I'll undo myself." The youngest daughter asked, "What did my father tell you?" He said, "The impossible. Impossible things. A ring was lost in the sea one hundred years ago, and now he has to have it tomorrow on the table at dinnertime." She said, "Hush! Hush! Now you're going to kill me. You have to kill me," she told him. "Oh, my! Kill you?" She said, "Yes. You have to kill me, you have to cut me into little pieces and put me in a bottle. But don't drop even a drop of my blood. Be sure not even a drop of my blood." He killed her, cut her into little pieces, and put her into the bottle. And ala! A drop of blood was dropped. A little drop. And a hole appeared in her little finger. He threw the bottle into the sea. "And you have to play the guitar at the edge of the sea." And the bottle turned and turned, and then he fell asleep. And she said, "Play, play, so you don't lose me. Play, play, so you don't lose me." She found the ring and brought it out of the sea.

And she said to him, "Look at the hole in my little finger. Now my parents are going to tell you that you have to marry one of the three of us. And my father is going to lock us in a room. My two older sisters are going to stick out their hands two times before I do. You'll recognize me by the little hole in my finger." That's what happened. The devil locked them up in a room and asked, "You'll want to marry one of my daughters, won't you?" He answered, "Yes, sir, why not." Good. The devil took out one hand. "Do you want this one?" "No." He took out the hand of the other one. "Do you want this one?" "No, sir. Not this one either." "And this one?" The boy said, "This one." "I knew it," the devil said. "Whether you're a devil or a saint, you're with one of my daughters."

They got married, and Blancaflor said, "Tonight my father is going to come to kill the two of us. Let's fill two sacks with straw and put them in the bed, because tonight he's coming to kill us." That's what they did. The devil and his wife came. Tras! Two knives. Plum! They stabbed them and wounded the sacks. "And now we've killed them." They left and Blancaflor said, "Go downstairs and take the thinnest horse there is. It must be the thinnest one, the one that staggers." He took one and left the other, which was so thin. "This one." Then in the morning the devil and his wife came into the bedroom and said, "Oh, my! They've filled two sacks with straw and fled."

The devil said, "We're fine, because he took the bad horse that doesn't run as fast." The devil mounted the faster horse and went in search of them. Blancaflor saw him from far away and said, "My father is coming to look for us. I'll become a garden, and you be the gardener." She became a garden of cabbage and lettuce, and he became the gardener. And the devil asked him, "Have you seen pass by here a married couple, a young woman and a . . . ?" The gardener said, "No, sir. Do you want lettuce? It's here for you to make a salad." "I'm not asking you that. I'm asking you if a woman and a man, a lady and a gentleman, passed by here." "Do you want cabbage? It can be cooked now." The devil said, "Enough. I'm going home because this man is a fool. I haven't gotten anything." He went home, and his wife asked, "Did you see anything?" "Yes. There was a garden and a gardener who asked if anyone wanted cabbage, if anyone wanted lettuce." "You fool, they were those things," the woman said to her husband.

He went back again, but they had left flying. Blancaflor wore a comb in her hair. She removed the comb and threw it behind her. It turned into a forest that was very thick, and her father couldn't pass through it. He went back home. "Oh, my!" he said to his wife. "Do you know what they threw? It turned into a forest that was very thick! Who could pass through it?" "Oh, what a stupid fool you are!" his wife said. "They were those things."

They went on. The devil went after them again on another horse, Thought. Or was it Air? Air was one and Thought was the other. He saw them from afar, and the daughter became a church, and the boy became a priest about to say mass. "Do you want to come in? The bell is going to ring for mass. Do you want to come in?" "These people drive me crazy with all of this," said the devil.

With that they went on, and the devil went away. He didn't look for them again. But before they arrived, Blancaflor told her husband, "When we come to your town, let no one embrace you. If you let someone embrace you, you'll forget about me. So when we come to your town, let no one embrace you." They arrived, and he let no one embrace him. No one, neither his father nor his mother, no one. But as he was sitting in a chair, his grandmother came from behind and said, "Oh, my son! How long it's been since I've seen you. I thought you were never going to return from the castle 'Where One Goes and Never Returns.' And now you're here." He completely forgot about his bride.

But he didn't forget about her forever, because if one says forever he wouldn't go back to her, right? Well, she made her home and lived alone. And no maiden was more beautiful than she. And there were three friends, her husband and two others, and one of them said, "Let's go court that beautiful maiden." Her husband was to go last, the other two first. The first came and there was conversation, and she said, "Well, good, let's go to bed." She had a tube of water there or a large jar, a *botijo*, and a glass. "But before we go to bed," she said, "you have to bring a glass of water." He spent all night with the glass of water on top of him. He was there all night. She was pouring the glass of water over him. He really wanted the day to come so he could get out of there! He couldn't do anything else. And then it was day, and he could go. The other one asked him, "How did it go for you?" "Oh, my! I spent a divine night. It was a stupendous night." The other one went, and the maiden said the same thing to him. They were there talking, maybe they had supper, and she said, "Let's go to bed." They went to bed. It was the last thing she really wanted to do. She went downstairs and closed the door. Well, the door was closed on his ribs all night. He wanted the day to come, and when it did he got up and went. And her husband went and he said, "How are you?" "Fine, fine." And when he came, she knew it was him. She sat down and took out a chair and set it down. And she took a glass of water and a glass of wine and put them on the table. The glass of water asked the glass of wine, "Don't you remember when you went to the castle 'Where You'll Go and Won't Return'?" And the glass of wine said, "Yes, I remember." And the man said to himself, "Yes, that happened to me." The glass of water said, "Don't you remember when you took the youngest maiden's clothes when the three maidens were bathing?" "Yes, I remember," answered the glass of wine. And the man remembered, "Yes, this happened to me." The glass of water said, "Don't you remember when you went to take care of the dogs, and I told you I was the little white dog?" He said, "Yes, I remember." The glass of water asked the glass of wine everything until they came to the end of everything that had happened. And he said to himself, "It all happened to me." And when they came to the last thing, they recognized each other. They got married again. They had a good wedding, and the story is over.

Gregoria, like all women, has heard many stories told by men who blame women for family problems, and so she responds by switching blame from the mother to the father to explain why their son must make a journey to hell. She describes the father as self-indulgently addicted to cards and selfishly promising his oldest son to the devil in exchange for a lucky deck. A man who requests lucky cards from the devil appears in other variants of "Blancaflor," but the father in these stories does not sell his oldest son to change his luck (Cortés Vázquez 1979: 2: 70–83). It is possible that Gregoria once heard a tale like Florencio's and reworked the imagery to make the point that women can blame men just as easily as men can blame women for family problems.

Gregoria persuades her listeners to see women as helpful intermediaries in a man's marriage by specifying the feminine identity of the helpful wolf who carries the hero to his bride. Men either do not specify the gender or they portray as masculine the helpful characters who transport the hero to Blancaflor. Leandro Jimenez of El Guijo de Santa Bárbara described a royal eagle of unspecified gender taking the hero to meet the heroine, and Eugenio Real Vázquez of Serradilla said the helpful character was the masculine wind. Gregoria, on the other hand, describes the helpful agent as a lame she-wolf who transports the hero to Blancaflor and tells him what he must do to survive his ordeals with the devil.

Narrators describe the first meeting between the hero and the heroine in various ways to make different points about beginning a courtship. Eugenio describes Blancaflor threatening the hero on their first encounter, representing the fear a man might feel when initiating a courtship. Leandro describes the heroine falling in love at first sight with the hero, expressing the masculine romantic wish that a courted maiden make a complete and total transfer of her loyalties and affections from her parents to the man who loves her. Gregoria, on the other hand, draws attention to the efforts of a vulnerable maiden to defend her premarital chastity. Her Blancaflor is vulnerable because the hero, acting on the advice of the she-wolf, has stolen her clothes, and she defends her chastity by offering to help the hero if he removes her from the situation that could threaten her moral reputation. This initial exchange is the beginning of the relationship between the hero and heroine that eventually turns into marriage. By portraying Blancaflor as concerned about her modesty, Gregoria persuades her listeners to see courted maidens as defending their virtue even in situations that appear to be otherwise. Gregoria, like all woman, has heard men jump to conclusions on the basis of appearances, meaning that any woman in the wrong place at the wrong time may be accused of failing to defend her feminine honor.

Gregoria, like Florencio, expresses in symbolic language the complementarity of gender relations. She describes the hero powerless to perform the impossible tasks without the supernatural power of the heroine, representing men's dependence on women. Gregoria's hero is more helpless and disheartened than Florencio's. Her imagery emphasizes woman's view of man as needy and weak without his wife's asistance and love. When her Blancaflor flees from her parents with her husband, she tells how the heroine uses her supernatural power to turn the couple into objects that have gender associations in Cáceres Spanish culture. Blancaflor becomes a chapel, vegetables, and the garden itself, and her husband becomes the priest and the gardener in accordance with the actual roles of men and women in the gender division of labor. Men, not women, are priests and men spend a great deal of time working in the fields, just as the husband is the gardener in Gregoria's story. Men work to produce vegetables, which they give to women to sell or prepare since they are the nurturers of their husband, children, and parents. The symbolic association of the woman with a chapel or a house fits the tendency of women with young children to perform domicile-based tasks and accords with the symbolic association of the woman with the home (Brandes 1975: 112–114). Gregoria, however, eliminates the symbolism in Florencio's tale of the destructive power of women as she emphasizes the constructive role of women in marital and family relationships. Florencio metaphorically expressed the destructive power of a woman's sexuality by describing the hero dissolving a pair of iron shoes and a bronze helmet in the urine and the flatulence of the she-mule.

Gregoria confronts what threatens men most in courtship and marriage: the woman who betrays her man. Men's fear of betrayal probably has an Oedipal basis in early childhood when a young man perceives his mother as betraying his wish to monopolize her affections and banish his father. Cáceres men express clearly the Oedipal themes in many stories of

courtship and marriage. A man projects Oedipal fears onto a courted
maiden when worrying in retrospect that she may have betrayed him with
another man or will betray him in the future. Men further project Oedipal
themes into courtship when they tell stories of courted maidens with conflicted loyalties and express the wish that a woman break with her parents
and transfer her affections to the man who courts her, much as a boy in
Oedipal entanglements might wish that his mother break with his father
and turn to her son. Gregoria confronts men's concern over the transfer
of a woman's loyalties by drawing the attention of her listeners away
from the conflict in loyalties for the courted maiden and focusing on the
conflict for the man. She shifts attention away from Blancaflor's conflict
in filial and conjugal loyalties by eliminating the curse, a feature that appears in a number of masculine stories to explain why the hero becomes
alienated from the heroine. Gregoria persuades her listeners to focus their
attention on the conflicts in men who also can be slow to transfer their
affections and loyalties from their mother to their spouse. She describes
her hero forgetting about Blancaflor because his grandmother embraces
him.

In her concluding episode, Gregoria persuades men and women to see
male slander of women as the result of men promoting their reputation
for manliness by lying about the women with whom they have had prior
courtships. Gregoria has undoubtedly heard many men tell how they believe that women courted by other men have probably lost their virginity
with their former sweethearts. She also knows that men are likely to draw
their own conclusions based on appearances. So she concludes her version of "Blancaflor" by describing the heroine courted by two men who
lie about their experiences to save face and enhance their own reputation
as the Don Juáns of their village. Gregoria describes two friends of the
hero courting Blancaflor and spending the night with her while she drips
water over one and closes a heavy wooden door on the ribs of the other.
They lie about what really happened to enhance their own esteem in the
eyes of each other and consequently slander the heroine. The message that
men lie about women to promote their reputation for manliness among
other men appears in other feminine "Blancaflor" stories from adjacent
provinces (Cortés Vázquez 1979: 2: 70–83), undoubtedly because male
slander is a widespread concern of women. The dialogue through storytelling may help make some men sympathetic to the vulnerable position
of women.[3] Men as well as women tell "The Innocent Slandered Maiden"
and "The Wager on the Wife's Chastity," which clearly affirm that men
lie about virtuous women. Gregoria ends her tale by expressing her faith
in the power of a woman to restore a broken marital tie, a faith shared
by many narrators of "Blancaflor." She describes Blancaflor using her su-

pernatural power to speak through a glass of water and a glass of wine in order to unlock her husband's memory and rekindle his love for her.

## THE POWER OF A WOMAN'S LOVE

The way Blancaflor uses her supernatural power to help a man is different than the way any heroes use supernatural power to aid a woman. The contrasting uses of supernatural power by women and men in stories of courtship and marriage accord with the roles of the genders in marriage and family life. Blancaflor uses her power continuously to help her husband perform a series of impossible tasks, flee from her pursuing father, and restore the marriage. Heroes use their supernatural power only to initiate marriage. The heroes in "The Grateful Animals" acquire power from animals to disenchant and marry a princess, but once the marriage takes place, the story comes to an end and we learn little about how the hero deals with maintaining his family relationships. I collected no story from any narrator in Cáceres about a hero who continuously used supernatural power to help a maiden through a series of difficulties or to restore a broken marriage. As mentioned in Chapter 8, I did not encounter any "Lost Wife" tales (AT 400) in Cáceres, and they are rare in Spanish oral tradition.

In general, the Cáceres tales of courtship and marriage attribute to women the power to heal social wounds, just as they heal through their nurturance the physical wounds and ailments of their children, their spouse, and their elderly parents. The power of women to restore broken family relationships appears in other stories of family life as well. For example, "The Queen and Her Marvelous Children" (AT 707), also known as "The Seven Heirs Apparent" (A. Espinosa 1924: 234–236), is a story about the disintegration and reformation of the nuclear family. I collected three variants from Felisa Sanchez Martín of Serradilla, Guillermo Castaño of Garganta la Olla, and Leonardo Sanchez Sanchez of Cabezuela, all of which are listed in the Appendix. The tale circulates widely in Cáceres oral tradition (Curiel Merchán 1944: 63–67, 273–275, 284–286) and appears in collections of folktales from Salamanca (Cortés Vázquez 1979: 2: 103–109), Cuenca (A. Espinosa 1924: 234–236), and Asturias (Llano Roza de Ampudia 1975: 48–53, 87–90). The folktale is probably very popular because it captures widespread views of family relationships.

The versions from northern and central Cáceres tell of a king married to a humble woman who gives birth to a daughter and one or more sons. The queen's sisters, jealous of her marriage to the king, falsely report that the queen gives birth to monstrosities rather than children. The king imprisons his wife, and the sisters send the children down the river in baskets. A miller adopts the children, who eventually inherit the miller's property, and when the boy(s) set out to find marvelous objects for their garden (a talking bird, a singing tree, a fountain with reeds of gold), they fall into enchantment. The stories are interesting expressions of how family unity is restored primarily by the actions of a woman rather than a man. In the versions by Felisa and Guillermo, the sister takes the crucial step of reuniting her family by disenchanting her brothers and acquiring the talking bird that reveals the truth to the king. Leonardo Sanchez Sanchez masculinizes the story by describing the brother disenchanting his sister, but his tale is unusual among the variants in this region of Spain, particularly if one takes into consideration the masculine and feminine versions with parallel episodes collected by Curiel Merchán in southern Cáceres (1944: 63–67) and Cortés Vázquez in the adjacent province of Salamanca (1979: 2: 107–109). Llano Roza de Ampudia also reported an Asturian variant collected from a young woman; it included the episode of siblings who become enchanted as they attempt to find marvelous objects for their palace. Once again, the sister disenchants her brothers and sets the stage for the complete restoration of her family (1975: 48–53).

Women, who are believed to hold the power to restore broken family relationships, express in other folktales a greater faith than men in achieving a harmonious blend of family loyalties. One example is "Hansel and Gretel" (AT 327), which, among other things, is a story about conflicting family loyalties expressed in terms of sharing and hoarding food. Florencia Herrero and Julio Lopez Curiel, both of Garganta, told very similar variants of this tale that illustrate the contrasting views of a man and a woman about achieving a harmonious balance in family relationships. The Garganta stories (listed in the Appendix)[4] begin with a presumed or specified state of family bliss because there is a natural and nurturing mother. Events that follow illustrate how family harmony breaks down when the natural mother dies and is replaced by a stepmother who insists that the father abandon his children in the forest. The children return home several times by following a trail of food, but eventually they become hopelessly lost and end up in the house of a cannibalistic witch bent on eating them. The little girl once again saves her brother, setting the stage for the restitution of the broken family relationships. Julio and Florencia, however, bring their tales to very different conclusions, expressing their contrasting views on the ability to harmoniously blend loyalties in a family. Julio's ending is skeptical about the possibility of combining filial and conjugal loyalties: he describes the father killing the stepmother after the children return home. Julio includes the brutal detail of the father slapping the head of his dead wife three times before going to bed and three times before getting up in the morning to punish her for demanding that he abandon his children in the forest. Florencia, by contrast, draws her tale to a conclusion with the idea that one can combine loyalties to a spouse and to children. She tells how the father finds his children in the old woman's house and brings them home, where the stepmother loves them as if she were their natural mother now that the difficulties of food scarcity are overcome. Women from other Cáceres villages told variants that conclude on the same hopeful note (their stories are listed in the Appendix). The greater faith of women in the successful resolution of conflicting family loyalties is an essential part of a woman's power to restore broken family ties. That power undoubtedly derives from the position of women in a family in which feminine filial as well as conjugal loyalties remain strong throughout the life course.

# CHAPTER TEN

# A Cross-Cultural Perspective

LONG COURTSHIPS, the creation of an illusion of romantic love, and dialogue through storytelling help to mediate sharp gender differences and fear between Cáceres men and women. Through the telling and retelling of similar stories, men and women tell each other how courtship and marriage can work and they affirm their strong, mutually held faith in the marital bond and the power of a woman's love to heal broken family relationships. The tellers of tales in rural Cáceres express their faith in conjugal love by concluding their stories with married couples living happily ever after. The faith in conjugal love held by the women and men of the Cáceres villages is not universally shared by all people in the Hispanic world. I now turn to other models of marriage and family relations presented through storytelling to place the Cáceres model in a broader cross-cultural perspective.

The Spaniards who colonized the New World told many of their tales of courtship and marriage to American Indians, who adapted the stories to their own oral tradition and changed the plots through retelling according to their own experiences.[1] The Indians broke some of the tales apart and recombined them with stories of non-European origin to create entirely new narratives. Many tales of Spanish origin, however, survive relatively intact in American Indian societies. Comparisons of Spanish and Hispanic-American stories can illustrate important differences in conceptions of the family, gender relations, courtship, and marriage in the two cultures.

American Indians who have experienced Spanish domination vary widely, and many could serve equally well to place the Cáceres model of gender relations in a broader cross-cultural perspective. I shall focus for comparative purposes on the Nahuat of Mexico because I carried out fieldwork in their culture over a ten-year period from 1968 to 1978 in the villages of Huitzilan de Serdán and Santiago Yaonáhuac.[2] The Nahuat are suitable for comparison to the Cáceres villagers because they tell many stories of Spanish origin modified according to a different marriage and family structure (Taggart 1983). Nahuat storytellers told seven different tales cognate with the stories of enchantment that were the focus of earlier chapters in this book; the tales are "Cinderella" (AT 510B), "Cupid and Psyche" (AT 425), "Blancaflor" (AT 313), "The Grateful Animals" (AT 302 and 554) combined with "The Dragon Slayer" (AT

300), "The Fisherman" (AT 303), "The Wager on the Wife's Chastity" (AT 882), and "Hansel and Gretel" (AT 327) also sometimes combined with "The Dragon Slayer" (AT 300).[3] Many of these stories are very popular throughout Mexico (Robe 1973) and have become incorporated into the oral tradition of other indigenous-language-speaking groups in Mexico (Radin 1944; Foster 1945a; Gossen 1974; Laughlin 1962, 1977; Burns 1983). I collected all the tales in Nahuat, which indicates that the stories have circulated in the indigenous oral tradition for a number of generations.

The Nahuat are an interesting case for comparative purposes because their configuration of family loyalties contrasts dramatically with that of the Spaniards in northern Extremadura. Men and women socialized in the Nahuat family develop a model of family relations that stresses the filial loyalties of men, takes the separation of a mother and daughter as an unpleasant fact of life, and anticipates a relatively weak conjugal bond particularly during the first years of a marriage. Nahuat narrators changed many stories of Spanish origin to express their model of family relations, emphasizing how women have weak or ambivalent loyalties to their parents and giving voice to men's fear that the women they love will betray them. Relative to the Spanish stories of courtship and marriage, Nahuat storytellers show relatively little faith in the power of a woman's love.

Nahuat men and women, like their counterparts in northern Extremadura, are socialized under different, gender-based social pressures, which create distance and suspicion in their relationship. The genders have a sharply defined division of labor, women keep strictly apart from men in public, and men deeply fear losing the sexual fidelity of their women. Romantic love and long courtships undoubtedly help many Nahuat couples overcome some of their fears of each other and make the transition to married life. Love (*tahsotalis*) is a very important consideration for choosing a marital partner, and an adolescent boy (*telpuč*) and girl (*ičpuč*) have many opportunities to meet and explore their feelings for each other when the girl goes to fetch water or makes trips to the village market. A boy normally declares his love to a girl and then conveys to his parents his wish to initiate a courtship. The details of courtship vary between Huitzilan and Yaonáhuac, but parents traditionally select an elderly and respected woman as a petitioner (*siwatanke*) to convey their son's wishes to the girl's father. The petitioner may make two or three trips before receiving a positive reply because the girl's father and mother want to consider the suitability of the request. They consult with their daughter about her wishes, they consider if the boy is a hard worker and will be a good provider, and they think about the reputation of his family. If they give their consent to the marriage, the boy and his family traditionally prepare for the betrothal ceremony, at which they will deliver a gift to the girl's parents to seal the agreement between the two families. The bridal gift in Huitzilan, where traditional betrothals were more common than in Yaonáhuac when I carried out my fieldwork, normally consists of one or two turkeys, a leg of pork, cigarettes and tobacco, aguardiente (rum), spices, and some cash. The Huitzilan betrothal ceremony is particularly dramatic and includes play-acted anger of the mother directed to the boy's family for taking her daughter and a moving ceremony in which the petitioner instructs the shy boy and girl to stand in front of the altar, exchange necklaces with gold crosses, and embrace while she surrounds the couple with a sacred web of incense.[4] Huitzilan couples normally begin living as husband and wife in the house of the boy's parents sometime after the betrothal ceremony, then marry in the church and hold a second celebration in honor of the godparents chosen for the sacrament of marriage. Couples in Santiago Yaonáhuac more frequently begin married life in the house of the groom's parents without a betrothal and they postpone their church marriage longer than their counterparts in Huitzilan de Serdán. Nevertheless, gender differences and the fears that come with such differences are not really worked out during courtship in either village. Few couples get to know each other well because adolescent boys and especially girls have little chance to spend much time together alone. Moreover, girls in both villages become wives right after puberty and before they have had time to individuate fully from their parents. In general, Nahuat girls marry at about the age of fourteen, whereas their Spanish counterparts from Cáceres marry at least four to five years later.

The sharp gender segregation and the overtly male-centered nature of Nahuat society are not conducive to developing a storytelling dialogue through which men and women might work through some of their differences. Reconstruction of the storytelling dialogue between women and men is difficult for the Nahuat because women generally do not feel comfortable telling stories in public and in the presence of men. Storytelling situations in the Nahuat communities resemble those in the villages of Cáceres: men tell stories at wakes, they may tell tales while drinking with their companions in bars, they frequently tell folktales while working in sugarcane processing groups, and men who migrate to the coastal plantations tell stories while relaxing in the evening. The gender patterns of storytelling may vary for different ethnic groups within Mexico. Laughlin (1962, 1977) found a similar pattern of male but not female public storytelling in a Mayan-speaking village that has a social structure similar to that of the Nahuat.[5] Spanish-speaking women in other parts of Mexico, however, seem more inclined to tell tales in public than their Nahuat and Mayan sisters (see Parsons 1932; Robe 1970; Paredes 1970).

A more private storytelling dialogue probably takes place between men and women in Nahuat villages because the few female storytellers I knew told tales that closely resemble the stories told by men. Moreover, male storytellers from other similar indigenous-language-speaking communities in Mexico report learning as many stories from their mother as from their father (Laughlin 1977: 5). The comparative absence of Nahuat women willing to tell tales in public and in the presence of men is probably symptomatic of the relatively weak role that women play in the public cultural construction of reality in their society. Nahuat women do not simply accept the cultural reality as constructed by men, and they have their own ways of creating a different reality through symbols. Their more muted public role in storytelling, however, accords with their publicly more subordinate position in gender relations in this part of Mexico. The Nahuat pattern of gender relations is related directly to a different model of marriage in which men express little faith in the strength of the marital bond.

## "CINDERELLA"

Because most of the Nahuat storytellers are men, their tales do not reveal the entire configuration of the male-female dialogue through which men and women might work out some of their differences. Comparison, however, of the masculine variants of similar stories from the Nahuat and Cáceres narrators can reveal how some aspects of that dialogue probably differ. Fernando Vega from Santiago Yaonáhuac told a variant of "Cinderella" (AT 510B) that expresses many themes that run through several stories told by men in Nahuat culture. Fernando was a married man of fifty when I collected his story, and he along with his brother are directors of traditional dance groups that perform at fiestas in Yaonáhuac and neighboring villages.[6] Many of the tales in Fernando's repertoire are of obvious Spanish origin, and the initial episodes of his "Cinderella," which begins with a father who proposes marriage to his daughter, have much in common with variants of the same story collected in Spain (A. Espinosa 1924: 204–209), Cuba, Puerto Rico, the Dominican Republic (Hansen 1957: 62–63), the Hispanic Southwest of the United States (Robe 1973: 89), and among Spanish-speaking communities in Mexico (Wheeler 1943: 100–103, 104–115). The first half of Fernando's tale resembles stories collected by Juán B. Real in the American Southwest (Real 1957: 1: 240–242) and by Howard T. Wheeler among Mexican Spanish speakers in Jalisco (Wheeler 1943: 114–115). They tell how the heroine escapes her father's marriage proposal by turning into a donkey, flees from the father, and finds shelter in the home of a king or rich man whose son falls in love with her when he sees her in human form. Although many of the "Cinderella" stories of this type conclude with the heroine marrying and living happily ever after, Fernando's tale ends in tragedy when the heroine parts company with the man who loves her. In this respect, Fernando's story concludes like the masculine tale of "Cinderella" told by Leandro Jimenez of El Guijo de Santa Bárbara in Chapter 6; there he describes how the prince came home from war to find that the woman he loved had perished when thrown off the balcony of the castle. Fernando's and Leandro's tragic endings express the idea that romantic love for a man can end suddenly, tragically, and forever. Fernando, however, gives his ending a particular Nahuat twist that accords with the very strong filial loyalties of men in his culture. He continues his story with an episode describing how Cinderella's son reestablishes his rightful place at the side of his father, much as Nahuat sons should remain close to their fathers according to the ideals imparted in the patrilineal extended family.

"THE LITTLE DONKEY MOTHER," BY FERNANDO VEGA[7]

Once there was a man who was a widower. He was not very old, about forty more or less. He had a daughter, and she was about fifteen. Her father decided to marry his daughter because he did not have a wife. But his daughter thought it was not a good thing to marry her father. She had heard the priest deliver a sermon in church saying it was a sin for a girl to marry her father. But her father was stubborn in wanting to marry his own child. The girl did not have a mother and so she decided to ask an old woman for advice. She went to the old woman's house and said, "I need you to give me some advice. My father wants me to sit with him [a euphemism for sex] and marry him. I can't marry him because he is my father. He kept me clean when I was small, and he and my mother fed me and reared me. For these reasons it would be a sin for me to sit with my father." The old woman replied, "Don't, little mother, because it *is* a big sin to sit with your father. Be patient for now. Go home and tell your father that you will not sit with him because you would be committing a big sin in the eyes of God, a great big sin. If your father still insists that you sit with him, then you come to me for more advice." The girl went back home. But her father said again, "I won't look for a wife because I decided to sit with my daughter." So the girl went once more, after four or five days, to the house of that little mother of ours and asked for more advice. She said, "Little mother, I've come because I want to ask you another question. My father still wants me to sit with him. Tell me if that is good or bad." The little old woman said, "It is not good. It is bad for you to sit with your father because he is your father. You told him that you could not sit with him. If your father still decides that you should sit with him, then you tell him that you'll do it only if he obtains three dresses for you: one of the sun, the other of the moon, and a dress of the stars. And if he does happen to get them, you still won't sit with him. He won't find them here in the plaza or in a store. But if he does find them, then you tell him that you will sit with him." The girl understood. She returned home and said once more, "Father, I cannot sit with you because it is a sin. But if you obtain for me the dress of the sun, the dress of the moon, and the dress of the stars, then I probably will sit with you." Her father went crazy with emotion because his daughter gave him her word that she would sit with him. He went crazy with emotion as he searched for the three dresses. He probably met the devil, who obtained the dresses, and the father returned saying, "Daughter of my soul, I've obtained the three dresses for you." "Good, father, you have met my condition."

The girl went once more to the house of that mother of ours, that little old woman, and said, "I've come our little mother. I've come, because my father obtained those three dresses. What am I going to do?" The old woman replied, "Well, daughter, tell your father yes. He brought the dresses, the dresses of three colors, and so you sit with him. But when you go to the church to marry him, you won't be alone. I will take the place of your mother because you don't have one, and you don't have an aunt. You go with me to the church. Let's see when he wants the marriage to take place. You go marry your father. But you go with me as your witness," she said to the girl. They agreed.

There used to be women who were like wise persons. She, who accompanied the girl to the church was a wise person. Then, at the moment the marriage was to take place and the priest was giving his blessing as the father knelt at the altar with his daughter, at that moment the old woman turned the girl into an animal, a she-donkey. The priest said that the girl had turned into an animal because she probably had sinned with her father. The priest did not bless the father with his daughter because she had become a pack animal. The old woman took the girl outside, and the daughter separated from her father because she had become a pack animal. Her father went one way, and the girl went another way with that little mother of ours. The girl was ashamed. Then our mother said to her, "You don't see your father now. It's better if you go with me." The girl understood and went with our little mother in another direction.

They took a different road. That girl was a she-donkey, a Christian converted into an animal. They came to a house, and our little mother asked for lodging. It was dark. She asked, "Won't you give me permission to stay here? I have a she-donkey. Let my she-donkey stay here." The owner of the house replied, "She can't stay inside. You stay inside, but your she-donkey cannot because she will soil the inside of the house. It's better for her to stay outside. I have some horses over there. Take her there to be with my pack animals. I'll feed her some grass. She can stay and have supper with the pack animals." "No," protested our little mother. "It would be better for me to sleep outside with her. Let me pay whatever you want for a room so she'll stay inside the house. I'll stay outside as if I were a pack animal. Let her stay in a safe place inside the house. She won't eat corn, she won't eat grass, she won't eat fodder, she doesn't eat any stubble. She will only eat tortillas. Give her tortillas, a meal for humans. She'll finish it and wash the plate." It couldn't be true that a pack animal would eat tortillas, a human meal, and wash the plate before she returned it. There must have been two kinds of animals. So that the owner of the house would know what kind of animal she was, that little mother of ours took the she-donkey in through the kitchen and left her in a room. It was a very clean room without a single dirty thing. Then our little mother prepared a good supper to feed the she-donkey inside the room. Then one of the children of that man, who was rich, secretly opened the door. He saw her eating, but she was not a she-donkey, she was a maiden, a beautiful girl! She was not a she-donkey; she was a Christian! She cleaned herself after eating, she washed the plate and returned it. But when she brought the plate, she was a she-donkey. Someone in the house exclaimed, "We gave dinner to a pack animal who is a Christian! The plate is clean! Dear me! She returned it all clean. Perhaps she licked it with her tongue or who knows what." The girl stayed in the room, where she rested. The next day, the owner's son liked the girl's face and wanted to persuade her to stay. He wanted her to stay not for his parents but for himself. But that little mother of ours said, "You cannot have her because I am taking her to another town. We have a trip to make, and you can't stay with her." But the owner of the house was very rich and convinced the girl to stay as a daughter-in-law. But the girl took the money and then tricked the son. They slept together two or three nights, and she left him after the third. She went where she had planned to go.

That girl, that trickster, after eight or nine months had a child. Her child was born in another house, and she gave him away because she didn't want to be ashamed. She wanted to continue as a maiden. She gave her child away in another place, and the child awoke. The child was born with the same face as his father. Everything from his eyes to his nose was identical to his father. The girl went her own way, and as she left she gave her son a gold ring. The ring had the name of the place where she had been with her child's father. The ring had the name of the boy who wanted to marry her. He had given it to her as a remembrance.

The child grew and grew and was eight years old, then ten, then twelve. And he asked, "Who is my father? I want to know who my father is." "We don't know," everyone said to him. But he had the gold ring with the name, and he went looking with that name for his birthplace. He went asking who his father was and where his father lived. And as he got closer and closer, little by little, to where his father was, he met a black boy who asked, "Where are you going?" "I'm looking for my father." The black boy asked, "Who is your father?" The white one replied, "I don't know who he is. I have only this ring with the name of my father. I'll know who he is with this ring." Then the black boy took the ring from the white boy, and the white boy was lost. The black boy went directly to where the white boy was headed. He went to present himself with the ring to the white boy's father. The black boy took the ring from the white boy because he was envious and so he could introduce himself as the son of the white boy's father. "Why do you come, son?" the father asked the black boy.

"Well, father, I am your son," replied the black boy. "Why are you my son?" The father looked at his own face in the mirror and then looked at the face of his "son." The boy was black, and the father was white, and so the boy couldn't be his son. "I don't think you are my son," said the father. "I am your son because I bring this ring, this remembrance from when you tricked my mother. You tricked her, and then she went on an errand. You gave this ring to my mother. My mother gave it to me when I was small, and I have come looking for you with the name on the ring. You live here, you are my father, and I am your son." The father had married another woman and said to her, "Let's see. My lady, give something to eat to this boy because he is my child. I did not think that woman would have any children, but she had one. But this child came out quite black. I wonder why."

The white boy went on and on and on. He complained as he went: "I came asking who my father is. I brought a gold ring with two letters. But as I came walking along the road, I met a black boy who was about the same age. And this black boy was very strong. He asked me where I was going, and after asking this question he took the ring off of my finger. He took the ring from me and fled. I did not follow him because, as I said, he was strong. I thought it would be better to let him have the ring so he would not hit me." The white boy thought it would be better to find out where the black boy went. "The boy introduced himself to my father with that ring. But he wasn't anything to my father. He just had the ring. It was I who was someone to him. So I kept looking for my father and I came to a strange house. 'Let me stay here and I'll leave tomorrow.' The owner of the house asked, 'Where are you going, son?' 'Sir, I am on a mission. Some time ago my mother—I don't know where she is now—gave birth to me in such and such a place. I come from where my mother gave me away and where I grew up. I grew and grew and I had a ring that my mother gave me. But this black boy took it from me when I walked along the road, and I am now in the dark. I was coming with this gold ring that was my guide to finding my father.' 'Well son, you stay here if you want and go on your way tomorrow.' "

That little man, the "father" of the black boy, told his wife, "Give tortillas to this boy." And then he said to the white boy, "We do this even though you won't pay us for them. Some day you will pay us." Then he said to his wife, "But right now we'll give a bit of food to this boy."

"So then the head of the house sat down with the black boy to his right, and I sitting to his left. I didn't know he was my father. He starting looking into the mirror. There was a big mirror where we were eating. I, the head of the house, and the black boy were there eating. My father looked at his face in the mirror and saw it was white. I am also white, and he saw the face of the black boy. The black boy's face did not look like my father's. I do have the same face as him. I didn't know that he was my father because I didn't know who lived in the house I had come to. It seemed as if he were not my father. Then he asked me, 'Where are you going?' 'Well I come looking for directions. I didn't know where I was until I found myself here. I am grateful to you for giving me this bit of food. May God give you strength so that you are not left with less because of this honored tortilla, this little bit of coffee. I am happy with it.' The head of the house questioned me further because he knew I was his son. I was also asking questions because the black boy had taken my ring with the writing. 'So then this boy took the ring from me, and I don't know where he went!' We finished supper and my father went into the kitchen and spoke to his wife. He said, 'María, things are not right.' 'Why?' the lady asked. 'Because the black boy who came with my ring is not my child. My child is the white boy. The black boy took the ring from him and said he is my child. You'll see what is going to happen because the boy is going to talk. I don't know if I'll make him talk by using a pistol or a carbine.' "

He took the ring from the black boy and showed it to the white boy. "Is this the ring you were bringing?" "That is the exact same ring I was bringing. He took if from me. I am your child. He is not your child." The father said, "The black boy does not know that I know who is my child." He took the black boy out of the house and said, "Go get the donkey and fetch a load of wood for tomorrow or the next day, when I'll hold a celebration. I'm going to give a banquet, a *mole* dinner[8] and invite some compadres. The wood will be needed to boil the meat and prepare the tortillas. So take the donkey and bring me thirty-five or forty cords of wood for the next five days." And the father really did hold a celebration. The little boy started bringing the loads of wood. Day after day he brought loads of wood with the donkey. He piled up twenty cords of wood. Then the father poured gasoline or kerosene on the wood and set it on fire. A huge blaze rose. So then he said, "Let's see, little black boy. If you really are my child, you will pass four times from here to the other side through the middle of the fire. If you can make four trips, then you are my child. If you don't, then you are not." But the black boy did not reach the other side because it was thirty meters across twenty cords of wood. The father told the black boy to jump so he would burn in the fire and come to his end. There the black boy died, and the white one stayed with his father. That is the story of the donkey mother.

Fernando related this story of "Cinderella" in a way that fits a masculine view of gender relations and the position of women and men in Nahuat society. He reduced the role of women as actors in the plot concordant to the more male-centered worldview of men, he described the heroine betraying the man who loves her in accord with Nahuat men's relatively weak faith in conjugal love; and he added final episodes that emphasize the filial loyalties of men who are part of the Nahuat patrilineal extended family. The features of Fernando's tale that fit the Nahuat family experience become particularly apparent if one compares his story with other variants of the same tale circulating in Mexican and Spanish oral tradition.

Fernando has reduced the role of women as prominent actors in the plot of his tale by removing the mention in the first episode of Cinderella's mother, who sets the stage for the father's incestuous marriage proposal. The heroine's dying mother tells her husband to marry someone who either looks like her or who can wear her wedding ring, and her wish ironically leads the father to ask his daughter to marry him in the Cáceres tales by Maximina Castaño and Leandro Jimenez (see Chapter 6) and the Mexican stories collected among Spanish speakers in Jalisco (Wheeler 1943: 100–103, 104–115). Fernando's shift in focus on male actors accords with a more sharply gender-segregated society likely to give rise to more separate male- and female-centered worldviews. Gender segregation most assuredly exists in village Spain and Spanish-speaking Mexico, but the Nahuat maintain a sharper and more rigid separation of the sexes in the organization of work and in public life. Nahuat husbands and wives, relative to their counterparts in northern Extremadura, spend much less time working together and performing complementary tasks in agriculture. Planting is entirely a male activity among the Nahuat, whereas both men and women work together planting fields in the villages of northern Extremadura. Spanish women, much more than their Nahuat sisters, will hoe and irrigate fields alongside men, and whereas Nahuat women help with the harvest of corn and coffee, their Spanish counterparts play a greater role by helping men collect wheat, olives, cherries, raspberries, paprika, cotton, and tobacco. Nahuat women apparently help men in agricultural labor less because they traditionally perform the domicile-based tasks of arduously grinding boiled corn into tortilla dough and weaving cloth, tasks that require huge expenditures of time. Greater Nahuat gender segregation is apparent in public life when women sit totally apart from men in family life crises ceremonies, including betrothals, marriages, baptisms, wakes, and family festivals held to celebrate the creation of a new ritual kinship relationship. One finds women clustering together around the hearth while men occupy the rest of the house sharing shot glasses of aguardiente, smoking cigarettes, and eating dishes of meat in ceremonial *mole* served with hot tortillas fresh from the women's grinding stones (*metates*) and griddles (*comales*). If, at a wake, a storyteller spins a tale, the teller is most likely a man narrating to other men or children. He may be within earshot of the women clustered around the hearth, but they will not be the main members of his audience. Similar patterns of separating women from men are evident on all other public occasions including celebrations held by ritual sponsors (*mayordomos*) in honor of household or community saints. The sharp separation of the genders undoubtedly contributes to more male- and female-centered rather than gender-integrated views of social relations depicted in stories. Fernando's elimination of the mother as the prime mover in the first episode of the plot is one example of seeing social situations from a male-centered perspective.

The heroine's efforts to flee from her father by consulting with an old woman, the request for three dresses, the heroine's metamorphosis into a donkey to escape from committing the sin of incest, and her arrival at the house of a rich man are features found in many versions of this tale in Spanish America (see Robe 1973: 89). Fernando's account of the heroine betraying the man who loves her, however, does not appear in any variant I know of that folklorists have found in Spain or Spanish-speaking groups in Mexico. Fernando tells how the heroine took the rich man's money, slept with his son for two or three nights, and then "left him after the third." She not only betrays her lover, but she also betrays her own son, to whom she gives birth eight or nine months later and whom she then gives away so she might appear to be a maiden.

Cáceres men, of course, sometimes tell tales with tragic endings to express metaphorically their brittle conception of romantic love. Leandro Jimenez of El Guijo de Santa Bárbara concluded his version of "Cinderella" with the death of the heroine, but he included no hint of the heroine's betrayal of the man who loved her. Moreover, not all Cáceres men present as pessimistic a scenario in their renditions of this tale. Leandro's variant closely resembles another masculine version from southern Cáceres (Curiel Merchán 1944: 321–323) that likewise describes servants accidentally throwing Cinderella out of the window because they believe she might be a thief. But the southern Cáceres narrator concluded his tale with a happy ending, illustrating how some men weave a more optimistic scenario than Leandro in their versions of the same story. The heroine in the southern Cáceres tale remains true to her prince, bears his sons, and reunites with her lover when she presents him his child in a basket of flowers.

Nahuat men change other stories of Spanish origin by describing how women betray the men who love them. They told "Blancaflor" (AT 313), a story about the power of a woman's love for a man, and one narrator from Yaonáhuac concluded his story by telling how the heroine betrays her lover by delivering him to her father, who is the devil![9] Nahuat narrators weave episodes of feminine betrayal into their accounts of the story of "Adam and Eve," and one changed the first episode of "The Fisherman" (AT 303) by describing the fisherman's wife bringing about the death of all of the fish by her adultery.[10]

Moreover, the Nahuat storytellers tell tales that resemble those told by men in other indigenous language groups in Mexico with a similar marriage and family structure. Robert Laughlin (1962) and Jane Collier

(1968, 1973: 180–217) have made a fascinating study of courtship and marriage and their reflection in folktales (Laughlin 1962) among Mayan speakers in Zinacantán, a *municipio* in the highlands of Chiapas. The Maya, like the Nahuat, negotiate their marriages through an elaborate coutrship process that involves the delivery of a bridal gift. Mayan brides, like their Nahuat sisters, usually begin their marriage living with their husband, who have strong filial loyalties and remain attached to their patrilineally extended family (Vogt 1969: 127-140). Laughlin (1962) found many storytellers, most men, who told a number of folktales of Spanish origin dealing with courtship and marriage. The men of Zinacantán, like their Nahuat brothers, told stories expressing relatively little faith in the conjugal bond, particularly for the early marital years. They told of heroes who lost their wife, sometimes to another man with whom the wife had been unfaithful (1962: 221, 228–231).

Nahuat men, to be sure, like their counterparts in Spain, tell "Lost Husband" tales (AT 425)[11] and "Blancaflor," describing how women restore broken marital ties and thus expressing how men in both cultures recognize that woman can heal social wounds. But Nahuat men of Huitzilan and Yaonáhuac[12] as well as Mayan men of Zinacantán (Laughlin 1962: 228–231) also tell "Lost Wife" (AT 400) tales that describe men who lose and then struggle arduously to find their mates. "Lost Wife" tales undoubtedly express Mayan and Nahuat men's anxiety about losing the nurturance of women on whom they heavily depend, and they capture the actual experiences of many young husbands whose wives have returned to their parents after a family quarrel. The early marital tie is brittle in both the Nahuat and the Mayan communities because girls are betrothed and marry very young and must adapt to a difficult family situation in which they work under the authority of a critical mother-in-law. Unlike her sisters in northern Cáceres, the Nahuat and the Mayan bride usually resides patrilocally, where she may conflict with her mother-in-law over her husband's loyalties. A young bride frequently runs home to her parents if she becomes ill, if her parents suspect her husband's family of witchcraft, if her husband rebukes or mistreats her, if her husband is unfaithful, or if she lacks food (see Laughlin 1962: 108; J. Collier 1973: 180–195). Nahuat and Mayan men need their wife—they rely on her for nurturance, agonize over the conflict in their loyalties to their mother and to their wife, and mourn the temporary loss of a bride who runs home to her parents. No wonder they tell "Lost Wife" tales in an effort to make sense of the difficult experiences of early marital adjustment.

Although men rely heavily on the nurturance of women in both cultures, no Cáceres narrator told a similar "Lost Wife" tale in which the hero undergoes an arduous search to find his lost mate. Moreover, "Lost Wife" tales are rare in Spanish oral tradition, perhaps because men generally have greater faith in the conjugal bond and the power of a woman's love for a man. I suspect that their greater faith stems from a different marriage and family structure in which women marry later and thus have more independent habits. Moreover, they more frequently begin their early marital years in an independent household (see Table 2) and consequently do not have to work under the critical eye of a mother-in-law.

Fernando's tale concludes with a particularly strong expression of the importance of filial loyalty to a Nahuat man. The last episodes of his tale describe the struggle of the heroine's son to find his father and gain his rightful position in his family. The boy uses a ring, which his father originally gave to his mother as a token of his love and his mother gave to her infant son just prior to abandoning him, in order to find his father. A ring appears in many versions of the "Cinderella" story from Spain and the Americas, including a variant of Cinderella and her jealous stepsisters told by a Mayan Indian woman from Zinacantan (Laughlin 1977: 204–212). The ring in many of the feminine Spanish variants is a device by means of which Cinderella gets her man to recognize her in other than beautiful form. In Fernando's story, however, the ring is a badge of a son's identity and is used by a usurper to claim falsely the position of son in

TABLE 2
Postmarital Residence of Married Couples in Garganta and Yaonáhuac

| | *Garganta* | | *Yaonáhuac* | |
|---|---|---|---|---|
| *Matrilocals* | *no.* | *%* | *no.* | *%* |
| Couples living with wife's parent(s) | 22 | | 12 | |
| Couples living in a house owned by wife's parent(s) | 6 | | 10 | |
| SUBTOTALS[a] | 28 | 70.0 | 22 | 22.0 |
| | *Garganta* | | *Yaonáhuac* | |
| *Patrilocals* | *no.* | *%* | *no.* | *%* |
| Couples living with husband's parent(s) | 7 | | 59 | |
| Couples living in a house owned by husband's parent(s) | 5 | | 19 | |
| SUBTOTAL[a] | 12 | 30.0 | 78 | 78.0 |
| TOTAL | 40 | 100.0 | 100 | 100.0 |

[a] Chi square for subtotals = 26.619 with 1 df, p < .001.

another man's family. By his narrative style, Fernando gives particular emphasis to the importance of the theme of a son's rightful place alongside his father. He changes from speaking in the voice of the narrator to that of the son who struggles to find and regain his position next to his father. Speaking in the voice of the struggling son expresses the degree to which a Nahuat man identifies with the importance of reestablishing a broken patrilineal tie.

The contrasting configurations of filial loyalties in the Cáceres and Nahuat villages are related to differences in family structure. The weak filial ties of men depicted in the Spanish stories accord with patterns of postmarital residence observed in Garganta la Olla that can be generalized to other communities in Cáceres. Although most couples reside neolocally in Garganta, some live with or in houses owned by one or both parents of the husband or wife. More Garganta couples reside with or in houses owned by the mother or father of the wife because men prefer to be independent of their father, and women prefer to remain close to their mother. For the Nahuat, who depict strong filial loyalties for men, the pattern is just the opposite. Far more couples in Huitzilan and Yaonáhuac live with or in houses of the husband's parents (see Table 2). Nahuat parents expect their sons to reside in the same or in neighboring dwellings after marriage because they value highly the labor of their grown sons, who contribute substantially to the economy of the household. Parents maintain close ties with their sons by inculcating the value of filial piety and promises of land inheritance. Nahuat parents act on their promises by bequeathing the bulk of their land to their sons, who are obedient to parental wishes. Parents also threaten to disinherit sons who show too much independence, and their expressions of favoritism toward their more obedient sons could be one source of the conflict between the black boy and the white boy in Fernando's story. The two boys could represent brothers who are rivals for their father's approval.

The Nahuat, however, generally idealize the loyalties among all closely related patrilineal men, particularly brothers, in their retelling of other stories of Spanish origin. Fernando Vega, for example, retold the first episode of "The Wager on the Wife's Chastity" (AT 882) by describing how two men who love each other as brothers create an extended family compound like many of those found in Huitzilan and Yaonáhuac. The men build the houses for their wives right next to each other, since Nahuat brothers are supposed to reside in contiguous dwellings. The story emphasizes how the selfish desires of one man lead to the disintegration of a familylike group based on male solidarity. Other Nahuat storytellers told variants of "The Fisherman" (AT 303) that likewise stress male sibling solidarity more than the Spanish versions of the same story. Fratricide occurs in a number of stories collected in the villages of Cáceres when the youngest brother reveals to his older brother that he has slept with the older brother's wife (see the versions by Bernardo Ramos, Miguel Chorro Hernández, Julio Lopez Curiel, and Julia Lobato Gil). No brother in any of the Nahuat versions, however, kills his brother for sleeping with his wife even when the brother fails to guard the woman's marital chastity by neglecting to place his sword on the bed.[13]

Male sibling solidarity, like filial piety, also undoubtedly appears in the Nahuat stories as a functional part of the patrilineally extended family. Accounts of family histories contain many expressions of concern about the conduct of male siblings on whom the unity of the extended family depends during the latter stages of the household developmental cycle. Widowed Nahuat mothers work hard to maintain family unity by holding their married sons together in a common household that functions as a unit of agricultural production. Widowed mothers attempt to hold their sons together by inculcating the value of sibling solidarity in conjunction with filial piety and managing family resources with equity to reduce rivalry. While men rival one another for women in Nahuat villages, the observance of strict avoidance rules and respectful behavior generally prevents male sexual rivalry from developing within the extended family. The weaker stress on the solidarity of male siblings in the parallel versions of the stories from Cáceres is part of a family system in which married sons are relatively but not absolutely more independent from their parents and, therefore, their siblings. Parents do not expect all their sons to reside in the same household or contribute to the household economy to the same degree in northern Extremadura. To be sure, many men in the Cáceres villages worked for their father as young unmarried men and they sharecrop their father's land after marriage. Cáceres parents, however, do not expect lifetime support from their sons and they rarely threaten to disinherit sons who cease to work on the patrimonial land.

### Other Differences in the Models of Family Relations

A comparison of other parallel stories reveals additional, related differences in models of family relations concordant with the relatively strong filial loyalties of mothers and daughters in Spain and fathers and sons in the Nahuat communities in Mexico. To some degree, feminine characters in tales from both cultures have complex, ambivalent relationships with their parental family. The women in masculine stories from Cáceres, however, have stronger loyalties to parents and brothers than do their counterparts in Nahuat stories, much as Spanish women from northern Extremadura actually remain closer to their parental family long after marriage. As mentioned, more couples in Garganta la Olla reside uxorilocally than virilocally. Moreover, women are not alienated by being cut out of the inheritance of family property. The inheritance of land in houses in the Cáceres villages, as in other parts of Spain (Pitt-Rivers 1966:103–104; Freeman 1970: 67–72; Brandes 1975: 120–123; Behar 1986: 68–88), is bilateral. Archival data on land transfers for Garganta la Olla contain an almost equal number of women and men who inherited land from their parents (see Table 3).

To be sure, some heroines in Cáceres and Nahuat stories are willing to turn against their parents and go with their husband when they face stiff parental opposition to their marriage. Blancaflor uses all of her magical power to help her husband complete impossible tasks and flee from her parents in the Cáceres and Nahuat versions of the tale. The contrasting masculine images of women's filial and fraternal loyalties, however, become apparent in a comparison of masculine variants of "The Grateful Animals" (AT 302 and 554) and "Hansel and Gretel" (AT 327), where one finds that heroines in the Spanish stories but not in the Nahuat ones remain loyal to parents and brothers.[14] The Nahuat daughter betrays her parents by committing parricide in "The Four Grateful Animals" (AT 302 and 554); she conspires with her chosen husband to blow up her father and mother on the way to the altar to marry a man preferred by her parents. The sister in the Nahuat "Hansel and Gretel" betrays her brother by offering him to the devil, who comes to eat her while her brother is up in a tree looking for a way out of the forest.[15]

The Nahuat images of young women as betrayers of parents and brothers may stem from the actual marginal position of women in their natal families because of patrilocality and patrilineality. It is interesting that sisters separate from their brothers in several versions of "Hansel and Gretel," much as patrilocality in the Nahuat villages actually scatters women and attenuates their connections with their male siblings and par-

TABLE 3
Land Inheritance in Garganta and Yaonáhuac

|  | Garganta | | Yaonáhuac | |
|  | no. | % | no. | % |
| --- | --- | --- | --- | --- |
| Women who acquired land | 69 | 48.9 | 141 | 34.1 |
| Men who acquired land | 72 | 51.1 | 273 | 65.9 |
| TOTAL[a] | 141 | 100.0 | 414 | 100.0 |

Source: This table is based on records of land transfers contained in the Registro de la Propiedad in Jarandilla de la Vera (Spain) and the Recaudación de Rentas in Tlatlauqui (Mexico).

[a] Chi Square = 9.28 with 1 df, .01 > p > .001.

ents. Nahuat mothers make regular visits to their daughters, but women become increasingly distant from their brothers, particularly after the death of the mother. Nahuat parents alienate their daughters further by promising to bequeath most of their land to their sons and hold them in the patrilineal extended family. Widowed mothers generally carry out bequeathals in accord with the wishes her husband expresses prior to his death. Mothers occasionally give residual land to their daughters when there is an adequate supply, but many Nahuat communities, including Huitzilan, face a severe shortage of land, and thus land goes to sons only. According to family histories collected in Huitzilan and Yaonáhuac, women acquire from one-fifth (19.9 percent in Huitzilan) to a little more than one-third (37.4 percent in Yaonáhuac) of the inherited land. The family histories correlate very closely with archival data on land transfers.

The transformation in masculine Nahuat stories of feminine characters into women with ambivalent loyalties to their own family is possibly connected to the image of women as the betrayers of the men who love them. Nahuat men probably project onto images of women as wives some of the same ambivalent loyalties they depict for women as daughters, sisters, mothers. Men may also project onto women their own weak conjugal loyalties attenuated by the pull of their strong filial ties. A very high percentage of sons begin their marriage in their parents' household, where they bring their bride to work in the kitchen under the authority of their mother, who has taught her sons the value of filial piety. Sons' loyalties are caught between two women—their mother and their wife—in a situation wrought with conflict. Nahuat consider the relationship between mother-in-law and daughter-in-law one of intense rivalry, which has the potential of tearing the extended family apart. Many first marriages end in separation despite complex betrothals designed to build ties between intermarried families and to support the marital union.

Nahuat men's relatively weak faith in feminine filial and conjugal loyalties leads a number of male storytellers to rework folktales of Spanish origin into scenarios of complete family disintegration. Two men from Huitzilan de Serdán told versions of "Hansel and Gretel" that depict the collapse of the nuclear family to a degree not found in parallel masculine stories from Cáceres.[16] Their stories start off like the Cáceres tales, with a widower who remarries and betrays his children out of loyalty to his new wife. By the conclusion of the Nahuat stories, the girl and boy are separated from each other, and one of the two has perished. One tale is filled from start to finish with acts of betrayal ending with the tragedy of filicide. The story begins when the father betrays the natural mother by breaking the ideal of monogamy when he carries on with a "promiscuous woman" (*siwat awilnemi*). The Nahuat use the term *siwat awilnemi* as a synecdoche standing for many other negative behaviors in women, including greediness and sloth. After the death of the natural (and presumably nurturant) mother, the father takes up with the *siwat awilnemi*, who selfishly demands that he abandon his children in the forest. The children fall into the hands of a diabolical and cannibalistic blind old woman and a diabolical mestizo man who wants them for "seed" to produce other children he can eat. A second mestizo man seduces the girl with an apple, causing the separation of the brother and sister. The tale concludes when the father finds his son and kills him with witchcraft after the son refuses to give his father large sums of money. Nuclear family disintegration occurs in other Mexican variants of "Hansel and Gretel" (see Radin and Espinosa 1917: 204–205; Paredes 1970: 89–91), but Huitzilan narrators carry the process to an extreme.

The economic pressures on the Huitzilan Nahuat family partially account for why both versions of "Hansel and Gretel" from this community end with the destruction of the nuclear family. The family is under great stress because of landlessness, a widespread condition in many Mexican Indian groups and especially pronounced for this group relative to the Nahuat of Yaonáhuac, who do not describe the total disintegration of the nuclear family in the one version of the "Hansel and Gretel" story I collected from them. The Huitzilan Nahuat have lost the bulk of their land to a mestizo minority that moved into the area around the turn of the century and acquired land with the Colonization Laws of 1883 and 1894. Only 35 percent of the married couples among the Nahuat in Huitzilan own land, and many must support themselves by working for very low wages for mestizo patrons. In Yaonáhuac, 72 percent of the married couples own some land, and many support themselves on their own estates rather than work for the mestizos. Landlessness among the Huitzilan Nahuat puts severe strains on family loyalties, a situation narrators express in their versions of "Hansel and Gretel." Men have a very difficult time providing food for their wife and children when they lack land for cultivating crops. They fear that mestizos will use their greater wealth to seduce women, much as a mestizo man and a priest seduced the sisters in the masculine variants of this tale from Huitzilan. Landlessness contributes to tension between fathers and sons because it makes older fathers more dependent on the labor of their grown sons. The episode of filicide at the conclusion of one Huitzilan variant could easily be related to actual tension between fathers and sons stemming from landlessness in Huitzilan.

To be sure, masculine Spanish narrators from the seven Cáceres communities often depict an irreconcilable conflict in filial and conjugal loyalties in their versions of "Hansel and Gretel" and other tales with themes more directly related to courtship and marriage. Few masculine storytellers from Cáceres, however, ended their tales with the degree of family disintegration found in the Nahuat stories, particularly those from Huitzilan. The Cáceres narrators from Serradilla are members of a landless agrarian working class and have experienced tremendous hardship that has undoubtedly put severe strains on family relationships. Some Serradilla narrators volunteered the observation that times of food scarcity, particularly after the Spanish Civil War, created stress in families like that described in "Hansel and Gretel" stories. The Serradilla variants of tales cognate with those circulating in Huitzilan oral tradition, however, generally depict more family unity throughout the story plot.

I suspect that one key difference between the landless Nahuat and their counterparts in Cáceres is the position of women in the social and cultural system of which storytelling is a functional part. Spanish narrators—women as well as men—express a great deal of faith in the power of a woman's love to hold a family together. This faith is particularly apparent in such stories as animal-groom tales and "Blancaflor," which describe tremendous hardships for a couple, including a conflict in filial and conjugal loyalties, but conclude with a harmonious and relatively complete nuclear family in place. These tales, some of which come from Serradilla, are specific expressions of a general belief that women have the supernatural power to heal family relationships. I suspect that this belief and its expression in stories are connected to a social structure in which the genders have more equality in the control of important strategic resources, more interdependence, and women—particularly mothers and daughters—have lifelong ties that give them strength. Cáceres women inherit land as often as men and thus have considerable control over the most important productive resource in the rural villages in this part of Spain. Their Nahuat sisters inherit little if any land because land scarcity promotes patrilineal inheritance, a norm that probably has antecedents in ancient Nahua culture, according to which patrilineally related men lived next to one another and formed the core of the farming group.[17] Cáceres men and women work side by side in agriculture much more than their counterparts in the Nahuat area of Mexico, where women spend a great deal more time in domicile-based tasks because of labor-intensive food processing. Moreover, few Nahuat women live near their mother, who can help them with child care and free them to participate in agricultural labor with men. The gender integration and close lifelong interdependence between mothers and daughters in the Cáceres village social structure contribute to communication through storytelling between men and women over their model of marriage and their faith in the healing power of a woman's love.

# CHAPTER ELEVEN

# Conclusions

WOMEN SPEAK with a muted public voice as part of their subordination in many societies throughout the world. Some anthropologists have generalized that women in nonliterate societies are silenced by a symbolic system controlled by men that draws attention to women's connection with animals. Sherry Ortner (1974) expressed this view by asserting that women are generally associated symbolically with nature and men with culture in a metaphorical relationship that emphasizes men's greater capacity for abstract thought and justifies their monopolization of cultural creativity. Women become distinguished from men because of their more obvious biological role in the production and rearing of children,[1] which draws attention to their common connections with nature. The relegation of women to nature is clearly one way that men can keep women in their subordinate position by maintaining male primacy through the public control of symbols.

Storytelling is the process of creating cultural reality through symbols, and Edwin Ardener (1977a, 1977b) has noted that anthropologists, most of whom have been men, frequently construct their picture of that reality for nonliterate societies through an examination of stories told by other men. Ardener suggests that male anthropologists have perceived other men as better than women at bridging the linguistic gap between the native and the outside observer, presumably because men are more accustomed to speaking in public. Male myths often describe in metaphorical language a worldview in which there is a human center and a wild non-human periphery; men place themselves in the center of cultural activity and women more toward the wild. It is not difficult to see that such worldviews as articulated by men work to silence women and maintain a male-dominated social order.

The Nahuat of Mexico fit the generalizations by Ortner (1974) and Ardener (1977a, 1977b) because they are, for the most part, a nonliterate society where men tell publicly most of the myths, placing themselves closer to the center of cultural activity to justify their primacy in the social and cultural order, and they describe woman as intrinsically more mute, justifying male control over the public construction of cultural reality. Male storytellers from the Nahuat community of Huitzilan de Serdán express the view, in their mythic account of human origins, that women have less capacity for speech than men. They tell a popular origin myth expressing the muteness of women in a tale that probably derives from the biblical story of "Noah's Ark" and the Spanish story of Cinderella in animal skins, which still circulates in Navaconcejo oral tradition (see "Cinderella" by Filomena Arivas Miguel in Chapter 6). According to the Nahuat myth, a fully human Noah enters the ark with his she-dog and survives the flood. Noah and his she-dog begin life anew with Noah cultivating his corn and bean plot and his she-dog preparing his meals. One day the she-dog removes her animal skin to grind tortilla dough, and Noah discovers that she, like Cinderella, is a beautiful woman. Noah prevents her from dressing in her animal skin, and he and the dog-turned-woman have children who become the current race of humankind, which includes the Nahuat of Huitzilan and speakers of other languages whom the Nahuat place below them in their hierarchy of values. Although elements of this story appear in the oral tradition of other societies in Latin America (see Drummond 1977: 847–848), Nahuat narrators add details that specifically express their ideas about women's capacity for speech. They use this story to explain how women and men, then as well as now, speak languages that are as different from each other as Nahuat is from Totonac, a Mayan language spoken in communities that neighbor Huitzilan to the north. Their tale carries the message that women's speech is like the barking of a dog and is fundamentally different from the speech of men.[2] The Nahuat view expressed in their origin myth is similar to that which Mayan men express more directly when they criticize the public storytelling ability of women by doubting their memory for words (Laughlin 1962: 53–54; 1977: 55).

Men who describe women's speech as like the barking of a dog and who doubt women's memory for words are attempting to silence women and maintain male primacy. The Mayan and Nahuat belief in male primacy is part of a social and cultural system placing priority on the relations among agnatically related men. Nahuat and Mayan families are based on ideals, taught through child rearing, that patrilineally related men should remain attached to their parents throughout the life course. Men undoubtedly scoff at women as competent narrators in an effort to control the public construction of reality by which they maintain the male-centered social structure of which their families are an important part. To the extent that Nahuat and Mayan women have internalized some of men's views, they socialize their children according to the values of the male-dominant public culture, and like women elsewhere, they are ironically the agents of their own subordination.

European women, who live in various kinds of family and social orders, are by no means always empowered with public speech. Linda Dégh (1969: 171) describes the typical storyteller in the Hungarian village where she did her fieldwork as "generally an experienced and widely traveled man." Spanish women, however, are storytellers of renown as often as men in northern and central Cáceres, southern Cáceres and Badajoz (Curiel Merchán 1944), Cádiz (Larrea Palacín 1959), Salamanca (Cortés Vázquez 1979: 1, 2), Asturias (Llano Roza de Ampudia 1975), and undoubtedly many other provinces. The Spanish case illustrates what happens when both men and women are comfortable speaking publicly in stories and carry on a storytelling dialogue to work through their differences and mitigate some of the problems in their relations derived from different but overlapping worldviews. Spanish women and men have different views of their social universe because they are socialized under different pressures. The genders grow up learning totally different expectations for sexual assertiveness and modesty, which are linked to ideas about masculinity and femininity that are firmly established in rural Spanish culture. Moreover, psychoanalytic theory, revised with feminist insight, predicts that boys and girls would develop different worldviews because they are raised by women more than men, and boys and girls grow into adults with different relationships to their same-gender parents. Chodorow (1974, 1978) suggests that boys become men after separating from women, devaluing the feminine world, and learning to identify with a distant father. Men consequently develop a "positional" identity in which they define themselves in terms of how they stand in relation to others. Girls separate less from their mother as they grow into women and develop a "relational identity" according to which they define themselves in terms of their connections to others. As a consequence of their early childhood experiences, men and women develop different conceptions of heterosexual love modeled on contrasting relationships with their parents developed in early childhood.

A comparison of the Cáceres feminine and masculine variants of the same stories of courtship and marriage yielded pictures of the male and female worldviews that accord with Chodorow's generalizations about the socialization of gender identity in families in which women spend more time than men rearing children. The feminine variants express women's struggle to separate while remaining connected to their mother, women's undulating conception of romantic love, women's changing perception of men, and their faith in the power of their love to heal family relationships. The masculine variants of the same tales express men's desire to separate more completely from their father, their heavy dependence on women's nurturance, competitive view of the world, brittle conception of romantic love, fear that the women they love will betray them, and almost total reliance on women to hold marriage and family together.

The storytelling dialogue between women and men from the northern and central Cáceres villages illustrates what happens when women and men play a joint public role in the creation of their culture through telling folktales. A woman may hear a tale from a man, but she does not necessarily accept the man's description of social reality described in the language of his story. Likewise, a man may hear a tale from a woman and will change the story plot to accord with his own version of reality. When men and women tell the same tale back to each other and share their different perspectives on social relations, they provide the basis for greater mutual understanding between the genders. Speaking through their stories strengthens the positions of men as well as women and contributes to an ongoing dialogue that has more public support than in the Nahuat and Mayan communities of Mexico. Women present themselves in stories as strong and important characters worried about ending their childhood and balancing their love of parents and husband, but ready to moderate the challenge for a man they love who also proves his love to them. Men emerge as fragile, human, multidimensional, and more than phallic aggressors concerned about competition for women and their masculine honor. They need women but fear the loss of their honor, rejection, and betrayal during courtship. Their aggressive and competitive posture is a defense that can drop away once their honor is intact in a good marriage to a faithful wife. Part of men's and women's opposition comes from antecedent pre-Oedipal and Oedipal themes that are universal and are worked out in a particular way because of the strength women gain from their enduring ties with their mother. The relative equality of Spanish women and men gives them a chance to mitigate their strong opposition and differences and bond into an enduring and complementary marriage.

The role of women and men in the public construction of cultural reality is changing in Spain, as in the rest of the world, with the growth of literacy and mass media. European folktales about courtship and marriage, which once were only circulated in oral tradition, have became part of literary tradition.[3] A written tradition has coexisted alongside an oral one for centuries in many parts of Europe, and Darnton (1984: 20) disputes the argument that "a literary line cuts through all history, dividing oral from 'written' or 'print' culture."[4] Rather, traditional storytelling can continue long after literacy has become the norm, and a written tradition may actually feed into an already existing oral one as some narrators, such as Mercedes Monroy from Cabezuela, illustrate. Mercedes heard stories read to her from books, committed them to memory, and then told them as oral narratives to her children. Nevertheless, the appearance of a written tradition makes things very different. Alan Dundes (1986: 259) points out that something happens to an oral tale when it becomes transcribed or a part of literature because lost are the "subtle nuances entailing significant body movements, eye expression, pregnant pauses, and the like from the inevitably flat and fixed written record of what was once a live and often compelling storytelling event." Many folklorists who have taken a careful look at the storytelling situation (see Dégh 1969; Georges 1969; Bauman 1986) describe the face-to-face contact between the storyteller and the audience. That contact changes or disappears entirely when stories are distributed through books and when fairy tales are imparted only through the mass media. Lost is the complex process of social interaction through which a story is shaped to have meaning to the members of a storytelling community. Those who listen to a storyteller's tale shape a story through repeated storytelling occasions by showing their approval or disapproval of the narrator's performance. Disapproval is apparent to any Spanish storyteller when the audience is too easily distracted, fails to utter the right word at the right time, breaks into heated discussion about the correct details or the plot, or criticizes a teller's choice of words and phraseology. A listener indicates approval with a pleased facial expression, rapt attention to the narrator's words and gestures, an exclamation at just the right point, or praise for the narrator's incredible memory at the conclusion of a performance. Men and women of small storytelling communities such as Garganta la Olla know one another well because they grew up together and have learned the common signs of approval that are part of their culture. When women and men publicly tell as well as listen to stories, they are engaged in a complicated social process through which they can reach an accord about the social situations portrayed in the plots of their stories according to their own perceptions of similar situations.

The appearance of a literary tradition and mass media is a part of a larger process of change that distances individuals and communities, particularly the powerless, from their once public role in the construction of their culture. Zipes (1979) argues that stories adopted into literary tradition become part of a culture industry managed by elite men who impose their values on women. Fairy tales in popular children's literature reinforce the sexist values of the capitalist and male-dominated society, and Zipes (1979: 171–173) illustrates his argument with a number of tales, including "Cinderella," a story with considerable importance because of its widespread distribution (see Dundes 1982). He sees the sexist values of European society expressed not only in the tales themselves but also in their modern interpretation, which focuses on the wickedness of the stepmother rather than the father, the heroine's passivity, girls quarreling over a man, and Cinderella's dutifulness, virginity, and passivity.[5]

The changes that Wilhem Grimm made to "Cinderella" in successive editions of *Nursery and Household Tales* between 1812 and 1857 illustrate what can happen when male authors change popular stories according to their tastes and the climate of their times. Ruth Bottigheimer (1987: 57–70) describes how Wilhelm Grimm silenced the female characters and put words in the mouth of the male ones. He cut down the number of direct speeches by Cinderella, her mother, and their allies; reduced the utterances by the stepmother and her daughters; and increased the speech of Cinderella's father and the prince. Bottigheimer (1987: 71–73) interprets the silencing of female characters as part of a common trend and suggests that it represents the "transformation and elevation of daily experience to folk literary status." In short, Wilhelm, like many men in his society, silenced women to keep them in their subordinate position. Wilhelm Grimm, however, is only one of the masculine purveyors of the "Cinderella" story in children's literature, and others, including Walt Disney, have perpetuated a pattern that probably began when oral versions of the tales were converted to print. The masculinization of stories that originally circulated in oral tradition when both genders publicly told them is likely to make folktales less appealing to women. Kay Stone (1975, 1985) discovered that North American women who heard as children the mass-media versions of "Cinderella" were disillusioned by the story's message and found it meaningless to their adult lives. We who live in literate societies, however, can find other guides to our experience, organized in narrative form, in the tales told by men and women such as those of village Spain.

# List of Supplementary Tales

THE INTERPRETATION of the storytelling dialogue is based on forty-five supplementary stories of courtship and marriage as well as the twenty-four texts that appear in Chapters 3 through 10. The high cost of printing all of the tales would have increased the price of this book and made it inaccessible to many readers. Scholars who wish to consult the supplementary tales may write to me for copies of the Spanish originals, which are listed below along with the names, ages, and communities of the storytellers.

1. "The Wager on the Wife's Chastity," by Natividad Corrales, age seventy-eight (Serradilla)
2. "The Wager on the Wife's Chastity," by Ulalia García Castaño, age seventy-eight (Garganta la Olla)
3. "The Wager on the Wife's Chastity," by Zacaria Iglesia, age seventy-four (Piornal)
4. "The Maidens and the Thieves," by Julia Perez, age fifty-one (Navaconcejo)
5. "The Poor Girl Seduced by Her Rich Sweetheart," by Isabel García, age eighteen (Ahigal)
6. "Snow White," by Eugenio Real Vázquez, age sixty-five (Serradilla)
7. "Snow White," by Amaranto Galallo Sanchez, in his early forties (Cabezuela)
8. "Snow White," by Julio Lopez Curiel, age seventy-four (Garganta la Olla)
9. "Cinderella" and "Snow White," by María Marco, in her early sixties (Navaconcejo)
10. "Cinderella," by Valentina Prieto, in her early fifties (Navaconcejo)
11. "Cinderella," by Domitila Prieto Perez, age sixty-seven (Piornal)
12. "Cinderella," by Filomena Arivas Miguel, age fifty-four (Navaconcejo)
13. "Cinderella," by Francisco García, in his mid-seventies (Cabezuela)
14. "Cinderella," by Mercedes Zamoro Monroy, age seventy-six (Cabezuela)
15. "The Three Grains of Anise," by Felisa Sanchez Martín, age seventy-two (Serradilla)
16. "The Grateful Animals," by Pedro Cuesta Martín, age eighty-nine (Tornavacas)

17. "The Grateful Animals," by Julia Lobato Gil, age sixty-nine (Serradilla)
18. "The Father and Son Who Went Out Looking for Work," by José Díaz Sanchez, in his early sixties (Serradilla)
19. "The Soldier," by Eugenio Real Vázquez, age sixty-five (Serradilla)
20. "The King Don Damadá," by Juán Julian Recuero, age seventy-four (Serradilla)
21. "Beauty and the Beast," by Florencia Real Cobos, in her mid-fifties (Serradilla)
22. "The Frog Prince," by Victoria Díaz, age in her mid-forties (Piornal)
23. "The Animal Groom 1," by Emilia Moreno Calle, age thirty-five (Piornal)
24. "The Animal Groom 2," as told by Emilia Moreno Calle
25. "The Two Ploughmen," by Alvino Bravo Sanchez, age sixty-four (Serradilla)
26. "The Two Ploughmen," by Casiano Miranda, age seventy-one (Garganta la Olla)
27. "The Two Ploughmen," by Esperanza Cozas, age seventy-five (Garganta la Olla)
28. "The Fisherman," by Florencio Ramos, age sixty (Navaconcejo)
29. "The Fisherman," by Bernardo Ramos, age thirty-four (Navaconcejo)
30. "The Fisherman," by Miguel Chorro Hernández, age seventy-four (Navaconcejo)
31. "The Fisherman," by José Díaz Sanchez, in his early sixties (Serradilla)
32. "The Fisherman," by Julio Lopez Curiel, age seventy-four (Garganta la Olla)
33. "The Fisherman," by Estrella Iglesia, age twenty-four (Navaconcejo)
34. "The Fisherman," by Julia Lobato Gil, age sixty-nine (Serradilla)
35. "Blancaflor," by Leandro Jimenez, age seventy-four (El Guijo de Santa Bárbara)
36. "Blancaflor," by Eugenio Real Vázquez, age sixty-five (Serradilla)
37. "Blancaflor," by José Díaz Sanchez, in his early sixties (Serradilla)
38. "Blancaflor," by Evarista Moreno, age thirty-three (Cabezuela)
39. "The Queen and Her Marvelous Children," by Felisa Sanchez Martín, age seventy-two (Serradilla)
40. "The Queen and Her Marvelous Children," by Guillermo Castaño, age seventy-seven (Garganta la Olla)
41. "The Queen and Her Marvelous Children," by Leonardo Sanchez Sanchez, in his late fifties (Cabezuela)
42. "Hansel and Gretel," by Julio Lopez Curiel, age seventy-four (Garganta la Olla)

43. "Hansel and Gretel," by Florencia Herrero, age sixty-eight (Garganta la Olla)
44. "Hansel and Gretel," by María de Pilar Corrales, age forty (Serradilla)
45. "Hansel and Gretel," by Isabel García, age eighteen (Ahigal)

# Notes

CHAPTER ONE
Introduction

1. Aurelio Espinosa (1924) devoted an entire volume to tales of enchantment, which are metaphors for courtship and marriage, collected from many different parts of Spain. Spanish folklorists have found local variants of stories like those collected by Espinosa in Andalusia (Larrea Palacín 1959), Extremadura (Curiel Merchán 1944), Salamanca (Cortés Vázquez 1979: 2), Zamora (Cortés Vázquez 1976), and Asturias (Cabal 1924; Llano Roza de Ampudia 1975).

2. Persistiany (1966) attempted to synthesize the concepts of honor and shame in Mediterranean society. See Davis (1977) and particularly Herzfeld (1984) for critical views and cautions against promoting false stereotypes of gender relations in this part of the world.

3. Carmelo Lison-Tolosana is a Spaniard trained in the British tradition.

4. Counihan (1985) describes how carnival ritual in Sardinia begins with an affirmation of gender difference and ends with a ritualistic expression of unity between men and women.

5. Nahuat oral tradition contains stories that have mixed Spanish and ancient Nahua antecedents, which I discuss in Taggart (1982a, 1982b, 1982c, 1983, and 1986).

6. All folklorists who have collected tales from Spanish storytellers and reported the gender of the narrators indicate that they have collected tales from women as well as men. For examples of collections in which folklorists identify the narrator's gender, see Larrea Palacín (1959), Curiel Merchán (1944), Cortés Vázquez (1976, 1979: 1, 2), and Llano Roza de Ampudia (1975). Aurelio Espinosa did not report the names or genders of the particular narrators from whom he collected his three volumes of stories, but he does mention that he collected tales from women as well as men in many parts of Spain. For accounts of his fieldwork in Spain, see A. Espinosa (1921) and J. Espinosa (1985: 35–49).

7. Folklorists and literary critics disagree on the precise terms used for folktales and fairy tales. Spanish narrators generally use the terms *cuento*, or *historia*, or occasionally *cuento de hada* for the stories discussed in this study. Hispanic American and Spanish folklorists, who have collected stories from Spanish oral tradition, generally prefer the terms *cuento* or *cuento popular* (see A. Espinosa 1924; Cabal 1924; Llano Roza de Ampudia 1975; Larrea Palacín 1959; Curiel Merchán 1944; and Cortés Vázquez 1976, 1979: 1, 2).

8. I have translated the Spanish titles when narrators generally concur on the the same story. Otherwise, I use the titles found in Boggs (1930), Hansen (1957), and Robe (1973) to facilitate tale identification.

9. Boggs (1930), Hansen (1957), and Robe (1973) base their classification of Spanish and Hispanic American folktales on Aarne (1928) and Aarne and Thompson (1961).

10. Bakhtin lays out his vision of narrative dialogue in many of his works (1968, 1981, 1984). Hill (1986) describes the relevance of Bakhtin's ideas for moving beyond structuralism in linguistics and anthropology.

11. Todd (1988: 19–32) actually identifies seven types of families, of which four are found in Europe. They include the exogamous community family characterized by equality between brothers and married sons living with their parents (1988: 33); the authoritarian family, in which an unbroken patrimony passes to one of the sons who lives with his parents after his marriage (1988: 55); the absolute nuclear family, which has no precise inheritance rules and no cohabitation of parents and their married children (1988: 99); and the egalitarian nuclear family, in which married children also reside apart from their parents, and brothers inherit equal amounts of the family property (1988: 99). The Cáceres family corresponds most closely to the egalitarian nuclear family, but it contains features, such as strong ties between a mother and daughter manifest in occasional matrilocality, that Todd does not consider in his classification of family types. Men and women living in the four types of families tell many of the same European folktales of courtship and marriage, and it would be an interesting study to compare the contours of their male-female storytelling dialogue on gender relations.

CHAPTER TWO
The Context

1. The map showing the provincial boundaries of Spain is based on Foster (1960: x), and the one describing the location of the storytellers' communities relative to rivers, roads, and railroads is derived from *Mapas Provinciales de Carreteras*, published by the Libreria y Casa Editorial Hernando, S.A. I thank my sister Beatrice Taggart for her artistic rendering of both maps.

2. Fernandez (1983: 166).

3. The statistics on current village populations come from the 1980 Spanish census (Instituto Nacional de Estadistica 1982: 42–44).

4. The populations based on the 1950 Spanish census (Instituto Nacional de Estadística 1957: 39–43), the rank order of population decline from 1950 to 1980, and the percent of change in parentheses for the eight communities are Navaconcejo, 2369 (−15.6 percent); Ahigal, 2347 (−18.5 percent); Cabezuela, 2820 (−18.9 percent); Piornal, 2263 (−28.8 percent); Tornavacas, 2292 (−33.5 percent); El Guijo de Santa Bárbara, 1039 (−33.5 percent); Garganta la Olla, 2089 (−43.4 percent); and Serradilla, 4907 (−53.4 percent).

5. Honorio Velasco (1981) described how northern Cáceres communities, including Garganta la Olla, express their differences in folklore, a practice that stems from a time when honor and shame were group concerns (Mitchell 1988).

6. The changes that took place in Spain with the collapse of the labor-intensive agrarian economy are discussed in Aceves and Douglass (1976).

7. Falassi (1980) describes storytelling taking place under very similar conditions in rural Tuscany, Italy.

CHAPTER THREE
"The Innocent Slandered Maiden"

1. In the context of Donjuanismo, the Don Juan is in many respects like the safe-appearing but dangerous man in the stories. Carmelo Lison-Tolosana (1983: 334–335) describes the Don Juan for his native community of Belmonte de los Cabelleros in Aragón, and his description applies equally well to Cáceres and to many other parts of Spain. "Young men define the Don Juan as one who is a *conquistador* ('lady-killer') of women. They never use the word seducer, which seems to indicate actual possession of the woman; in this sense there would be very few Don Juans indeed in the *pueblo*. . . . He is self-confident and regards success with girls as something quite easy; he believes that they are constantly talking about him, that they never refer to him as tonto. He goes straight up to a group of girls in the main street on Sunday afternoons and greets them all courteously. He lets them go first, opens doors for them, pulls up chairs for them— only a Don Juan can do this sort of thing gracefully in the pueblo—and invites them to the bar. His conversation is agreeable, he pays compliments to all of them, remarks at once on their dresses, hair-styles, necklaces, bracelets, and so on. The girls are excited by his presence and his gallantry, feeling unable to cope with him but pleased by his company."

CHAPTER FOUR
Maidens and Thieves

1. See Dwyer (1978), who describes sexual ideology of Moroccan men and women expressed in popular folktales, some of which are like those circulating in Spanish oral tradition.
2. Cáceres narrators frequently use the expression "pin pan, pin pan" to describe a man or a woman making a long journey on foot or horseback.
3. The expression "¡ala!" means "pull!" or "haul!" or perhaps "go to it!" or "come and get it!" depending on the context.
4. "Tran, tran, tran, tran" is also a common way to represent someone traveling a long distance on horseback or foot.

CHAPTER FIVE
"Snow White"

1. See Buechler and Buechler (1981) for a fascinating account of a woman's relationship with her mother in Galicia.
2. The Italianas regularly perform for the festival of Santa Isabel, which takes place from the first to the fourth of July.

CHAPTER SIX
"Cinderella"

1. The types of "Cinderella" stories circulating in Spanish oral tradition resemble those in Cox's (1893) classification of 435 tales.

2. Marie Louise von Franz (1988: 143–157) offers an interesting Jungian interpretation of a Russian Cinderella story, known as "The Beautiful Wassilissa." She emphasizes how the story "takes place in the feminine realm" (1988: 147) and suggests that it represents a girl individuating from her mother.

3. Maximina used the term *guarda cochino asqueroso* (filthy pigkeeper) to associate the heroine with filth, particularly excrement. The heroine's metonymical association with excrement is a poetic device that draws attention to her ugliness when dressed as a pelican.

4. The maiden who hides inside a golden bull to escape from a difficult situation appears in other folktales in Cáceres oral tradition. Curiel Merchán (1944: 321–323) collected a masculine tale with this episode in the southern Cáceres town of Trujillo.

CHAPTER SEVEN
Disenchanting a Princess

1. See Boggs (1930: 40–41, 42–43, 71), Hansen (1957: 23–24, 25–26, 70–71), and Robe (1973: 42–44, 48–49, 99–100).

2. José Díaz Sanchez actually said "la laguna de los Gredos," referring to one of the six lakes known as La Laguna Grande de Gredos (Big Gredos Lake) and Las Cinco Lagunas (The Five Little Lakes) located near the summit of Mount Almanzor, the highest peak in the Gredos mountain chain on the border of Cáceres and Avila. The reference to water from one of the Gredos lakes metonymically associates the serpent with a force of nature because all of the Gredos lakes are in an uninhabited wilderness area.

3. See Taggart (1982a) for the text and an interpretation of the metaphors of male socialization in "Juanito el Oso" as told by Julio Lopez Curiel in Garganta la Olla.

CHAPTER EIGHT
The Animal Groom

1. See Opie and Opie (1974).

2. Robe (1973: 68–70) lists a number of "Lost Wife" tales from Mexico told primarily by Spanish speakers. Laughlin (1962: 228–231) discusses variants of this story told in the Mayan community of Zinacantán in highland Chiapas; Burns (1983: 121–143) presents an Orpheus or "Lost Wife" tale as told by a Mayan speaker from the Yucatán peninsula; and Taggart (1977: 282–284; 1983: 133-135) contains and discusses two variants of similar stories as told by Nahuat-speaking narrators from Huitzilan de Serdán and Santiago Yaonáhuac in the northern sierra of Puebla.

CHAPTER NINE
"Blancaflor"

1. While Cáceres narrators often depict wealthy and powerful fathers in opposition to the men who court and marry their daughters, they represent the re-

lationship between the girl's father and his son-in-law in a variety of ways. For example, Eugenio Real Vázquez and Juán Julian Recuero from Serradilla represent very differently the wealthy and powerful father in their stories about men who search for enchanted princesses. Eugenio told a tale he called "The Soldier," which appears to be a variant of AT 301B, known as the "Quest for a Vanished Princess" (Robe 1973: 46–47), in which the hero uses helpful dogs to find a princess enchanted by her father and mother. Juán Julian Recuero, however, told a story he called "The King Don Damadá," also a variant of stolen or vanished princess tales AT 301, 301A, and 301B (Robe 1973: 44–47), in which the hero never encounters his father-in-law's overt opposition. Eugenio's "The Soldier" and Juán's "The King Don Damadá" are listed in the Appendix.

2. Florencio describes Ursula in ways that fit his description of himself; both raise calves (*chotos*) belonging to others and are reminded of their poverty in the context of courtship and marriage. As mentioned, Florencio's first courtship came to an end before marriage because he was considered too poor by the maiden's mother. Florencio's apparent identification with the heroine is explained by psychoanalytical (Bettelheim 1977: 78–83) and Jungian critics (von Franz 1982: 99–120) as the projection onto a folktale of the feminine side of a man's personality.

3. Curiel Merchán (1944: 82–86) collected a "Lost Husband" tale from a school-age boy in southern Cáceres that tells of men lying about their experiences with a maiden who only appears to compromise her marital chastity.

4. English translations of the "Hansel and Gretel" stories by Florencia Herrero and Julio Lopez Curiel appear in Taggart (1986: 438–441).

CHAPTER TEN
A Cross-Cultural Perspective

1. Franz Boas (1912) argued that most folktales in Mexican and North American Indian oral tradition came from Spain, France, and Africa, and he collected a number of tales of Spanish origin from Zuñi (Boas 1922) and Nahuatl storytellers in Mexico (Boas and Arreola 1920; Boas and Haeberlin 1924). George Foster (1945b) placed Boas's argument in broader perspective by describing how Mexican folktales contain story elements from Spain and indigenous sources mixed to form new story hybrids in accord with the experience of Mexican Indians after the Spanish conquest.

2. Fieldwork took place in the Nahuat-speaking communities of Huitzilan de Serdán and Santiago Yaonáhuac during two extended periods (1968 to 1970 in Huitzilan and 1977 to 1978 in Yaonáhuac) and several summers between 1971 and 1976.

3. A comparison of the Spanish and Nahuat variants of "Cupid and Psyche" (AT 425), "Cinderella" (AT 510B), and "Hansel and Gretel" (AT 327) is in Taggart (1982b, 1982c, 1986, 1988).

4. A detailed description of Huitzilan Nahuat betrothal ceremonies is in Taggart (1975: 97–103).

5. Robert Laughlin (1977) collected a large number of Tzotzil narratives in the Mexican *municipio* of Zinacantán from nine storytellers, of whom eight were men and one was a woman. See Laughlin (1962: 15–16; 1977: 164–321) for a

sensitive and illuminating portrait of a Tzotzil woman storyteller and an excellent translation of her stories into English.

6. A brief biography of Fernando Vega appears in Taggart (1983: 255–256).

7. Interested readers may write me for the interlinear Nahuat-English translation of Fernando's "Little Donkey Mother."

8. *Mole* is a ceremonial sauce prepared with chiles, tomatoes, and other spices usually served with turkey or pork on ritual kinship and other religious occasions.

9. The "Blancaflor" tale in which the heroine returns her lover to her father, the devil, was told by Luciano Vega of Yaonáhuac. His story and short biography appear in Taggart (1983: 227–228, 256–257).

10. The "Adam and Eve" and "Fisherman" tales describing a woman's adultery appear in Taggart (1983: 175–188, 231–233).

11. A Spanish translation of a Nahuat "Lost Husband" tale as told by Mariano Isidro appears in Taggart (1982c), and Mariano's brief biography is in Taggart (1983: 253–254).

12. "Lost Wife" tales from Huitzilan and Yaonáhuac appear in Taggart (1977: 282–284, 1983: 133–135).

13. Four "Fisherman" tales appear in Taggart (1983: 231–238).

14. Readers may write me for an interlinear translation of "The Grateful Animals" (AT 302 and 554) by Mariano Isidro of Yaonáhuac. Summaries of the Nahuat "Hansel and Gretel" stories are in Taggart (1986).

15. The episode of the sister betraying her brother appears in a "Hansel and Gretel" story told by Mariano Isidro of Yaonáhuac, which is in Taggart (1986: 448–451). Radin and Espinosa (1917: 205) report another "Hansel and Gretel" story from Ixtlan, Oaxaca, where the sister similarly betrays her brother. Radin and Espinosa are not clear about the exact source of their tale and do not report the family structure of their informant's community. Parsons (1936: 66–153) gives ample evidence for a patrilineal and patrilocal family structure in the Oaxacan village of Mitla, which, if like that of Ixtlan, could explain the sister's betrayal in the variant collected by Radin and Espinosa.

16. The Nahuat stories describing the complete breakdown of the nuclear family were told by Juán Hernández and Nacho Angel. Texts of their tales appear in Taggart (1986: 451–453), and their brief biographies are in Taggart (1983: 248–250).

17. Carrasco (1964, 1976) described virilocal postmarital residence and a predominantly agnatic household structure of the Nahua living in central Mexico during the sixteenth century.

CHAPTER ELEVEN
Conclusions

1. Antonio Veracruz's version of "Noah's Ark" features the woman dressed in a dog's skin. An English translation of his story and a short biography of Antonio appear in Taggart (1983: 194–197, 252–253).

2. See Barry and Paxson (1971) and Barry et al. (1977) for a classification of societies in terms of the roles of women and men in rearing children.

3. Charles Perrault's *Contes du temps passé*, published in 1697, and the sev-

enteen editions of Jacob and Wilhelm Grimm's *Kinder- und Hansmärchen*, which came out between 1812 and 1858, were two of the early and popular literary editions of European folktales (Bottigheimer 1987: 6–7) resembling those discussed in this book

4. Darnton refers to an argument developed by Jack Goody (1968, 1977).

5. Zipes takes a Marxist approach and is very critical of Bettelheim's (1977) psychoanalytic interpretation of "Cinderella."

# Bibliography

Aarne, Antti. 1928. *Types of the Folktale*. Folklore Fellows Communication, no. 74. Helsinki.

Aarne, Antti, and Stith Thompson. 1961. *The Types of the Folktale*. 2d rev. ed. Folklore Fellows Communication, no. 184. Helsinki.

Aceves, Joseph. 1971. *Social Change in a Spanish Village*. Cambridge, Mass.: Schenkman.

Aceves, Joseph B., and William Douglass, eds. 1976. *The Changing Faces of Rural Spain*. New York: Wiley.

Ardener, Edwin. 1977a. "Belief and the Problem of Women." In *Perceiving Women*, edited by Shirley Ardener, 1–17. New York: Halsted Press.

———. 1977b. "The 'Problem' Revisited." In *Perceiving Women*, edited by Shirley Ardener, 18–27. New York: Halsted Press.

Bakhtin, Mikhail. 1968. *Rabelais and His World*. Cambridge: MIT Press.

———. 1981. *The Dialogic Imagination: Four Essays*. Austin: University of Texas Press.

———. 1984. *Problems of Dostoevsky's Poetics*. Minneapolis: University of Minnesota Press.

Baldwin, Karen. 1985. " 'Whoof!' A Word on Women's Roles in Family Storytelling." In *Women's Folklore, Women's Culture*, edited by Rosan A. Jordan and Susan J. Kalčik, 149–162. Philadelphia: University of Pennsylvania Press.

Barry, Herbert III, and Leonora M. Paxson. 1971. "Infancy and Early Childhood: Cross-Cultural Codes." *Ethnology* 10: 466–508.

Barry, Herbert III, Lili Josephson, Edith Lauer, and Catherine Marshall. 1977. "Agents and Techniques for Child Training: Cross-Cultural Codes 6." *Ethnology* 16: 191–230.

Bauman, Richard. 1986. *Story, Performance, and Event: Contextual Studies of Oral Narrative*. Cambridge: Cambridge University Press.

Behar, Ruth. 1986. *Santia María del Monte: The Presence of the Past in a Spanish Village*. Princeton: Princeton University Press.

———. In press. "The Struggle for the Church: Popular Anticlericalism and Religiosity in Post-Franco Spain." In *Religious Orthodoxy and Folk Belief in European Society*, edited by Ellen Badone. Princeton: Princeton University Press.

———. 1988. Personal communication: reader's report for Princeton University Press.

Behar, Ruth, and David Frye. 1988. "Property, Progeny, and Emotion: Family History in a Leonese Village." *Journal of Family History* 13: 13–32.

Bettelheim, Bruno. 1977. *The Uses of Enchantment: The Meaning and Importance of Fairy Tales*. New York: Vintage Books.

Boas, Franz. 1912. "Notes on Mexican Folk-lore." *Journal of American Folklore* 25: 204–260.

Boas, Franz. 1922. "Tales of Spanish Provenience from Zuñi." *Journal of American Folklore* 35: 62–98.

Boas, Franz, and José María Arreola. 1920. "Cuentos en mexicano de Milpa Alta, D.F." *Journal of American Folklore* 33: 1–24.

Boas, Franz, and Hermann K. Haeberlin. 1924. "Ten Folktales in Modern Nahuatl." *Journal of American Folkore* 37: 345–370.

Boggs, Ralph S. 1930. *Index of Spanish Folktales*. Folklore Fellows Communication, no. 90. Helsinki.

Bottigheimer, Ruth B. 1987. *Grimms' Bad Girls and Bold Boys: The Moral and Social Vision of the Tales*. New Haven: Yale University Press.

Brandes, Stanley H. 1975. *Migration, Kinship, and Community: Tradition and Transition in a Spanish Village*. New York: Academic Press.

———. 1980. *Metaphors of Masculinity: Sex and Status in Andalusian Folklore*. Philadelphia: University of Pennsylvania Press.

Buechler, Hans C., and Judith-Maria Buechler. 1981. *Carmen: The Autobiography of a Spanish Galician Woman*. Cambridge, Mass.: Schenkman.

Burns, Allen F. 1983. *An Epoch of Miracles: Oral Literature of the Yucatec Maya*. Austin: University of Texas Press.

Cabal, Constantino. 1924. *Los cuentos tradicionales Asturianos*. Madrid: Editorial Voluntad.

Caro Baroja, Julio. 1957. *Razas, pueblos y linajes*. Madrid: Revista de Occidente.

———. 1973. *The World of Witches*. Chicago: University of Chicago Press.

Carrasco, Pedro. 1964. "Family Structure in Sixteenth Century Tepoztlán." In *Process and Pattern in Culture: Essays in Honor of Julian H. Steward*, edited by Robert J. Manners, 185–210. Chicago: Aldine.

———. 1976. "The Joint Family in Ancient Mexico: The Case of Molotla." In *Essays on Mexican Kinship*, edited by Hugo G. Nutini, Pedro Carrasco, and James M. Taggart, 45–64. Pittsburgh: University of Pittsburgh Press.

Chang, Kenne H.-K. 1970. "The Inkyo System in Southwestern Japan: Its Functional Utility in the Household Setting." *Ethnology* 9: 342–357.

Chodorow, Nancy. 1974. "Family Structure and Feminine Personality." In *Women, Culture and Society*, edited by Michelle Zimbalist Rosaldo and Louise Lamphere, 43–66. Palo Alto: Stanford University Press.

———. 1978. *The Reproduction of Mothering: Psychoanalysis and the Sociology of Gender*. Berkeley: University of California Press.

Christian, William A. 1981. *Apparitions in Late Medieval and Renaissance Spain*. Princeton: Princeton University Press.

Collier, George A. 1987. *Social of Rural Andalusia: Unacknowledged Revolutionaries of the Second Republic*. Stanford: Stanford University Press.

Collier, Jane F. 1968. "Courtship and Marraige in Zinacantán, Chiapas, Mexico." *Middle American Research Institute Publication* 25: 139–201.

———. 1973. *Law and Social Change in Zinacantán*. Stanford: Stanford University Press.

———. 1986. "From Mary to Modern Woman: The Material Basis of Marianismo and its Transformation in a Spanish Village." *American Ethnologist* 13: 100–107.

Cortés Vázquez, Luis. 1976. *Leyendas, cuentos y romances de Sanadria: Textos leoneses y gallegos*. Salamanca: Gráficas Cervantes.

———. 1979. *Cuentos populares salmantinos*. 2 vols. Salamanca: Libreria Cervantes.

Counihan, Carole M. 1985. "Transvestism and Gender in a Sardinian Carnival." *Anthropology* 9: 11–24.

Cox, Marian Roalfe. 1893. *Cinderella: Three Hundred and Forty-five Variants*. London: Folk-Lore Society.

Curiel Merchán, Marciano. 1944. *Cuentos extremeños*. Madrid: Consejo Superior de Investigaciones Científicas Instituto Antonio de Negrija.

Darnton, Robert. 1984. *The Great Cat Massacre and Other Episodes in French Cultural History*. New York: Basic Books.

Davis, John. 1977. *People of the Mediterranean*. London: Routledge and Kegan Paul.

Dégh, Linda. 1969. *Folktales and Society: Story-Telling in a Hungarian Peasant Community*. Bloomington: Indiana University Press.

Drummond, Lee. 1977. "Structure and Process in the Interpretation of South American Myth: The Arawak Dog Spirit People." *American Anthropologist* 79: 842–868.

Dundes, Alan, ed. 1982. *Cinderella: A Folklore Casebook*. New York: Garland.

———. 1986. "Fairy Tales from a Folkloristic Perspective." In *Fairy Tales and Society: Illusion, Allusion, and Paradigm*, edited by Ruth B. Bottigheimer, 259–269. Philadelphia: University of Pennsylvania Press.

Dwyer, Daisy Hilse. 1978. *Images and Self–Images: Male and Female in Morocco*. New York: Columbia University Press.

Ellis, John M. 1983. *One Fairy Story Too Many: The Brothers Grimm and Their Tales*. Chicago: University of Chicago Press.

Espinosa, Aurelio M. 1921. "A Folk-lore Expedition to Spain." *Journal of American Folklore* 34, no. 132: 127–142.

———. 1923. *Cuentos populares españoles*. Vol. 1. Palo Alto: Stanford University Press.

———. 1924. *Cuentos populares españoles*. Vol. 2. Palo Alto: Stanford University Press.

Espinosa, J. Manuel. 1985. "Aurelio M. Espinosa: New Mexico's Pioneer Folklorist." In *The Folklore of Spain in the American Southwest*, edited by Aurelio M. Espinosa and J. Manuel Espinosa, 1–64. Norman: University of Oklahoma Press.

Falassi, Alessandro. 1980. *Folklore by the Fireside: Text and Context of the Tuscan Veglia*. Austin: University of Texas Press.

Fernandez, James W. 1983. "Consciousness and Class in Southern Spain." *American Ethnologist* 10: 165–173.

———. 1986. *Persuasions and Performances: The Play of Tropes in Culture*. Bloomington: University of Indiana Press.

Fernandez, Renate. 1986. "Ethnography of Nutritional Deficiency in a Spanish Mountain Village: Analysis of Public Health's Delay in Preventing Iodine Deficiency Disorders." Ph.D. diss., Rutgers University.

Fischer, J. L. 1966. "A Ponapean Oedipus Tale: Structural and Sociopsychological Analysis." *Journal of American Folklore* 79: 109–129.

Foster, George M. 1945a. "Sierra Popolucan Folklore and Beliefs." *University of California Publications in American Archaeology and Ethnology* 42: 177–250.

———. 1945b. "Some Characteristics of Mexican Indian Folklore." *Journal of American Folklore* 58: 225–235.

———. 1948. *Empire's Children: The People of Tzintzuntzan*. Smithsonian Institution, Institute of Social Anthropology Publication 6. Washington, D.C.

———. 1960. *Culture and Conquest: America's Spanish Heritage*. Viking Fund Publication in Anthropology 27. New York: Wenner-Gren Foundation for Anthropological Research.

Freeman, Susan Tax. 1970. *The Social Contract in a Castilian Hamlet*. Chicago: University of Chicago Press.

———. 1979. *The Pasiegos: Spaniards in No Man's Land*. Chicago: University of Chicago Press.

Freud, Sigmund. 1968. *The Standard Edition of the Complete Psychological Works of Sigmund Freud*. Vol. 9. Translated and edited by James Strachey. London: Hogarth Press and the Institute of Psycho-Analysis.

———. 1978. *The Interpretation of Dreams*. New York: Random House.

García y García, Segundo. 1955. *Flores de mi tierra: Historia, costumbres y leyendas de Ahigal*. Cáceres: Publications de Departamento de Seminarios de la Jefatura Provincial del Movimiento.

Georges, Robert A. 1969. "Toward an Understanding of Storytelling Events." *Journal of American Folklore* 82: 313–328.

Gilligan, Carol. 1982. *In a Different Voice: Psychological Theory and Women's Development*. Cambridge: Harvard University Press.

Gilmore, David D. 1987a. *Aggression and Community: Paradoxes of Andalusian Culture*. New Haven: Yale University Press.

———. 1987b. "Introduction: The Shame of Dishonor." In *Honor and Shame and the Unity of the Mediterranean*, edited by David D. Gilmore, 2–21. Special Publication of the American Anthropological Association 22. Washington, D.C.

Gilmore, David D., and Sarah C. Uhl. 1987. "Further Notes on Andalusian Machismo." *Journal of Psychoanalytic Anthropology* 10: 341–360.

Goody, Jack. 1968. *Literacy in Traditional Societies*. Cambridge: Cambridge University Press.

———. 1977. *The Domestication of the Savage Mind*. Cambridge: Cambridge University Press.

Gossen, Gary H. 1974. *Chamulas in the World of the Sun: Time and Space in a Maya Oral Tradition*. Cambridge: Harvard University Press.

Hansen, Terrence Leslie. 1957. *The Types of the Folktale in Cuba, Puerto Rico, the Dominican Republic, and Spanish South America*. Berkeley: University of California Press.

Harding, Susan Friend. 1975. "Women and Words in a Spanish Village." In *Toward an Anthropology of Women*, edited by Rayna R. Reiter, 283–308. New York: Monthly Review Press.

———. 1984. *Remaking Ibieca: Rural Life in Aragon Under Franco*. Chapel Hill: University of North Carolina Press.

Herzfeld, Michael. 1984. "The Horns of the Mediterreanist Dilemma." *American Ethnologist* 11: 439–454.

Hill, Jane H. 1986. "The Refiguration of the Anthropology of Language." *Cultural Anthropology* 1: 89–102.

Instituto Nacional de Estadistica. 1957. *Reseña estadistica de la provincia de Cáceres*. Madrid: Presidencia del Gobierno.

———. 1982. *Poblaciones de derecho y de hecho de los municipios españoles*. Madrid: Ministerio de Economía y Comercio.

Kenny, Michael. 1969. *A Spanish Tapestry: Town and Country in Castile*. Gloucester, Mass.: Peter Smith.

Larrea Palacín, Arcadio de. 1959. *Cuentos Gaditanos I: Cuentos Populares de Andalucia*. Madrid: Consejo Superior de Investigaciones Científicas.

Laughlin, Robert M. 1962 "Through the Looking Glass: Reflections on Zinacantán Courtship and Marriage." Ph.D. diss., Harvard University.

———. 1977. *Of Cabbages and Kings: Tales from Zinacantán*. Washington, D.C. Smithsonian Institution Press.

Lewis, Oscar. 1951. *Life in a Mexican Village: Tepoztlán Restudied*. Urbana: University of Illinois Press.

Lison-Tolosana, Carmelo. 1983. *Belmonte de los Caballeros: Anthropology and HIstory in an Aragonese Community*. Princeton: Princeton University Press.

Llano Roza de Ampudia, Aurelio de. 1975. *Cuentos Asturianos: Recogidos de la tradición oral*. Oviedo: Editorial la Nueva España.

Lüthi, Max. 1984. *The Fairytale as Art Form and Portrait of Man*. Bloomington: Indiana University Press.

Malinowski, Bronislaw. 1929 (reprint, 1975). *Sex and Repression in Savage Society*. Chicago: University of Chicago Press.

Mark, Vera. 1987. "Women and Texts in Gascon Tall Tales." *Journal of American Folklore* 100: 504–527.

Mitchell, Carol. 1985. "Some Differences in Male and Female Joke–Telling." In *Women's Folklore, Women's Culture*, edited by Rosan A. Jordan and Susan J. Kalčik, 163–186. Philadelphia: University of Pennsylvania Press.

Mitchell, Timothy J. 1988. *Violence and Piety in Spanish Folklore*. Philadelphia: University of Pennsylvania Press.

Murphy, Michael D. 1983a. "Coming of Age in Sevilla: The Structuring of a Riteless Passage to Manhood." *Journal of Anthropological Research* 39: 376–392.

———. 1983b. "Emotional Confrontations between Sevillano Fathers and Sons: Cultural Foundations and Social Consequences." *American Ethnologist* 10: 650–664.

Nutini, Hugo. 1968. *San Bernardino Contla: Marriage and Family Structure in a Tlaxcalan Municipio*. Pittsburgh: University of Pittsburgh Press.

Opie, Iona, and Peter Opie. 1974. *The Classic Fairy Tales*. London: Oxford University Press.

Ortner, Sherry B. 1974. "Is Female to Male as Nature Is to Culture?" In *Women,*

*Culture and Society*, edited by Michelle Zimbalist Rosaldo and Louise Lamphere, 67–87. Palo Alto: Stanford University Press.

Paredes, Américo. 1970. *Folktales of Mexico*. Chicago: University of Chicago Press.

Parsons, Elsie Clews. 1932. "Folklore from Santa Ana Xalmimilulco, Puebla, Mexico." *Journal of American Folklore* 45: 318–359.

————. 1936. *Mitla: Town of the Souls and Other Zapoteco-Speaking Pueblos of Oaxaca, Mexico*. Chicago: University of Chicago Press.

Persistiany, J. G., ed. 1966. *Honour and Shame: The Values of Mediterranean Society*. Chicago: University of Chicago Press.

Pitt-Rivers, J. A. 1966. *The People of the Sierra*. Chicago: University of Chicago Press.

Price, Richard, and Sally Price. 1966a. "Noviazgo in an Andalusian Pueblo." *Southwestern Journal of Anthropology* 22: 302–322.

————. 1966b. "Stratification and Courtship in an Andalusian Village." *Man* (ns) 1: 526–533.

Propp, Vladimir. 1979. *Morphology of the Folktale*. Austin: University of Texas Press.

Radin, Paul. 1944. "Cuentos y leyendas de los Zapotecos." *Tlalocan* 1, no. 3: 194–226.

Radin, Paul, and Aurelio M. Espinosa. 1917. *El folklore de Oaxaca*. México: Escuela Internacional de Arqueología y Etnología Americana.

Real, Juán B. 1957. *Cuentos Españoles de Colorado y Nuevo Méjico*. 2 vols. Stanford: Stanford University Press.

Robe, Stanley L. 1970. *Mexican Tales and Legends from Los Altos*. Berkeley: University of California Press.

————. 1973. *Index of Mexican Folktales*. Berkeley: University of California Press.

Rowe, Karen E. 1986. "To Spin a Yarn: The Female Voice in Folklore and Fairy Tale." In *Fairy Tales and Society: Illusion, Allusion, and Paradigm*, edited by Ruth B. Bottigheimer, 53–74. Philadelphia: University of Pennsylvania Press.

Schneider, Jane. 1971. "Of Vigilance and Virgins." *Ethnology* 10: 1–24.

Schneider, Jane, and Peter Schneider. 1976. *Culture and Political Economy in Western Sicily*. New York: Academic Press.

Spiro, Melford E. 1982. *Oedipus in the Trobriands*. Chicago: University of Chicago Press.

Stone, Kay. 1975. "Things Walt Disney Never Told Us." In *Women and Folklore: Images and Genres*, edited by Claire R. Farrer, 42–50. Prospect Heights: Waveland Press.

————. 1985. "The Misuses of Enchantment: Controversies on the Significance of Fairy Tales." In *Women's Folklore, Women's Culture*, edited by Rosan A. Jordan and Susan J. Kalčik, 125–145. Philadelphia: University of Pennsylvania Press.

Taggart, James M. 1975. *Estructura de los grupos domésticos de una comunidad de habla nahuat de Puebla, México*. Mexico: Instituto Naciona Indigenista.

——. 1977. "Metaphors and Symbols of Deviance in Nahuat Narratives." *Journal of Latin American Lore* 3: 279–308.

——. 1979. "Men's Changing Images of Women in Nahuat Oral Tradition." *American Ethnologist* 6: 723–741.

——. 1982a. "Animal Metaphors in Spanish and Mexican Oral Tradition." *Journal of American Folklore* 95: 280–303.

——. 1982b. "Class and Sex in Spanish and Mexican Oral Tradition." *Ethnology* 21: 39–53.

——. 1982c. "Metáforas de espacio y tiempo en la tradición oral de España y México." *Ethnica* 18: 169–189.

——. 1983. *Nahuat Myth and Social Structure.* Austin: University of Texas Press.

——. 1986. " 'Hansel and Gretel' in Spain and Mexico." *Journal of American Folklore* 99: 435–460.

Tatar, Maria. 1987. *The Hard Facts of the Grimms' Fairy Tales.* Princeton: Princeton University Press.

Todd, Emmanuel. 1988. *The Explanation of Ideology: Family Structures and Social Systems.* Oxford: Basil Blackwell.

Velasco, Honorio M. 1981. "Textos sociocéntricos: Los mensajes de identificación y diferenciación entre comunidades rurales." *Revista de Dialectología y Tradiciones Popuplares* 36: 85–103.

Vogt, Evon Z. 1969. *Zincantán: A Maya Community in the Highlands of Chiapas.* Cambridge: Harvard University Press.

Von Franz, Marie Louise. 1982. *An Introduction to the Interpretation of Fairytales.* Dallas: Spring Publications.

——. 1988. *The Feminine in Fairytales.* Dallas: Spring Publications.

Weiner, Annette B. 1976. *Women of Value, Men of Renown: New Perspectives in Trobriand Exchange.* Austin: University of Texas Press.

Wheeler, Howard T. 1943. *Tales from Jalisco Mexico.* Philadelphia: American Folk-Lore Society.

Zipes, Jack. 1979. *Breaking the Magic Spell: Radical Theories of Folk and Fairy Tales.* Austin: University of Texas Press.

# Index

Aarne, Antti, 229n.9

Aarne-Thompson tale type, 10

Aarne-Thompson (AT) tale type numbers for Spanish folktales

AT 301A, "The Quest for a Vanished Princess" or "The King Don Damadá," 33, 232–233n.1, and "The Soldier," 232–233n.1

AT 302, "Juanito el Oso," 136–137

AT 302 and 554, "The Grateful Animals," 132, 133, 134–136, 140–143, 215

AT 303, "Blood Brothers" or "The Fisherman," 37, 144, 165–166, 180–181, 213–214

AT 313, "Blancaflor," 33–34, 38, 170–180, 180–194

AT 325, "The Magician and His Pupil" or "The Father and Son Who Went Looking for Work," 139–140

AT 327, "Hansel and Gretel," 32–33, 34, 38, 198–199, 233n.4 (chap. 9)

AT 361, "The Soldier," 34, 150–155

AT 400, "The Lost Wife," 164, 211, 232n.2 (chap. 8)

AT 425, "The Lost Husband," 146–149, 157–163, 211, 233n.3 (chap. 9)

AT 461, "The Griffin Bird" or "The Three Hairs of the Devil," 118–131

AT 510, "Cinderella," 94–98, 100–114, 203–208, 223–224, 232n.2 (chap. 6)

AT 707, "The Queen and Her Marvelous Children," 197–198

AT 709, "Snow White," 33, 80–83, 86–88, 91–92, 111, 130

AT 759, "God's Justice Vindicated" or "The Two Ploughmen," 169–170

AT 882, "The Wager on the Wife's Chastity," 38, 57–58, 213

AT 883A, "The Innocent Slandered Maiden," 32, 43–46, 49–55

AT 956 and 970, "The Maidens and Thieves," 59–60, 65–68, 70–73

Aceves, Joseph, 4, 116, 230n.6

agrarian working class symbols, 168–169

agrotowns, 4

Ahigal, xii; courtship in, 22; location of, 17; population of, 17, 230n.4; wedding rituals in, 24–25

Alcalá, 27

Andalusia: courtship in, 7–8; gender division of labor in, 5; gender relations in, 4–5; honor and shame in, 4; matrilocality in, 27

anticlericalism, 47–48

Aragón: honor and shame in, 4; socialization of gender in, 41

Ardener, Edwin, 219

Arivas Miguel, Filomena: folktale sources of, 60; marital history of, 60; residential history of, 35

Arreola, José María, 233n.1

Arroyomolinos, 117–118

Asturias folklore. See Cabal, Constantino; Llano Roza de Ampudia, Aurelio de

avoidance behavior, 28, 116, 132. See also father; father-in-law; son

Bakhtin, Mikhail, 11, 230n.10

Baldwin, Karen, 11, 168

Barrado, 117–118

Barry, Herbert III, 234n.2

Bauman, Richard, 10, 11, 38, 223

Bazagona, 37, 117

beauty: symbolism of, 93, 110–111

Becedas, 77

Behar, Ruth, xii, 4, 6, 8, 23, 30, 47–48, 215

Belmonte de los Caballeros, 41

Bettelheim, Bruno, 10, 11, 63, 80, 85, 93–94, 105, 131–132, 136, 146, 148, 150, 160, 186, 233n.2 (chap. 9), 235n.5

Big Heads, 84–85

blasphemy: expressions of, 47; justification of, 169–170; men's use of, 75, 169; obscenity as, 169; Oedipal meaning of, 169; scatology in, 169; women's use of, 169

Boas, Franz, 233n.1

Boggs, Ralph, 10, 150, 229nn. 8 and 9, 232n.1 (chap. 7)

Bottigheimer, Ruth B., 11, 223–224, 235n.3

Brandes, Stanley H., xi, 4–6, 21, 23–24, 38, 41, 59, 63, 67, 74, 76–77, 84–85, 90, 100, 103, 105, 116, 139, 150, 169, 195, 215

bridal gift, 202

brother: disenchants sister, 198; sister betrays, 215, 234n.15; sister disenchants, 198

Buechler, Hans C., 6, 27, 231n.1 (chap. 5)

Buechler, Judith-Maria, 6, 27, 231n.1 (chap. 5)

Buñuel, Luis, 17

Burns, Allen F., 201, 232n.2 (chap. 8)

Cabal, Constantino, 94–95, 146, 229nn. 1 and 7

Cabezuela, 31; fieldwork in, xii; location of, 17; population of, 17, 230n.4

cabrón, 116. See also cuckold

cannibals, 59, 69, 91, 160, 198

Cantabrian region, 4

carnival, 38, 229n.4

Caro Baroja, Julio, 184

Carrasco, Pedro, 234n.17

Castaño, Guillermo: courtship of, 22; sharecropping history of, 37

Castile, 4

castration, 63, 105, 112

Chang, Kenne H.-K., 27

child care, 4, 78–79

Chodorow, Nancy, 12, 81, 89, 99, 105, 112, 221

Christ, 101

Christian, William A., 156

class. See social class

Collier, George A., 19, 28

Collier, Jane F., 19, 28–29, 210–211

conjugal bond: faith in, 7, 100, 185–186, 189, 211–212, 218; portrayal of by anthropologists, 4; sentimentality in, 8–9; stability of, 7. See also marriage

Contes du temps passé, 234n.3

Corrales Sánchez, María de Pilar: storytelling style of, 38; teaching her daughter stories, 32–33; views on stories held by, 38

Cortés Vázquez, Luis, 57–58, 60, 67, 94–95, 118, 120, 129–130, 137, 146, 150, 161, 165–166, 180, 187–188, 194, 196–198, 221, 229nn. 1, 6, and 7

Counihan, Carole M., xiii, 38, 229n.4

courtship: breaking of, 21, 42–43; changes in, 19, 28–29; conjugal relations following, 7–8; development of trust during, 7–8; distrust between families during, 66–67; functions of elaborate rules in, 116; gallantry in, 20, 23; informal relationships preceding, 21–22; initiation of, 22–23; length of, 23; manliness in, 20; Mayan practices of, 211; men's fears in, 59; Nahuat practices of, 201–202; Oedipal rivalry during, 138–139; parental opposition to, 116–118; pregnancy during, 42–43; social class in, 116–117, 133–134; timeless themes in, 30–31; virginity of women during, 21, 23; wealth as a factor in, 19, 116–117, 136–137; women's fears in, 59

Cox, Marian Roalfe, 231n.1 (chap. 6)

cuckold: Spanish term for, 116. See also cabrón

Cuesta Martín, Pedro: occupational history of, 138

Curiel Merchán, Marciano, 33, 57–60, 94, 133, 138, 144, 146, 150, 161, 163, 180, 197, 198, 210, 221, 229nn. 1, 6, and 7, 232n.4, 233n.3 (chap. 9)

dance groups, 84

Darnton, Robert, 8, 222, 235n.4

daughter: individuation of, 101; maternal ties of, 77–80, 88–89, 99–100; parental ties of, 26. See also mother

daughter-in-law: conflict of with mother-in-law, 27, 69, 74

Davis, John, 20, 229n.2

defloration, 59, 64, 66, 149, 181, 187

Dégh, Linda, 10, 11, 220, 223

del Pino Díaz, Fermín, xi

Díaz Sanchez, José: courtship of, 133–134; folktale sources of, 53; social class themes of, 186–188

disenchantment, 130

division of labor: gender roles in, 5, 78–79

divorce, 7

Donjuanismo, 41, 231n.1 (chap. 3)

Douglass, William, 230n.6

Drummond, Lee, 220
Dundes, Alan, 222–223
dwarfs: phallic symbolism of, 84–85; relationship of to Big Heads, 84–85; thieves as, 91–92
Dwyer, Daisy Hilse, 231n.1 (chap. 4)

eagle, 186
El Gui jo de Santa Bárbara: fieldwork in, xi; location of, 17; population of, 17, 230n.4
Ellis, John M., 81
enchantment, 23, 85–86, 149, 161
erotic aggression, 116
Espinosa, Aurelio M., 9–10, 43, 60, 81, 91, 94–95, 101, 105, 133, 137, 146, 150, 161, 165, 180–181, 187, 197, 203, 217, 229nn. 1, 6, and 7, 234n.15
Espinosa, J. Manuel, 229n.6
excrement, 111

Falassi, Alessandro, 230n.7
family structure, 13, 201; European variants of, 230n.11; relationship of to storytelling, 12–13; symbolic portrayal of, 184
fasting women, 156
father: censored images of, 138–139, 166–168; filial piety toward, 138–139, 166–168; recast as father-in-law, 138–139; recast as ogre, 137; role in daughter's courtship, 110, 148–149, 159–160, 163; son's avoidance of, 28; son's conflict with, 28; split images of, 138–139
father-in-law: avoiding son-in-law, 116, 132; bad father as, 138–139; images of, 232–233n.1. See also father
feminism, 6, 12
Fernandez, James W., 4, 230n.2
Fernandez, Renate, 95
fieldwork, xi–xii, 39–40, 200, 233n.2
filial piety, 138–139, 166–168. See also father
filicide, 216–217
Fischer, J. L., 94
fish, 180–181
flight motif, 185
Flores, Vito: folktale sources of, 86
folklore, 31
folktales: classification of, 229n.9; number of in study, 6; obtaining Nahuat originals, 7; obtaining Spanish originals, 7; Spanish terms for, 229n.7; titles of, 229n.8; types of for children, 38
food: metaphors of, 64, 81, 85, 156, 198–199; sexual symbolism of, 69; as symbol for love, 103: wife nurturing with, 111
forest, 85
formulaic endings: function of, 46, 52; scatology in, 109
Foster, George M., xii, 24, 27, 201, 230n.1, 233n.1
Franco regime: anticlericalism during, 47; courtship during, 19; imprisonment of socialists by, 78
Freeman, Susan Tax, 4, 6, 23, 215
Freud, 11, 94; feminist critiques of, 12
Frye, David, 8

Galisteo: sharecropping in, 37
García Castaño, Ulalia: folktale sources of, 94; sharecropping history of, 37
García y García, Segundo, 22, 24–25
Garganta la Olla: dance groups in, 84; fieldwork in, xi–xii; inheritance of land in, 28; location of, 17; patron saint of, 84; population of, 17, 230n.4; postmarital residence in, 25–28; storytelling performance in, 34–35
gender: division of labor by, 36, 183; symbolism of, 182–184, 195
gender relations: antagonism in, 5, 38; anthropological portrayal of, 4; anthropological studies of, 5–6; in Extremadura, 4–5; gallantry in, 20; mediation in courtship of, 7–8
gender segregation, 5, 209–210
Georges, Robert A., 10, 11, 38, 223
Giants, 84–85
Gilligan, Carol, 12, 105
Gilmore, David D., 4–6, 20–21, 50, 59, 66, 77, 89, 116, 138, 155
godparents, 24–25, 202
goiter, 94–95. See also iodine deficiency
Goody, Jack, 235n.4
Gossen, Gary H., 201
grace (gracia), 5, 183
Grimm, Jacob, 235n.3
Grimm, Wilhelm, 223–224, 235n.3
Grimms, the (brothers), 10–11, 80
Gutiérrez Estévez, Manuel, xii

Haeberlin, Hermann K., 233n.1
Hansen, Terrence Leslie, 10, 203, 229nn. 8 and 9, 232n.1 (chap. 7)
Harding, Susan Friend, 6
helpful characters, 131
hero: dumb brother as, 130–131; youngest brother as, 130–131
heroine: youngest daughter as, 63
Herrero, Florencia: courting behavior of, 22; land inheritance of, 28, 79–80; marriage of, 25; on premarital chastity, 29, 41–42; relationship of with mother, 77–78; storytelling performance by, 34; storytelling style of, 38
Herrero, Teresa: folktale sources of, 147
Herzfeld, Michael, 229n.2
Hill, Jane H., 230n.10
honor: definitions of, 28; man's loss of, 116
honor and shame, 229n.2; in courtship, 19; history of, 20–21; variation in, 4
Huitzilan de Serdán: fieldwork in, 200, 233n.2 (chap. 10)

idealization of women, 98–99, 111, 156
Iglesia, Zacaria: folktale sources of, 35, 161
ilusión, la, 93. See also romantic love
incest, 104
inheritance: among Nahuat, 213, 216; in Spain, 28, 79–80, 214–215
iodine deficiency, 95. See also goiter
irony, 47, 52, 75, 119–120
Italianas, the, 84, 231n.2 (chap. 5). See also dance groups

Jaraíz de la Vera, 94
Jungian school. See von Franz, Marie Louise
Justo Perez, Narcisa: on folktales for children, 38; folktale sources of, 32, 49

Kenny, Michael, 4
Kinder- und Hansmärchen, 235n.3

Larrea Palacín, Arcadio de, 31, 60, 67, 137, 146, 161, 221, 229nn. 1, 6, and 7
Laughlin, Robert M., xii, 201–202, 210–212, 220, 232n.2 (chap. 8), 233n.5
León: anticlericalism in, 47–48; changing morality in, 30; conjugal relations in, 8–9; honor and shame in, 4

Lewis, Oscar, 27
Lison-Tolosana, Carmelo, 4, 8, 20–21, 41, 48, 229n.3, 231n.1 (chap. 3)
Llano Roza de Ampudia, Aurelio de, 57, 81, 91, 94–95, 133, 146, 163–166, 181, 187, 197–198, 221, 229nn. 1, 6, and 7
Lopez Curiel, Julio: folktale sources of, 32; idealization of women by, 111, 156; sharecropping history of, 37; storytelling performance by, 34–35
Los Olivos, 19
Lüthi, Max, 10, 63, 93, 130

machismo. See manliness
McKee, Lauris, xii
maiden: identity symbols of, 64; mother's image of, 143; peer groups of, 84. See also daughter; mother; women
male competition, 119, 139–140, 143–144, 167–168
Malinowski, Bronislaw, 6, 12, 169
manliness, 20
Mark, Vera, 31
marriage: age of women at, 202; banns of, 24; brittle nature of, 211; collection of money during ritual of, 24–25; consummation of, 25; godparents' role in, 24–25; groom's mother's role in, 24; making the rounds in, 24; practical jokes during, 25; rituals in, 24–25; setting the date of, 24. See also conjugal bond; courtship
masculinity: studies of, 5
mass media, 222–224
matrilocality, 26, 27–28
Maya: brittle marriage among, 211; courtship of, 211; patrilocality among, 211; storytellers among, 202–203, 220, 233–234n.5
men: agricultural roles of, 36, 183; betrayed by women, 210–211; enchantment of, 155; fears in conjugal relations, 75, 195–196; fears in courtship, 155; filial loyalties of, 212–213; filial piety of, 138–139, 166–168; idealizing women, 98–99, 111, 156; identifying with female characters, 233n.2 (chap. 9); moral views of, 57; parental attachments after marriage of, 28; possessiveness of, 163; reading magic from books, 140; slandering women, 43–58, 196, 233n.3 (chap. 9); socialization metaphors for, 136–

137; split paternal images of, 137–139; storytellers as, 6, 31–39, 202–203, 220, 233–234n.5; supernatural power of, 5, 119; work groups of, 35–37. *See also* father; father-in-law; son; wiseman (*sabio*)

menstrual magic, 5, 110–111

metonymy, 75, 111, 149, 232n.3 (chap. 6) and 2 (chap. 7)

Mitchell, Carol, 11, 168

Mitchell, Timothy J., 20, 230n.5

modesty, 29–30. *See also* women

*mole*, 234n.8

Monteros, 5

moon, 160

Moreno, Evarista: folktale sources of, 33–34, 86

Moreno, Juana: folktale sources of, 161; sharecropping history of, 37

mother: ambivalent position of in son's courtship, 100; complex images of, 140, 180–181; daughter's relationship with, 77–80, 88–89, 99–100; images of by gender, 89–90, 140; influencing daughter's courtship, 116–117; narcissism of, 80, 110; promoting son's marriage, 180; recastings of, 83–84; removal of as poetic device, 148; son's relationship with, 89–90; split images of, 80–82, 109–110

mother-in-law: daughter-in-law's conflict with, 27, 69, 74

mother's brother: Spanish term for, 80

Murphy, Michael D., xii, 28, 30

Nahuat: brittle marriage among, 211; courtship practices of, 201–202; family structure of, 201; fieldwork among, 200; gender segregation among, 202; landless of, 217; patrilocality of, 211; romantic love among, 201; storytellers' biographies, 234nn. 6, 9, and 11 (chap. 10) and 1 (chap. 11); storytellers' gender among, 202–203; storytelling situations of, 202

narcissism. *See* mother

nature: personifications of, 186. *See also* moon; sun; wind

Navaconcejo: courtship practices in, 22; fieldwork in, xii; location of, 17; migration from Piornal to, 35; population of, 17, 230n.4

neolocality: rates of, 25

Nutini, Hugo G., 27

obscenities: blasphemous expressions as, 169; men's use of, 168–169. *See also* blasphemy

Oedipal complex: boys' ties to mother during, 99; folktale evidence of, 15, 94, 120; gender differences in, 105, 130; girls' ties to mother during, 99; men's resolution of, 105, 131; men's wishes during, 130; mother's narcissism as a factor in, 110; paternal images in, 132–133, 166; recastings of, 131; relationship of to social class, 129–130, 137–139; universality of, 94; women's resolution of, 105; women's transference in, 148–149. *See also* Bettelheim, Bruno; Chodorow, Nancy; Spiro, Melford E.

Opie, Iona, 232n.1 (chap. 8)

Opie, Peter, 232n.1 (chap. 8)

Ortner, Sherry B., 219

paprika harvesting groups: division of labor in, 36; gender composition of, 35–36; Jaraíz as center for, 35–36; storytelling in, 35–37

Paredes, Américo, 202, 217

parents. *See* daughter; father; mother; son

parricide, 215

Parsons, Elsie Clews, 202, 234n.15

pastoralism, 79

patriarchal family, 184

patrilocal residence: in folktales, 69, 213–214; rates of, 26, 30, 202

Paxson, Leonora M., 234n.2

pelican, 94–95

Perrault, Charles, 234n.3

Persistiany, J. G., 20, 229n.2

phallic symbols, 64, 66

Piornal: courtship in, 22–23; dance groups in, 85; fieldwork in, xi–xii; Giants and Big Heads in, 85; location of, 17; population of, 17, 230n.4; wedding ritual in, 25

Pitt-Rivers, Julian A., 4–5, 7–8, 20–21, 23, 27–28, 41–42, 59, 77, 93, 111, 116, 132, 150, 183–84, 188, 215

Plasencia, 17

political economy, 19

postmarital residence: explanation of, 27–28; among Maya and Nahuat, 211; in Spain, 25–28, 30, 202. *See also* matrilocality; neolocality; patrilocal residence

pregnancy, 42–43
premarital chastity: changing attitudes toward, 29–30; storytellers' values of, 19–
20
Price, Richard, 8, 19, 21, 29
Price, Sally, 8, 19, 21, 29
priest, 46, 52
Propp, Vladimir, 10
psychoanalytic school. *See* Bettelheim,
Bruno; Chodorow, Nancy; Freud, Sigmund; Spiro, Melford E.

Radin, Paul, 217, 234n.15
Ramos, Florencio: courtship of, 21–23, 31,
116–117; folktale sources of, 32; narrative style of, 168–169; relationship of
with father, 166–167; telling folktales to
sons, 37; views of on courtship, 42;
views of on morality, 29
rape, 70
Real, Juán B., 203
Real Vázquez, Eugenio: folktale sources of,
33
Recuero, Juán Julian, 28, 78–79; folktale
sources of, 33
Robe, Stanley L., 10, 139, 151, 169, 201–
203, 210, 229nn. 8 and 9, 232n.1 (chap.
7) and 2 (chap. 8), 233n.1
*romances*, 34, 36
romantic love: conceptions of by gender,
104–105, 111–112, 204, 210; doubts of,
103; functions of, 93; Nahuat belief in,
201; Nahuat word for, 201; shared by
woman and man, 101; Spanish word for,
93; waxing and waning of, 100–101,
110–111
rounds, the (*la ronda*). *See* marriage
Rowe, Karen E., 11

Sanchez Martín, Felisa: folktale sources of,
32, 140; storytelling groups of, 140
Santa María. *See* León
Santiago Yaonáhuac: fieldwork in, 200,
233n.2 (chap. 10)
scatology: expressions of, 47; in formulaic
endings, 109; justification of, 169–170;
men's use of, 169; women's use of, 111,
169
Schneider, Jane, 20
Schwartz, Norman B., xii
seduction, 68

Serradilla: fathers and sons in, 28; fieldwork in, xii; landlessness in, 218; location of, 17; population of, 17, 230n.4
sexual anxieties, 150, 160
sexual symbolism, 63–64
shame. *See* honor and shame
sharecropping, 17
she-wolf, 194
sister: betrays brother, 215, 234n.15; disenchants brother, 198
*Sneewittchen. See* Aarne-Thompson (AT)
tale type numbers: AT 709, "Snow
White"
social class: in courtship, 70, 129; as factor
in women's images, 187–188; in folktales, 92, 186–188; height as symbol of,
139, 143; Oedipal complex related to,
129–130, 137–139
socialization, 41, 59, 221
son: avoiding father, 28; changing relationship with father, 30; filial piety of, 138–
139, 166–168; mother's relationship
with, 89–90; parental attachments of,
28; sharecropping father's land, 28. *See
also* father; men; mother; Oedipal complex
Spanish Civil War, 19, 23, 78–79
Spanish folktales: American Indian variants of, 200–201; Nahuat variants of,
200–201. *See* Aarne-Thompson (AT)
tale type numbers for individual Spanish
folktales
spatial symbolism, 75
Spiro, Melford E., 12, 81, 90, 94, 111, 187
split images. *See* Oedipal complex
stars, 160
Stone, Kay, 224
storytellers: borrowing folktale elements,
140; courtship practices of, 8–9; gender
of, 6, 32, 140, 202–203, 220, 233–
234n.5; literary sources of, 31–32; number of, 6; oral sources of, 31–32; premarital chastity values of, 19–20; report-
ing gender of, 229n.6; village locations
of, 17–19
storytelling: consensus in, 37; descriptions
of, 34–35, 209; gender participation in,
6, 32, 140, 202–203, 220, 233–234n.5;
indirect dialogue in, 13, 38–39; intergen-
erational dialogue in, 8, 69–70; social

settings for, 31–37, 202; styles of, 39, 168–169
sun, 160
synecdoche, 216–217

Taggart, Beatrice, xii, 230n.1
Taggart, Benjamin Counihan, xiii
Taggart, James M., 200, 229n.5, 232n.3 (chap. 7) and 2 (chap. 8), 233nn. 3 and 4 (chap. 10), 234nn. 6 and 9–16 (chap. 10) and 1 (chap. 11)
Taggart, Marisela Cristina, xii
Talavera de la Reina, 37
Tatar, Maria, 10–11
thieves, 63
Thompson, Stith, 229n.9
tobacco harvesting groups: gender division of labor in, 36; storytelling in, 35–37
Todd, Emmanuel, 12–13, 230n.11
Tornavacas: fieldwork in, xii; location of, 17; population of, 17, 230n.4
transference. See Oedipal complex
trousseau (ajuar), 23–24

ugliness, 93, 111
Uhl, Sarah C., 5, 21

Vega, Fernando, 203
Velasco Maillo, Honorio, xi, 230n.5
villages: economic changes in, 18–19; folkloric identity of, 230n.5; locations of, 17; number of in study, 6; populations of, 17, 230n.4
virginity. See women
Virgin Mary, 101; enchanted maiden as, 129–130; helpful figure as, 131; idealized woman as, 111
Vogt, Evon Z., 27, 211
von Franz, Marie Louise, 10, 185, 232n.2 (chap. 6), 233n.2 (chap. 9)

wedding. See marriage
Weiner, Annette, 6
Wheeler, Howard T., 203, 209
wind, 160, 186
wiseman (sabio), 119
wisewoman (sabia), 5, 183–184, 205
witch, 131
witchcraft, 184–185
women: age of at marriage, 202; agricultural roles of, 36, 183; ambivalence of in courtship, 98–100, 111; ambivalent family loyalties of, 214–217; beauty of, 93, 100–102; betraying man, 210–211; blamed by man, 194; caring for children, 4, 78–79; changing modesty of, 29; conflicting with parents-in-law, 53; destructive powers of, 182–183; faith of in family unity, 198–199; filial loyalties of, 26, 159, 185, 188; grace (gracia) of, 183; helpful characters as, 194; idealization of, 98–99, 115, 156; maintaining marital tie, 164, 188, 211; men's images of, 114–115, 187–188; menstrual magic of, 183–184; muting of, 219; nurturant role of, 27, 111, 211; power of love of, 138; restoring family relationships, 197; searching for lost husband, 169; sexual rivalry of, 160–161; speech capacity of, 220–221; split images of, 156, 187–188; supernatural power of, 5, 183–184, 205; virginity of, 21, 182; work groups (cuadrillas) of, 35–37. See also daughter; mother; mother-in-law; sister; wisewoman (sabia)

Zamoro Monroy, Mercedes: literary sources of, 31–32
Zinacantán. See Maya
Zipes, Jack, 223, 235n.5